Rebels and Whips

Rebels and Whips

AN ANALYSIS OF DISSENSION,
DISCIPLINE AND COHESION
IN BRITISH POLITICAL PARTIES

Robert J. Jackson

Macmillan
LONDON · MELBOURNE · TORONTO
St Martin's Press
NEW YORK
1 9 6 8

© Robert J. Jackson 1968

Published by
MACMILLAN AND CO LTD
Little Essex Street London WC2
and also at Bombay Calcutta and Madras
Macmillan South Africa (Publishers) Pty Ltd Johannesburg
The Macmillan Company of Australia Pty Ltd Melbourne
The Macmillan Company of Canada Ltd Toronto
St Martin's Press Inc New York

Library of Congress catalog card no. 68–19078

Printed in Great Britain by
ROBERT MACLEHOSE AND CO LTD
The University Press, Glasgow

To Doreen

To Dereen

Contents

Contents

Statistical Tables

Preface

In the nineteen years between the first Attlee government and the Wilson administration the major British parties were alternately assailed or applauded because of their high degree of cohesiveness in parliamentary affairs. These views were often overstated because Members of Parliament continued to dissent from party policy on many occasions regardless of the activity of disciplinarians. This book explains the dynamic relationships between dissension, discipline and cohesion by a detailed examination of the attitudes, beliefs and political behaviour of MPs during the years 1945 to 1964. Rebels and Whips still play an integral role in British politics. Consequently, outstanding events which have occurred since the period of this study have been incorporated in the text or footnotes, and these recent events seem to confirm the ideas put forward for the earlier five parliaments.

Everyone who writes about British politics for both American and British audiences faces a persistent dilemma. If he stresses historical events and individual personalities, he is apt to be criticized by Americans for his lack of sociological analysis and political science perspective, and if he stresses theories and broad gauge approaches to his subject, the British will be tempted to say that the author lacks the 'feel' of British politics. The following chapters try to employ both of these methods, but to stress the approach that seems more fruitful for any given problem. The scientific method consists in disinterested attempts to further man's knowledge, not in the approaches themselves. Nothing could mark the unscientific man more than a slavish acceptance of any one approach to the study of politics.

Theories may help to provide explanations which, as David Hume proffered, are where the mind comes to rest, but it is to individuals that an author owes his most significant debts. The accumulation of intellectual debts is particularly great in a study such as this where the book is on a country of which the writer is not a citizen. How can one adequately thank the anonymous political correspondents from such important sources as *The Times, The Guardian,* and *The Economist*? How can one cite those hundreds of politicians and ministers who gave up their valuable time to talk with, and often entertain, an interviewer from overseas? And, lastly, how can one impart the gratitude that one feels to one's Oxford friends who patiently listened to countless stories of British politics? My answer to these questions can only be that each of these groups has added considerably to my understanding of Britain and her people.

Particularly helpful were Philip Williams and Anthony King, each of whom read the entire manuscript and saved the author from significant errors of fact and interpretation. Hugh Berrington and Professor S. E. Finer gave me considerable help with deciding which Early Day Motions to study. To David Butler, indefatigable expert on British politics, I am indebted for his constant source of information and ideas about both the mainstream and idiosyncrasies of British life. The research was carried out with generous financial support from the Canada Council and Carleton University.

My most sincere thanks belong to Doreen, who worked tirelessly on this book and affectionately on comforting the author. The dedication is only an inadequate symbol of my gratitude to her.

ROBERT J. JACKSON

Carleton University, Ottawa
June 1967

Part I

Part I

1 Introduction

> Our alternating Cabinets, though belonging to different
> Parties, have never differed about the foundations of
> society. And it is evident that our whole political
> machinery pre-supposes a people so fundamentally at one
> that they can safely afford to bicker; and so sure of their
> own moderation that they are not dangerously disturbed
> by the never-ending din of political conflict. May it
> always be so.[1]

Since the decline of the Liberal party in the turbulent war and
depression years between 1914 and 1935, British politics has
been completely dominated by two mammoth political
machines known as the Conservative and Labour parties. Only
these two organizations have been able to retain enough popularity during general elections to allow their leaders to sit on
the government front benches or to form Her Majesty's Loyal
Opposition. This development of a somewhat rigid two-party
system was coupled with several changes in parliamentary
democracy which are still having disquieting effects in the
Britain of the late 1960s.

The evolution of British parties has been a subject of continual examination by scholars. The origin of the British two-
party system has been traced back for almost three centuries to
the great contests between the Whigs and Tories. Mass parties
with oligarchical structures and professional bureaucracies
evolved during the last half of the nineteenth century, but it
was almost a hundred years before electoral habits ossified to
the extent that almost no Independents could be elected to the

[1] Earl Balfour, 'Introduction' to Walter Bagehot, *The
English Constitution*, p. xxiv. The footnotes have been
shortened as much as possible in order to accommodate
a great number of them. A complete bibliography can
be found at pp. 317 ff.

mother of parliaments. By 1945, these three events – the development of a two-party system, the highly organized party structure, and the hardening of voting habits – gave rise to the election to parliament of Members who were rarely willing to take the risk of making public their opposition to the policies of their own party. This significant occurrence in British politics reinforced the tendency to rigidity in the British political system and marked the final stage in the history of party discipline in which British party leaders could obtain obedience from their followers in divisions, in other parliamentary activities, and, to a lesser degree, outside parliament.

The growth of party discipline was a significant development in the evolution of British politics. One indicator of the changing nature of parties was to be seen in the decrease in the number of governments that were forced to resign because of party dissension. On numerous occasions in the eighteenth and nineteenth centuries governments handed over the reins of administration to other parliamentary leaders because there had been a breakdown in party cohesion. In contrast the twentieth century has experienced very few such government defeats and the last such event took place over thirty years ago when Neville Chamberlain was forced to resign after a party revolt on the disastrous Norway campaign. A second related signpost was the gradual increase in party cohesiveness during parliamentary divisions. In *The Government of England*, A. L. Lowell compiled statistics for party voting from 1836 to 1899.[1] Whenever nine-tenths of a party voted together, Lowell called it a party vote. He calculated that in 1836 the percentage of divisions where both parties cast party votes on opposite sides was 23, and that by 1899 this percentage had increased to 69. Another student of politics later tabulated that between 1924 and 1928 the percentage of party votes remained constantly at 95%, and by 1945 this was

---

[1] A. L. Lowell, *The Government of England*, pp. 71–81. Disraeli complained about a 'mechanical majority' in 1869. See Sir Edward Boyle, 'No, Not Quite . . .', p. 17.

found to have increased to 98 per cent.[1] A Member was by then called a rebel whenever he voted against his party or abstained in the division lobbies, and it had become generally believed that some special means or techniques were required for retaining such a high degree of cohesion.

In spite of this increased awareness of party discipline, it has not received the same systematic study as elections, party organizations, or the civil service.[2] There are at least two reasons for this deficiency. First, it is difficult to obtain information. Leaders, Whips, and even recalcitrant Members rarely want the public to know what forms of discipline have been employed. Second, very few case studies have been made of party discipline, and this has meant that nearly all the cases had to be analysed before a systematic study could be undertaken.

In the last twenty years there has been periodic concern about the consequences of party discipline. Some critics, lamenting the rigidity of party discipline, have made statements about the 'passing of parliament' and the 'decline of the individual backbencher'. They have asked whether parliament can survive with disciplined parties.[3] Other critics, less dramatically, have called the British political system a Cabinet government rather

---

[1] Russell Jones, 'Party Voting in the English House of Commons' (unpublished M.A. Thesis, University of Chicago, 1933), p. 24, and Samuel H. Beer, *Modern British Politics*, p. 184 (American ed. entitled *British Politics in the Collectivist Age*).

[2] This argument is also suggested by R. E. Dowse and Trevor Smith in 'Party Discipline in the House of Commons – A Comment', p. 159. 'Parliamentary party discipline has not received much attention from students of British politics. It remains a subject about which little is known.'

[3] The most extreme of these critics is typified by Christopher Hollis in his *Can Parliament Survive?*; 'Can Parliament Survive?'; 'Has Parliament a Future?'; 'Parliament and the Establishment' in *The Establishment*, ed. Hugh Thomas. See also G. W. Keeton, *The Passing of Parliament*, and Michael Foot, *Parliament in Danger!*

than a Parliamentary government, and recently there has been concern that Britain may be evolving into a Prime Ministerial government.[1] All of these theories assumed cohesive and well disciplined parties. The difficulty is that some of the answers given for improving British government flow from false assumptions about the nature of party discipline. A cursory reading of the major texts on British government reveals that party discipline has seldom been either carefully defined or studied empirically.

TOWARD A CLARIFICATION OF TERMINOLOGY

No definition of party discipline eliminates all problems in terminology, but possibly some limits can be set to what the few contentious words imply. It is stipulated, therefore, that party discipline refers both to the existence of a high degree of cohesion, and to the methods of maintaining this cohesion in a political party. The existence of solidarity in British parties is evidenced by the relatively few splits in the mass party organizations and even more by the paucity of backbench revolts during divisions in the House of Commons. When the term 'party discipline' refers to the methods for retaining cohesion in any organization, it has many connotations. It can mean, for example, 'bringing under control' or 'trained condition' or 'system of rules for conduct'. When used with reference to politics, the term refers to the whole pattern of rewards and punishments that the leadership of a political party can award

[1] This last group includes a large number of historians and political scientists. The clearest statement that Britain is developing into a Prime Ministerial government is given by R. H. S. Crossman in his lucid introduction to a recent edition of Bagehot, *The English Constitution*. See also Max Beloff's letter to *The Times*, 3 Jul 1963.

to its membership. If coercion and persuasion are regarded as the two extremes of a spectrum it is clear that the disciplinary measures used by British political parties fall somewhere between the two. Persuasion is always attempted but other means are available.

Another somewhat ambiguous word is 'influence'. Party leaders attempt to influence backbench behaviour before divisions and other rebellious situations. They cannot discipline backbenchers (in the sense of employing rewards or punishments), for their actions are not yet known – they are only anticipated. Thus, it might help to employ a model in order to examine how influence and the anticipation of possible discipline affects the behaviour of backbenchers. Of course, it is usually impossible to employ the model in actual historical situations because of the lack of information.

The situation can be defined in the following terms:

(*a*) The leaders' prediction as to how backbenchers will behave in a given situation in the absence of an attempt to influence them. This involves the sounding mechanisms that leaders have for ascertaining their followers' future behaviour.

(*b*) The leaders' preference regarding the behaviour of backbenchers. This is assumed to be a united party based on official party policy.

(*c*) The techniques and resources leaders utilize to make (*a*) and (*b*) coincide as nearly as possible.

(*d*) The accuracy of the leaders' prior prediction.

(*e*) The backbenchers' own values and preference systems.

(*f*) The backbenchers' estimate of the probabilities of various contemplated outcomes. This involves, for example, both a calculation of the possibilities of damaging the party, and of the potential sanctions that could be used against backbenchers.

(*g*) The backbenchers' resistance (or counter-influence), techniques, and resources.

7

(*h*) The effects of the environment. This involves, for example, such variables as the nearness of an election.[1]

One factor (or weapon) which determines backbench behaviour is the leaders' control of future rewards and punishments. MPs will be influenced by their calculus of potential sanctions following what Carl Friedrich has called the 'rule of anticipated reactions'. That is, influence rests upon the capacity of humans to anticipate the reactions of those affected by their actions. Friedrich declared: 'Influence flows into the human relation whenever the influencer's reaction might spell disadvantage and even disaster for the actor, who foresees the effect the action might have and alters it more or less in accordance with his foresight.'[2]

What do recalcitrant MPs fear? There could be several answers to this question because virtually anything that Members value could be the basis of a power relationship. Members usually desire to remain in the House of Commons, and, as long as this is true, leaders have considerable influence. Moreover, leaders have control of many rewards which MPs desire such as government office and patronage. These factors advance the tentative hypothesis that life is easier and more pleasant for MPs who conform than for those who rebel. This assumption must be handled carefully because MPs are sometimes more interested in maintaining good relationships with other individuals than with their party leaders.

PREVIOUS STUDIES OF PARTY DISCIPLINE

Many ideas have been advanced about party discipline, and at least three basic types of explanation have been offered as

[1] The inspiration for this model came from J. David Singer, 'Inter-Nation Influence: A Formal Model', p. 421.
[2] C. J. Friedrich, *Man and His Government: An Empirical Theory of Politics*, p. 201.

causal factors of this important facet of British politics. The explanations have included: the significance of the structure of the political system, the development of centralized mass party organizations, and the nature of British political culture. It is necessary at this stage to outline and discuss some of these widely held and instructive ideas.

For centuries, the British political system, whether character-ized as Parliamentary, Cabinet, or Prime Ministerial, has been noted for its union of the executive with the legislative branch of government. This fusion has necessitated that the government be formed out of the majority party, with the Commons there-fore being composed of government and opposition Members. This fact led Members to regard their role in parliament as being limited to choosing between two simple alternatives; to vote with the 'ins' or the 'outs'. Government backbenchers were forced either to support their ministers to prevent a government defeat or to oppose it and allow the opposition leaders to form the government. Opposition backbenchers faced precisely the opposite dilemma. Although the basic structure of British government is, therefore, significant for any appraisal of the history and evolution of party discipline, the more immediate causal factor is the way in which British MPs perceive their role within the confines of governmental structure.

A second structural argument has been built on a constitu-tional provision which allows the Prime Minister, with the concurrence of the Monarch, to dissolve parliament at any time. It is said that party discipline is maintained by leaders threaten-ing backbenchers with dissolution.[1] That is, when rebels do

---

[1] Examples are numerous, but the classic statements are found in Sir Ivor Jennings, *Parliament*, p. 7; Maurice Duverger, *Political Parties*, p. 404; Roland Young, *The British Parliament*, p. 229; Herbert Morrison, *Government and Parliament*, p. 94; Lowell, *The Government of England*, p. 467; Hiram Miller Stout, *British Government*, p. 31. It is stated in its simplest terms in Jennings, *Parliament*, p. 7: 'The choice for a private member on the Government side is between support for the Government,

not acquiesce, their leaders force them to fight an election. This idea has been so widely accepted that many commentators have advocated that the power of dissolution should be exported to countries which have had difficulty in developing cohesive parties.

The most obvious limitation to the theory about dissolution causing party cohesion is that it does not account for the internal discipline of the opposition.[1] In the days when the majority in parliament was composed of changing groups, the power of dissolution was used as a check on parliamentary behaviour. But now that parties maintain almost complete control over their MPs, there is rarely any conflict between the executive and the House of Commons as a whole. The conflict that does exist takes place within each party, and the only possible meaning to party discipline in this circumstance is internal party discipline. Since only the government can dissolve parliament, opposition leaders cannot use this threat with their backbenchers. Therefore, nearly half of the MPs cannot be controlled by the threat of a dissolution of parliament.

There are also reasons why the threat of dissolution is not used as a weapon by the government party. First, dissolution is not known to have been used for this purpose since 1922, and it may have atrophied as a weapon.[2] As Martin Redmayne, Conservative Chief Whip, 1959–64, commented, 'One does not, I think, threaten a dissolution. It's too big a thing.'[3] On occasion Prime Ministers will, of course, make references to the possibility of dissolution, but backbenchers need have little fear

on the one hand, and, on the other hand, either a resignation or a dissolution at the choice of the Prime Minister.'

[1] The following argument assumes that there is a normal majority government, but for minority government and the power of dissolution see Harold J. Laski, 'The Position of Parties and the Right of Dissolution'.

[2] John P. Mackintosh, *The British Cabinet*, p. 498.

[3] Martin Redmayne, interviewed by Norman Hunt in *The Listener*, p. 1057.

of this action unless an election is imminent for other reasons. Even Harold Wilson's stern denunciation of 63 backbenchers who rebelled on the Defence White Paper in early March 1967 was not taken too seriously by most backbenchers, in spite of his reference to dissolution.[1] Second, a Prime Minister has more to lose from an election than does an ordinary MP, and he is more likely to be replaced as Prime Minister than a backbencher is to lose an election.[2]

Technically the executive can dismiss parliament simply by asking for a dissolution.[3] This power exists even if it is never used to discipline a party, and a Prime Minister might dissolve parliament if he was confident of winning an election, and wished to demonstrate that his policies had popular support. However, the most important argument against the use of dissolution is that it usually brings an attempt by the government to consolidate its ranks against the opposition. Any party which wants to be elected makes a determined effort to present a united front to the electorate.[4] Parties attempt to impress upon the public that their policies are best, and that if elected they will stand united to ensure that their programme is enacted.[5]

[1] See *The Times*, 3 Mar 1967.
[2] William G. Andrews, 'Some Thoughts on the Power of Dissolution', pp. 286–9.
[3] Max Beloff commented, 'What the power of dissolution during the normal five-year term of Parliament really means, is that where the balance of Parties in Parliament appears unlikely to afford support for a stable ministry of any kind, the ultimate sovereign, the electorate can be appealed to without delay to put an end to the situation.' 'Executive and Legislature in Britain', pp. 164–5.
[4] This was shown in the case of Aneurin Bevan and his followers in both 1951 and 1955, and again in 1963 when five unilateralist rebels had the whip restored.
[5] See, for example, the Conservative party's *Daily Notes* for both the 1950 and 1951 elections. Also interesting are the Conservative *Campaign Guides* which recorded much of the dissension which occurred in the Labour and Liberal parties.

Only if party leaders stood aside and allowed their dissident followers to be defeated would there be a case for dissolution as a form of party discipline. This does not happen in Britain, and the electors are not given an opportunity to decide between the views of the leaders of a particular party and their rebellious followers.

If MPs believe that dissolution is a check on their freedom, they can be influenced by the threat of it; the mere belief provides the basis for its significance. Many MPs are amused by the idea that the threat of dissolution is a factor in party discipline, but some believe it is a genuine check,[1] and for these individuals it undoubtedly is a factor in their obedience to the party whip. Regardless of whether the threat of dissolution is a causal factor in Members' behaviour, it cannot alter the following facts: (1) The opposition's cohesion, or lack of it, cannot be affected by a threat of dissolution by their leaders. (2) Dissolution has not been used to discipline the government party since 1922. (3) Dissolution does not force a contest between government leaders and their rebellious followers unless the dissident Members are excluded from their party.

The idea that party discipline is maintained by the threat of dissolution is a carry-over of terminology from the early nineteenth century and loose party organization. Its general acceptance may have played a part in keeping party discipline from being systematically explored. One perceptive Chief Whip reported that: 'On one occasion I actually used the promise of dissolution to obtain cohesion. This certainly was the opposite side of the coin. The threat is of little importance, take the revolt over Resale Price Maintenance in the Conservative party. It did not help them as they still only got a majority of one. It can't be effective in theory or practice.'

The second causal explanation for party discipline stems from the idea that the development of mass party organization

---

[1] MPs have expressed the two conflicting opinions in many interviews.

affected the behaviour of Members of the House of Commons. This thesis, propounded by M. Ostrogorski, A. L. Lowell and R. T. McKenzie, among others, put forward the argument that the development of constituency party machinery, linked vertically with some form of central party machinery, placed an extraordinary amount of power in the hands of such extra-parliamentary leaders as local party officials and professional party workers. Because of this development, the individual MP would find himself indebted to the extra-parliamentary party, since without its support he would have had considerably more difficulty in being elected.

Like all social formations, British parties developed a life of their own with a hierarchical structure and norms of behaviour. Unity and cohesion were quickly accepted as basic ideals by all members of the parties. MPs were encouraged to support the leaders of their parliamentary party and to regard party cohesion as more important than freedom of action in the House of Commons. Moreover, the development of parties with platforms and general policies for fighting elections, which began around the turn of the century, bound MPs of each party either to support their party's policies in parliament or to be accused of not supporting the leaders who were trying to enact those policies on which the individual MPs had been elected.

It followed from the development of mass parties that there would have to be institutionalized methods of maintaining party cohesion. Thus, the constitutions of both parties permitted party officials to construct lists of acceptable candidates and permitted constituency parties/associations to refuse to re-adopt their sitting Members. In view of the accepted norms in the party and the institutionalized weapons in the hands of the mass party organization, the Member could only safely rebel (without facing a powerful alliance of the mass party and the parliamentary leadership which he could not hope to defeat) when the membership of the mass party and the parliamentary leaders were in disagreement.

There is no doubt that there was an historical correlation

between the evolution of mass party organization and the increase of party solidarity in the House of Commons, but much of the causal link between these two phenomena was supplied by the hardening of electoral habits. As the British voters lined themselves up behind parties and refused to support Independent candidates, the mass party organizations which controlled the selection of candidates and the readoption of Members became more important *vis-à-vis* the individual MP and the Members found themselves being influenced by the fear of unpleasant reprisals if they deviated too far from the party line. Thus, although only a rough causal chain can be constructed because of the multitude of historical variables, there is general agreement that the development of party solidarity in the House was causally linked to the development of mass party organizations reinforced by the public's electoral habits.

A second form of argument concerning mass parties is that British mass parties are centralized and, therefore, they are more cohesive than American decentralized parties. In order to prove this, it would be necessary to show the effects of centralization on party discipline. The causal connection is not established by positing that one country with centralized parties happens to have well-disciplined parties while another country with decentralized parties happens to have little party discipline. This is not to state that this argument is false, only that no proof is usually given. If British parties are compared with those of another Parliamentary government such as Australia or Canada, quite different results are discovered.

The third theory about how party discipline is maintained consists of two parts each of which is concerned with a different aspect of political culture. One explanation is that the general political culture of Britain is a factor determining that Members will obey their party whips, and the other is that each party is based on certain principles or ideas which form a party culture within which party leaders and followers must operate.

The importance of general British culture as an explanatory variable in the maintenance of party discipline has been hinted at by many writers. Leon D. Epstein, an American political scientist, recently stated that one reason for disciplined parties was 'a respect for the British belief in the value of a cohesive parliamentary party.'[1] In much the same vein, William G. Andrews wrote that disciplined parties resulted from '. . . grafting the principle of universal suffrage on to traditional British governmental concepts and practices . . .', and from '. . . the implicit acknowledgement by the backbenchers of the legitimacy of popular sovereignty within a framework of parliamentary, non-representative government . . .'.[2] The implication of these statements is that individual MPs refrain from cross-voting or abstaining because they believe that it would not be in line with the best traditions of British government.

Although these statements of Epstein and Andrews are not conclusive, they are suggestive about the relationship between general culture and the activities of MPs in the House. Moreover, although it is a truism to say that MPs vote for their leader's policies because they usually do so, if MPs believe that they must keep their activities in line with certain traditions in British culture, this will act as a causal link. However, no complete survey of parliamentarians' attitudes has yet been completed and, until this is accomplished, this link between political culture and parliamentarians' behaviour will have to be phrased in the hypothetical.

Some of the arguments based on the development of British political culture are more tenuous. Two students of politics recently argued that academic commentators have concentrated too much on the formal machinery (i.e. the Whips) and on the fact that the individual MP is significantly weaker than the party machine.[3] They concluded that this was an 'un-

[1] Leon D. Epstein, 'Cohesion of British Parliamentary Parties', p. 364.
[2] Andrews, 'Some Thoughts on the Power of Dissolution', p. 290.
[3] Robert E. Dowse and Trevor Smith, 'Party Discipline in the House of Commons – A Comment'.

helpful' approach, and suggested that a new answer was required. Their answer can be best summarized in their own words:

> That the government of the day or the opposition has little real difficulty in controlling its supporters, as is evidenced by the astonishingly small number of intra-party revolts, may be taken as evidence that the pre-introductory stages of a bill ensure that its more contentious elements have been eliminated.[1]

The pre-introductory stages are taken to include interest representation, backbench committees, and in general the private discussions that precede the introduction of a bill. The authors provide adequate bibliographical references to prove that the government consults and is consulted by interest groups before legislation is tabled in the House. In the light of this they ask: 'What more effective plea can a Minister make to potentially hostile MPs than that the interests which are affected by a measure have been consulted and have given their approval?'[2] However, it is necessary to ask if all interests in the community have effective and equal representation. Will they all be consulted? Probably the answer is 'no' to both questions. Even when the government wants to consult all interests, it cannot always do so.[3] Moreover, is there nothing left that MPs represent simply because they are 'the people's' representatives? This argument is important for democracy,[4] but it is not

[1] *Ibid.*, p. 163. [2] *Ibid.*, p. 164.

[3] An enlightening statement was made by the Minister of Transport, A. T. Lennox-Boyd, when he answered a question on the denationalization of Road Haulage. 'Almost the first thing I did when I became Minister was to ask the Unions if they would have consultations with me, before the Bill was completed, on what form it ought to take. Acting on what advice or thoughts I do not know, they replied that they would prefer to wait until the Bill was published.' 503 *H.C. Deb.*, col. 1799.

[4] W. G. Runciman touches on this problem in his *Social Science and Political Theory*, pp. 82–4.

essential to discuss it here. More to the point is the fact that Dowse and Smith's argument counters the ideas of those authors who concentrate solely on what happens during a division. However, their discussion does not stress enough the fact that there is often considerable disagreement both before and after the introduction of legislation. If all interests could be accommodated and all backbenchers satisfied, obviously there would be no rebellions. The difficulty is that many types of legislation cannot be formulated in a way which solves all conflict, and Members sometimes admit publicly that they have voted for legislation which they found unacceptable.[1] If legislation could be composed so that it would be unanimously accepted, there would not be any need for democracy, let alone political parties. Moreover, Dowse and Smith's argument does not even attempt to account for the cohesion of the opposition party. There are other more plausible reasons for party discipline than an increase in uncontentious legislation.

The best explanation of party cohesion being caused by party ideology is given by Professor Samuel H. Beer in his *Modern British Politics*. He convincingly argues that within both the Labour and Conservative parties there has been a substantial consensus on values and beliefs, and that this consensus allows little room for dispute within the parties. Since the Members accept the reigning ideas of their own party, they are not very apt to revolt against their parliamentary leaders who are attempting to put these ideals into practice. Although conflict is still expected to occur, this is muted by basic agreement on certain moral ideas about society and politics.

This view has important explanatory value for British politics

[1] See R. H. S. Crossman's explanation of his vote in favour of German rearmament which he passionately opposed. 533 *H.C. Deb.*, col. 477. Also see Beverley Baxter's statement concerning the introduction of commercial television. He expressed his embarrassment at voting with his own party when he agreed with Labour. 502 *H.C. Deb.*, col. 275.

in some decades, but it can be overstated. One exaggeration has been that British parties are more ideological than American parties, and therefore more disciplined. If this is true, it is surprising to find that the Labour party, which supposedly is more ideological, has usually had less parliamentary cohesion than the Conservative party.[1] There is also a strong case for suggesting that ideological parties have more arguments over policy than those based on pragmatic philosophies. This argument, based on ideology, has not been proven, and even theoretically does not appear to explain the differences in the cohesiveness of British parties.

SOURCES OF PARTY DISCIPLINE

There are many reasons for parliamentary party solidarity, and the following chapters do not attempt to isolate any single cause. The aim is to make a detailed study of party rebellions, and to consider the rewards and punishments which leaders have employed for maintaining party cohesion. The relationship between rebellions and discipline provides a dynamic explanation of party cohesion in terms of a highly sensitive communication system.

Political parties have not been as cohesive as many commentators have suggested. Although a system has developed which involves nearly perfect solidarity in divisions, this cohesion is illusory. There are many occasions in both parties when individuals or groups ostentatiously abstain from voting with their parties, table critical Early Day Motions, publish grave pamphlets with an attempt to reformulate party policy, make

[1] For a criticism of the degree to which British parties are ideological and committed to a specific programme, see D. E. Butler, 'American Myths About British Parties', and Austin Ranney and Willmoore Kendall, *Democracy and the American Party System*, pp. 528 ff.

abusive speeches outside the House, and less often cross-vote. No amount of party discipline has prevented parliamentarians from publicly expressing conflicting opinions.[1] Of course, there is even more controversy in private. In committees and private informal groups the expression of dissatisfaction is continual. The controversies are so well concealed that one party often fails to notice them in the other. Enoch Powell has commented:

> Over and over I have seen cases where the Government were forced to swallow their pride and back down on some issue under the pressure of back-bench action and where, neverthe- less, the whole operation, which seemed so embarrassingly obvious to the participants in it, entirely escaped the Opposi- tion's notice.[2]

Nevertheless, there is considerable published evidence about party rebellions. The most difficult problem is how to classify this variety of facts. Whereas David Truman, in his classic study of cohesion in the United States Congress, asked 'How much of pattern and regularity can be found beneath an appearance of unpredictability or even chaos?'[3] the opposite question must be asked about British party cohesion. How much dissent and rebellion can be found beneath an appearance of party solidarity?

In the following chapters rebellions are taken to be any Member's public actions inside or outside parliament which are in direct opposition to party policy.[4] This is necessary because

---

[1] See Lord Morrison, *Herbert Morrison, An Autobiography*, p. 253; and Harold Laski, *Parliamentary Government in England*, p. 143.

[2] Enoch Powell, '1951–1959 Labour in Opposition', p. 336.

[3] David B. Truman, *The Congressional Party*, p. 9.

[4] See appendix I. Political parties do not always have clearly-defined policies, and MPs who oppose such policies cannot be considered rebellious. For a comparison of Early Day Motions which illustrate this point see Annex 3 of S. E. Finer, *et al. Backbench Opinion in the House of Commons 1955–1959*.

of the rumours and counter-rumours about party rebellion, many of which cannot be accepted as valid. If a rebellion is not made public, there is a strong case for asserting that no party discipline will be involved. Leaders and Whips believe, rightly or wrongly, that quarrelling in public has serious electoral consequences, but they do not employ reprisals such as withdrawal of the whip for private disagreement. Furthermore, on many occasions political commentators can acquire evidence only after there has been a public dispute.[1]

The following chapters survey the internal party rebellions which occurred from 1945 to 1964. Many forms of MPs' behaviour are included, such as cross-votes, public abstentions, critical Early Day Motions, and other activities condemned by party leaders. Although there are significant differences in the various forms of rebellion, it is impossible to assign relative weights to them in the statistics. There are some methodological problems to the approach used here, but they are not as great as in other methods. These technical problems are analysed in appendix I.

When the records of individual and group rebellions are examined, it is possible to determine which party elements have been most rebellious and which have been most loyal. Around each party leadership were supporters, adherents, critics and rebels who formed a series of concentric circles of ever-decreasing party solidarity and ever-decreasing reluctance to accept party discipline. Members changed circles depending on the issues involved, but supporters and rebels rarely changed places. There was movement toward or away from the centre, but only

[1] This disadvantage applies to many studies about politics, but this author agrees with a statement of James B. Christoph in *Capital Punishment and British Politics*, p. 8. 'One can argue that more can be learned about a political system by examining its behaviour under stress than from the search after the average case.' This is also argued by Ely Devons, in 'Government on the Inner Circle'.

rarely was there a radical jump from outside to inside or vice-versa. Old loyalties and beliefs tied Members closely to their usual circle, and there remained a hard core on both the inside and the outside circle until the leaders were changed. The records of revolt are used to discover whether or not such factors as education, sponsorship, and the year of entry to the House are significant in explaining which individuals rebel and why they do so. The statistics are also employed to suggest the importance of such mechanical factors as the size of the government's majority in determining the magnitude and style of revolts.

Along with this spectrum of party revolt, there are also various forms of party discipline. Leaders make use of both punishments and rewards to keep their parties cohesive. Negative devices include expulsion, withdrawal of the whip, and the non-readoption of sitting Members. Positive devices consist of such rewards as government office, patronage, and even trips abroad. The rewards and punishments were then related to the record of every MP's rebelliousness to see if there were any persistent relationships.

The conclusions suggest that rebellions are more frequent and discipline is less frequent than is generally assumed; that there is not a very clear relationship between rewards and punishment and party cohesion; and, lastly, that both rebellions and discipline are part of the communication system within the parties. Whereas the three types of explanation of cohesive parties mentioned above – the significance of the structure of the political system, the development of centralized mass party organizations and the nature of British political culture – were all necessary conditions in the development of the type of present-day parties, they are not sufficient causes of cohesive parties. The conclusions suggest that a fourth explanation based on a party with adequate adjustment or accommodation processes is required to maintain a stable and cohesive party. This ability to accommodate is very considerably due to the beliefs and attitudes of British politicians.

The history of party rebellions was found in the *House of Commons Debates*, *Notices of Motions*, party literature, and daily and weekly newspapers. Local newspapers were examined in the cases of individuals who were recipients of party discipline. When possible, interviews were used. Well over a hundred individuals were interviewed, and these included most MPs who were expelled, lost the whip, or had readoption problems, as well as most Whips and the main party professionals who were in charge of party discipline. Moreover, many of these individuals made their private papers available to the author.[1]

In conclusion, Part II of this study examines the history of party rebellions from 1945 to 1964, and Part III analyses the cases of individuals who experienced party discipline. The conclusions to Part III relate rebelliousness to rewards and punishments and attempt to provide an explanation of cohesion in British parties. However, these chapters must be placed in the context of party organization, and the next chapter explores that aspect of party discipline.

[1] For a detailed list of sources see the Bibliography.

2 Party Discipline and Formal Organization

> The fact is that in political, as in other forms of warfare, the leader must be able to rely on his troops when he is fighting his opponents. The more that discipline is self-imposed the better, but discipline there must be unless one is prepared to lose the battle.[1]

The Labour and Conservative party constitutions and organizations for maintaining party discipline deserve an important place in any study of British politics. Formal rules provide the framework within which authoritative decisions are made for a party and may reflect fairly rigid attitudes toward methods of making decisions. Moreover, certain types of party organizations may lead to effective functioning while other forms may actually lessen the effectiveness of the party. This chapter, therefore, discusses the formal rules which affect parliamentarian's behavior in the House of Commons, and then outlines the structure and functions of the Whips' Offices for both major parties.

Various authors have asserted that the Conservative party was forced to develop a disciplined party because of the strict disciplinary tactics of the Labour party. Actually the increase of party cohesion began in the nineteenth century, before the advent of the Labour party. Labour's innovation was the enforcement of written regulations. In contrast to the Conservative party, the Labour party has often employed Standing Orders to describe the degree and quality of dissidence allowed, and the machinery for punishing rebels. Written regulations were introduced in the party as early as 1906 and by 1931 the regulations were substantially in their present-day form, with

[1] Earl Attlee, 'Party Discipline is Paramount', p. 16.

all candidates compelled to sign a pledge declaring their
obedience to the Standing Orders of the PLP.[1] At the 1931
conference, Labour leaders demanded strict adherence to the
regulations because ILP Members had voted against the
MacDonald government. Arthur Henderson asserted that he
would accept individual abstentions based on conscience, but
not cross-votes. He objected to the ILP '. . . having a meeting,
despite the meeting of the Parliamentary Party, and saying they
are going to oppose something by organized vote that is against
the decisions of the Parliamentary Party'.[2] Michael Foot, a
recent critic of Labour Standing Orders, described Henderson's
argument in the following words: '. . . a Labour M.P. was
entitled to have a conscience, so long as he revealed it only in
isolated abstentions. But the sin against the Holy Ghost of the
Party machine was the "organized conscience", the attempt
of two or three or more gathered together to make their conscientious scruples effective in action.'[3]

Although many MPs condemned Henderson's dictum, the
conference approved the Standing Orders by 2,117,000 votes
to only 193,000.[4] Both Josiah Wedgwood and Fred Jowett
complained because the new conscience clause did not apply
to promises made to electors, and raised many other complaints
about the Standing Orders. They drew attention to the fact that
126 of the 287 Labour MPs had voted against their party on at
least one occasion in the preceding parliament, and Jowett therefore declared that it was dishonest to sign such regulations. He
said that 'If the policy of relieving Members of responsibility
for their vote as public representatives should finally be accepted

[1] A copy of this form is found in appendix II.
[2] *Labour Party Conference Report (LPCR)*, 1931, p. 176. A
study of the earlier history of these regulations can be
found in R. T. McKenzie, *British Political Parties*, pp.
388 ff, and in R. K. Alderman, 'The Conscience Clause
of the Parliamentary Labour Party'.
[3] Michael Foot, *Aneurin Bevan*, p. 149.
[4] *LPCR*, 1931, p. 176, and see also pp. 33, 93 and 174 ff.

by the Labour Party ... the whole purpose of the system of representative government will have been challenged!'[1]

The imposition of Standing Orders may not have been the chief reason for the split between the ILP and the Labour party, but some ILP Members thought it was.[2] Nineteen ILP candidates refused to sign the Standing Orders and were deprived of Labour party sponsorship, and eventually in 1932 the ILP critics disaffiliated from the Labour party. In the 1935 general election they sponsored seventeen candidates, four of whom were successful. Although the ILP made overtures in 1939 for a union of the two parties, no agreement was established. In 1945 James Maxton, John McGovern, and Campbell Stephen were elected for the ILP. The next year Maxton died and James Carmichael took his place. Shortly afterwards all three ILP MPs joined the Labour party and received the whip. By 29 March 1948 the ILP organization decided to end all electoral activities for a time. This decision was later reversed when four left-wing Labour Members were expelled by the NEC. The ILP offered support to all of them, but they were defeated in the 1950 general election.[3] Such was the fortune of one group which opposed the Standing Orders.

The Co-operative party, another significant group within the Labour movement, was also forced to accept the Standing Orders. In 1939 Co-operative sponsored candidates were allowed to pledge loyalty to the Labour party, but after the Hastings Agreement of 1946 all Co-operative sponsored candidates were required to accept the Standing Orders and Labour party discipline.[4]

The Labour party Standing Orders were revised in 1945,

[1] Fenner Brockway, *Socialism Over Sixty Years: The Life of Jowett of Bradford*, p. 298.
[2] McKenzie, *British Political Parties*, pp. 443–5. Also see Brockway, *Socialism*, pp. 297 ff.
[3] See chapters 3 and 8.
[4] See Barbara Smith and Geoffrey Ostergaard, *Constitutional Relations Between the Labour and Co-operative Parties*.

1952, 1959 and 1961.[1] The 1945 regulations gave the PLP authority to withdraw the whip from MPs for 'things said or done by Members of the Party in the House'.[2] The Liaison Committee was to notify the PLP about persistent rebels, and to report them to the NEC. The rebels then had the right to be heard by both the PLP and the NEC before a decision was taken.[3] MPs were required to consult party leaders before tabling any motion, amendment or prayer. They were not allowed to vote contrary to PLP decisions, but they were allowed to abstain on matters of conscience such as 'religion and temperance'.[4] This was more strict than the 1944 Standing Orders which had permitted abstention 'on any matter' involving conscientious scruples.[5]

The 1945 Standing Orders were suspended for a trial period in 1946, on the initiative of Herbert Morrison who thought that the party was cohesive and had a large enough majority to offset any difficulties.[6] Although there is little doubt that two of the reasons for the suspension were the size of the majority and elation over Labour's tremendous electoral victory, the motive behind the suspension was expressed idealistically at the 1946 Labour conference. The *Report* states that 'the building of a tradition of free discussion, combined with a true spirit of good fellowship, co-operation and comradeship in a great cause is to be preferred to written Standing Orders'.[7]

The suspension was applauded by many political commentators and made light of by some others. J. M. Burns declared

[1] Only very slight changes have occurred since 1961.
[2] *LPCR*, 1946, p. 221. A complete set of the regulations is found in appendix III.
[3] Herbert Morrison, interview. *LPCR*, 1944, p. 221.
[4] *Ibid.*   [5] *LPCR*, 1944, p. 199.
[6] Herbert Morrison reported that he thought the term discipline was too crude and unsympathetic, and that the Standing Orders were suspended in order to encourage freedom of action and expression without 'upsetting the applecart'. Morrison, *Autobiography*, p. 254.
[7] *LPCR*, 1946, p. 57.

it 'was a concession to the idea of debate and dissent noteworthy for a Government holding full power for the first time'.[1] However, the Standing Orders prevented neither debate nor dissent, and although the suspension was a gesture toward individual freedom, it had limited practical effect. There was not an inordinate increase in party rebellion, and Labour leaders retained the power to withdraw the whip in 'extreme cases'.[2] One critic, Ivor Bulmer-Thomas, argued that Labour's Standing Orders were suspended in 1946 because they could not be enforced.[3] This suggestion does not take into account the fact that rebellions have usually resulted in the imposition rather than with withdrawal of Standing Orders. In both 1952 and 1961, the Standing Orders were revived because of considerable party dissension.

While the Standing Orders were suspended the procedure for dealing with rebels was altered. Ordinarily, the PLP withdrew the whip before the NEC took action, but during the suspension the NEC expelled Members first and then the PLP withdrew the whip. When the Standing Orders were in effect, the NEC theoretically did not discuss the cases of rebel MPs until they received a report from the PLP.

The Standing Orders were reinstated in 1952 after a six year suspension. The immediate reason was a backbench revolt on the government's Defence Bill. The PLP decided to abstain on the main motion dealing with British rearmament, and when 57 Labour MPs voted against the bill, it was considered a direct challenge to party leaders.[4] An attempt by some backbench loyalists to have the whip withdrawn from the 57 rebels was defeated, but the leaders' desire for new Standing Orders was accepted by the PLP on 19 March 1952.[5]

[1] J. M. Burns, 'The Parliamentary Labor Party', p. 864.
[2] Morrison, *Government and Parliament*, p. 129.
[3] Ivor Bulmer-Thomas, *The Party System in Great Britain*, p. 128.
[4] See chapter 5 for details of this revolt.
[5] Herbert Morrison said that he did not want the Stand-

The 1952 regulations did not include a religion and temperance clause, and this omission implied that the rules permitting abstention could apply to any issue.[1] Furthermore, there was a note attached to the Standing Orders which stated that 'outside activities of Members in writing or speech which are contrary to the discipline or constitution of the Labour party shall be dealt with by the National Executive'.[2] This provocative statement later played a minor part in the Bevanite controversy.

In 1959 there was continual backbench pressure for suspension of the written regulations. Although the leaders were suspicious, the PLP rescinded the Standing Orders, and substituted a new Code of Conduct.[3] Some Labour backbenchers opposed the Code because they wanted complete freedom, and thought that it might prove more restrictive than the Standing Orders. A small more realistic group asserted that in spite of all the discussion there had been little change. Although the new Code appealed for spontaneous party loyalty it retained the right of the PLP to withdraw the whip and to act in its own self-interest.[4]

The Code was rescinded in 1961 because of a Labour backbench revolt on the Armed Forces Estimates.[5] On 13 December 1961 the PLP accepted a new and more detailed set of Standing Orders.[6] These new regulations stated that Labour Members had to obey PLP decisions. Again Members were allowed to abstain on matters of personal conviction, but were instructed

ing Orders reintroduced, but that he feared disunity in the party. Herbert Morrison, interview, *The Times*, 12 Mar 1952, and 20 Mar 1952, and *Daily Herald*, 12 Mar 1952.
[1] *LPCR*, 1952, p. 201. See appendix III for the complete Standing Orders.   [2] *Daily Telegraph*, 18 Mar 1952.
[3] *The Times*, 23 Nov 1959.   [4] See appendix III.
[5] See chapter 7.
[6] These Standing Orders were neither renewed nor suspended officially when Labour took office in 1964 and 1966. Controversies ensued because of this vagueness and in February 1968 the PLP began to prepare a new code of behaviour.

that this did not '. . . entitle Members to cast votes contrary to a decision of the Party Meeting'.[1] This restriction was aimed at preventing MPs from voting after the PLP ruled in favour of abstention. Moreover, a rule was added which compelled Members to consult officers of the PLP before tabling a motion, amendment, or prayer, and forced them to delay these for 'one sitting day should the officers so request'.[2]

Members were cautioned that poor attendance records in divisions would be considered an abuse of party membership. They were also informed that if party officials had not given approval for the tabling of a motion, amendment, or prayer, this disapproval had to be made known to all MPs from whom the sponsors sought signatures. This was introduced to prevent MPs from obtaining signatures from unsuspecting colleagues for ventures which only appeared to have official approval.[3]

The Standing Orders, which derive their force from the fact that every Labour candidate is required to sign them, have often been criticized on the ground that they cause harsh party discipline. R. H. S. Crossman has said that they transform 'debates on great issues into arid arguments about procedure, as well as hardening disagreement into a conflict between loyalists and critics'.[4] According to this view, the existence of Standing Orders means that any dissension automatically raises the question of how to punish the rebels. However, Labour leaders have usually believed that Standing Orders lessen party rebellion. They have agreed with Attlee, who wrote:

> In fact it [the pledge] is only a recognition of the duty of a member to represent his constituents. A Labour Candidate stands for certain definite principles, and is supported by men

[1] *LPCR*, 1962, p. 85.
[2] There has not been an equivalent rule in the Conservative party.
[3] *LPCR*, 1962, p. 85. The PLP also decided to make public the fact that it kept records of its meetings.
[4] R. H. S. Crossman, 'Socialism and the New Despotism', p. 23. Michael Foot, interview.

and women who have chosen him to represent them and to carry out these principles. They have, therefore, the right to expect that he will faithfully carry them out.[1]

The basic difference between Labour and Conservative parties with regard to formal rules has been that the latter party has neither required candidates to make a pledge of party loyalty nor employed written regulations. Members of the Conservative party have always considered the party to be based on certain hierarchical ideas of authority combined with beliefs about individual freedom and initiative. They have argued that acceptance of these norms negates any need for strict rules and regulations. Individuals ought to decide for themselves what behaviour is proper in any particular situation, and leaders should be free to decide what action or actions are reasonable for members of the party to undertake, given the need for unity in the organization. Rules and regulations prevent the flexibility required to keep a party united and happy. Tories appear to believe that, given proper leadership, cohesion and unity can be maintained even within a party composed of independent actors. Conservatives also stress that the members of their party come from relatively homogeneous backgrounds and this makes for close personal relationships that mitigate against cleavages which would require written norms of behaviour.

The lack of written regulations is in harmony with the general poverty of formal institutions in the Tory party and with the power and authority accorded to their leader. Whereas the Labour party since its inception has had a constitution which prescribed the ideals of the party and the decision-making machinery, the Conservatives have never had such a document. As is well known, the Conservative leader has always been recognized as the supreme rule-maker for the party, and until 1965, there was not even any machinery for selecting him. Ideas like the 'emergence' of the leader belong to a traditional

[1] C. R. Attlee, *The Labour Party in Perspective – And Twelve Years Later*, p. 87.

approach to parties which is outside that suggested by the language of formal rules and regulations.[1]

The absence of written regulations means that Conservative leaders can make more flexible decisions in dealing with problems of party rebellion, and also suggests that the question of punishment does not constantly arise in response to dissension. The following chapters provide considerable data to suggest that the Conservative party has often had less trouble than Labour in managing rebellion. But the information also points out that the Labour party has been very flexible in interpreting its rules and regulations. Flexibility may be provided through lack of specific rules or through interpretation of the rules. However, the attitudes associated with Labour methods seem to be somewhat more rigid than those associated with the Conservative approach to party discipline.

Regardless of the actual behaviour of MPs, they have neither subscribed to the idea that they have relinquished their consciences to their party machines, nor have they allowed their parties to make such claims. Both Labour and Conservative parties have permitted a slight amount of flexibility in parliamentary behaviour when conscientious scruples have been involved. While Labour has had a statement of principle in its written regulations, Tories have believed in certain norms which allowed for a degree of freedom.

Members of the PLP have usually been allowed the right to abstain on issues involving personal conscientious convictions. There has, for example, been a conscience clause in the party's written regulations since 1906. However, this right has to be interpreted by a majority of the PLP, and is not a matter of individual discretion. Leon D. Epstein commented that, 'In practice, extension has been allowed on issues touching the pacifism or the alcoholic temperance of Labour Members.'[2] This conclusion,

[1] See McKenzie's *British Political Parties*, for specific historical details.
[2] Epstein, 'Cohesion of British Parliamentary Parties', p. 367.

which echoed the 1945 Standing Orders, does not seem to be a valid assessment because the decision of the PLP to punish a rebel depends on more circumstances than simply a definition of which acts involve personal convictions and which do not. The decision to punish a rebel is a political one, involving such factors as the size of the rebel group, the publicity that it receives, the importance of the issue to the leaders, the background and rebellious nature of the MPs involved, and the nearness of an election. All of these may be more important in the final decision than the explicit statement in the Standing Orders.

This problem was illustrated during the controversy over the United States' loan in 1945.[1] Many Labour MPs opposed the extent of the loan, and finally Attlee said there would probably not be any disciplinary action because the dissidents felt 'conscientiously bound to vote against the Government'.[2] In fact, Labour leaders were dissatisfied with many of the conditions of the loan and welcomed a show of dissatisfaction.[3] Attlee's misuse of the word conscience to apply to the intensity with which the rebels held their views points both to the problem of definition and to the fact that political leaders have to consider the circumstances in any decision about discipline. Nevertheless, the ideal of allowing Members to abstain on issues affecting personal convictions has remained part of the Labour party's Standing Orders. As Attlee argued after his retirement:

> In the Labour Party there are certain subjects which are held to be matters of conscientious conviction, such as religion, temperance and pacificism, on which latitude has always been allowed – though conscience must not be stretched to cover the unconscientious.[4]

The flaw in the conscience clause is evident. Individuals were not allowed to decide which issues involved moral convictions.

[1] For details see chapter 3.   [2] *The Times*, 13 Dec 1945.
[3] Discussed in chapter 3.
[4] Attlee, 'Party Discipline is Paramount'.

Moreover, the PLP often decided to abstain in divisions, and considered it a breach of the Standing Orders when Members voted. This is analysed more fully in the following chapters, but it should be remembered that until 1961 the Standing Orders did not explicitly prevent Members from voting when the PLP ruled that they were to abstain.[1]

Although the Conservative parliamentary party has never had written regulations, it has always claimed that Conservative MPs are free to obey their conscience on any issue. It has claimed that a Member's loyalty is first to his conscience, second to his constituency, and only last to the national party. This ideal is not often applied in practice. Although leniency is allowed on certain matters of constituency interest, when a Conservative MP rebels in a major crisis he may be rebuked either by the parliamentary party or by his local constituency association.

In the Labour party the existence of Standing Orders means that a minority can disagree in private, but after a vote is taken in the PLP the right to rebel no longer exists. It is similar in the Conservative party. Although there are no Standing Orders, minorities can disagree in private, but after the Tory leader decides on a particular policy the right to rebel no longer exists. The significant problem in the Labour party is based on a classic argument about democracy. Should the party have limited or unlimited majority rule?[2] If limited majority rule is accepted then there would be some political issues which would not be controlled by the PLP, and on these issues Members would be free to follow their conscience. However, in the Labour party the idea of unlimited majority rule has always been accepted. The individual MP has never been allowed to follow

[1] Cf. Sydney Silverman, 'Standing Orders and Democracy'.
[2] For more detailed arguments on these two theories of democracy see Ranney and Kendall, *Democracy and the American Party System*, and Henry B. Mayo, *An Introduction to Democratic Theory*.

his conscience on a set of issues except possibly on matters concerning religion and temperance. Labour rebels have always argued for the individual rights of MPs, but they have never been able to convince a majority of their colleagues to accept this viewpoint. In the Conservative party majority rule on policy decisions is not generally thought to exist at all.[1]

The right to withdraw the whip from Conservative MPs is controlled by the party leader. No formal regulations exist, and decisions are made on an *ad hoc* basis. Of course, the leader does not have to report his decision to any higher institution. On the other hand, if a Labour MP is to have the whip withdrawn he has the right to be heard by both the Parliamentary Committee of the PLP (or the Liaison Committee), and the PLP meeting. The decision to withdraw the whip requires a majority vote of the PLP. If the whip is withdrawn the NEC must be informed, and it may take further action. The party constitution states that the NEC shall:

> . . . enforce the Constitution, Standing Orders, and the Rules of the Party and . . . take any action it deems necessary for such purpose, whether by way of disaffiliation of an organization or expulsion of an individual, or otherwise. Any such action shall be reported to the next Annual Conference of the Party.[2]

Of course, the formal rules do not determine everything about party discipline. Conclusions based on party constitutions often produce formal and sometimes misleading accounts of what is in fact a subtle and dynamic process. When the history of party rebellions is examined in the following chapters, the parties' positions become more clear.

[1] Now that the Conservative party has adopted a set of rules for electing their party leader, this principle may be slowly eroded.
[2] *LPCR*, 1945, p. 155.

THE WHIPS' OFFICE

The Whips' Offices are vital links in the parliamentary organizations of both parties. The Whips date from the eighteenth century and since then the efficient running of the Westminster machine has depended largely upon them. Whips act as a channel for information flowing from party leaders to backbenchers, and also collect information about backbench opinions which may be of value to party leaders. The organization of the Whips' Office is therefore significant for a study of party discipline.[1]

Each party has a Chief Whip, Deputy Chief Whip, and several junior Whips. In the Labour party the Chief Whip is elected annually by the PLP, and he appoints the junior Whips, but the Conservative Whips' Office submits a list of proposed new Whips to the leader and he makes the official decision. Technically the government Chief Whip is both Patronage Secretary and Parliamentary Secretary to the Treasury. In the former capacity he is in charge of awarding honours, and in the latter, he works in conjunction with the Leader of the House to arrange House of Commons Business, keeps the leaders aware of backbench opinion, and bears responsibility for his party's attendance and voting in the House.[2] The opposition Chief Whip

[1] The author has been aided in writing this section by extended interviews with many former Whips and MPs, including Herbert Morrison, Sir Charles Harris (Private Secretary to the government Chief Whip 1919–61), A. H. Warren (Private Secretary to the government Chief Whip 1961–), Anthony Fletcher (Private Secretary to the Conservative Chief Whip 1964–66), Frank Barlow (Secretary to the PLP 1959–), Patrick Buchan-Hepburn (Conservative Chief Whip 1948–55), Martin Redmayne (Conservative Chief Whip 1959–64), Edward Short (Labour Chief Whip 1964–66), John Silkin (Labour Chief Whip 1966–), William Whitelaw (Conservative Chief Whip 1964–), and twenty Assistant Whips.

[2] Norman Hunt's interview with Martin Redmayne

performs many of the same functions as his government counterpart, and since 1964 has joined the Leader of the Opposition in receiving a salary. The Chief Whips of the various parties constitute what is called the 'usual channels', through which business and other matters are discussed, and are, therefore, very important for a smooth-running parliament.

The Chief Whips hold the most 'political' of all jobs outside the Leader of the Opposition and the Prime Minister. They maintain important informal contacts with the party outside parliament, and they always have close connections with the party chairman in the Conservative party, and with the party leader in the Labour party. In government, the Chief Whip is usually the Prime Minister's closest adviser. The Chief Whips also act as communication links between the broadcasting authorities and their parties. The leader of the Conservative party decides what party committees will be attended by the Chief Whip, but in the Labour party the Chief Whip may go to all meetings of the NEC and the Organization Sub-Committee of the NEC. Although the Labour Chief Whip may not vote at these meetings, he makes his opinions known on all questions and, in particular, with reference to discipline and the approval of individuals to be allowed on the official candidates list.[1]

The government Chief Whip's position is further enhanced because although he is not a member of the Cabinet he has regularly attended its meetings since approximately 1956.[2] In

in *The Listener* evaluated the Chief Whip's position in regard to these various functions.

[1] See chapter 10.

[2] No constitutional convention has yet developed on this point, and any Prime Minister could easily stop the practice. The role of the Chief Whip in the Conservative party may be increasing. Lord Windlesham concluded a study of the Conservative party by reporting that, 'Indeed from May, 1964, until the Election Mr. Redmayne stands out as one of the central figures in the communication of Conservative policy 1963–4,' 'The Communication of Conservative Policy 1963–64', p. 174.

the Conservative party, the Chief Whip does not speak at Cabinet meetings unless he is asked to present his views on the political implications of a policy. The Labour Chief Whip may have been allowed more initiative in Cabinet debates. He certainly has been accorded the right to attend and state his opinions at all meetings, and has cast his vote whenever the Cabinet decided an issue by a show of hands.

The Deputy Chief Whip aids the Chief Whip by replacing him at party meetings and directing much of the daily routine of the Whips' Office. He is solely responsible for delegating Whips to attend the House of Commons' standing committees. The other Whips work directly for the Deputy Chief Whip. In 1963, for example, there were thirteen Assistant Whips in the Conservative party. Seven of them held office as Lord Commissioners of the Treasury and three as officers of the Royal Household. The remainder of the government Whips and all of the opposition Assistant Whips were unpaid, but the relative stability of personnel in the Whips' Office meant that unpaid Whips could expect steady advancement up the Whips' promotion ladder.[1] However, the Ministerial Salaries Act changed the law regarding the payment of government Whips and since 1965 all of them, including the Assistant Whips who hold no particular office, have been paid.[2] In 1966 the Labour government employed fifteen Whips and the Conservative opposition had ten.

Although no one apparently solicits for an appointment to the Whips' Office, most of those chosen do seem to like their work. They believe that besides being paid as junior ministers, they have an excellent position for learning the procedure of the

[1] There may have been too much stability in the Labour party because for many years after the Second World War it was almost impossible for a Whip to be promoted to a position outside the Whips' Office. Michael Stewart was a rare exception.

[2] Ministerial Salaries Act, 1965, consolidated into the Ministerial Salaries (Consolidation) Act, 1965.

D

House of Commons, and that they acquire special relationships with other MPs. Their greatest satisfaction seems to come from being at what they describe as 'the nerve-centre' of the party where it can be seen that a party works on 'agreement and disagreement'. One Chief Whip declared romantically, 'Whips feel brushed by the winds of history. Our views on policy are often carried out and we feel that we are playing a significant part in communicating views.' There are, of course, some complaints. Most Whips feel that the major disadvantages are in their loss of freedom to speak on constituency problems and in always having to be on duty in the House. The latter can become very dreary and a Whip said that eventually you feel like all you have to do is 'nod your head, shout aye or nay, and make sure you touch the right piece of paper'. The most bitter criticism however came from a former Chief Whip who insisted that: 'It is a thankless job. You have to be able to play the job dirty and clean. The Chief Whip has to be very tough and the rewards are very few.'

Each Whips' Office has a small detachment of professional assistants. The government Whips' Office has rooms both inside the House of Commons and at 12 Downing Street. It is staffed by four civil servants called office assistants, who are directed by a Private Secretary, and each party brings its own small retinue of party workers to the office when it is elected.[1] The Private Secretary and his staff retain their position regardless of which party is in power, a practice which began in 1939 with the approval of Neville Chamberlain, C. R. Attlee, and Sir A. Sinclair. All government office assistants, including the party workers, are paid by the Treasury. When the party in power is defeated the civil servants remain in the new government Chief Whips' Office, and the party workers depart. The opposition Whips' Office is established in the House of Commons, and is staffed by paid party workers. The Labour Whips' Office differs from that of the Conservative party by having an

---

[1] The 1959 Conservative government had four party workers, and the 1964 Labour government had three.

additional party official act as secretary to the PLP in both opposition and government.[1]

Every Friday backbenchers are sent a confidential documentary whip to inform them which divisions their party considers important and which require attendance. Each statement is underscored with one, two, or three lines according to the importance of the division. One-line whips usually mean that there will not be a division and are common on Fridays, two-line whips oblige Members to attend the House but allow them to pair, and three-line whips call for compulsory attendance at important divisions. Two-line whips are more flexible than those with three lines, and have been used to avoid public revolts on contentious issues. Two-line whips allow Members who are critical of party policy to pair and quietly abstain. The wording on the whip only summons Members to attend the House, but it has much more significance. The whip actually calls Members to vote with their party or be known as rebels and perhaps be punished.[2]

If Members are out of the country when a three-line whip is issued there is a general understanding that they must return at their own expense if it is necessary. Sometimes it is possible for special transportation arrangements to be made; for example, the Whips' Office can occasionally get Members on service flights. There have also been a few exceptional circumstances when Members were given financial assistance to return for a division. In one very exceptional case, a Conservative Prime Minister ordered a liner to stop in the ocean to allow a backbencher to board another ship heading for England. Although this proved very costly for the passenger ship, the MP arrived back in London in time to add to the government's majority in the division lobbies.

[1] He is responsible to the chairman of the PLP. Carol Johnson held this position from 1943–59, and he was replaced by Frank Barlow.
[2] See chapter 7 for a study of recent discussions about the meaning of whips.

SECRET

ON MONDAY, 5th April, 1965, the House will meet at 2.30 p.m.

Rent Bill: 2nd Reading and Committee stage of the Money Resolution.
(Money Resolution – EXEMPTED BUSINESS for 45 minutes)

A Division will take place and your attendance is essential.

Industrial and Provident Societies Bill (Lords): 2nd Reading.
(Consolidation Measure)

Consideration of the Motion on the South East Asia Treaty Organisation (Immunities and Privileges) Order.
(EXEMPTED BUSINESS)

Opposition Prayer to annul the Ministers of the Crown Order (S.I. 1965, No. 319). (EXEMPTED BUSINESS)

Divisions may take place and your attendance until the Business is concluded is essential, unless you have registered a firm pair.

Note A Motion to Suspend the Ten O'Clock Rule for the Industrial and Provident Societies Bill (Lords) will be moved at 10 p.m.

ON TUESDAY, 6th April, the House will meet at 2.30 p.m.

The Chancellor of the Exchequer will open his Budget.

Your attendance is essential until the Budget Resolutions have been passed.

EDWARD SHORT
(LABOUR WHIP)
1965

<u>ON WEDNESDAY</u>, 2nd August, the House will meet at 2.30 p.m.

If necessary, a Motion to Suspend the Ten O'Clock Rule for the Licensing Bill will be moved at 10 p.m.

A Debate will take place on a Government Motion relating to the Common Market. (1st Day)

A good attendance throughout the Debate is particularly requested.

Licensing Bill: Further consideration of Lords Amendments
(if not completed).

Divisions will take place and your attendance at 10 p.m. prompt and until the Business is concluded is particularly requested, unless you have obtained a pair.

<u>ON THURSDAY</u>, 3rd August, the House will meet at 2.30 p.m.

Conclusion of the Debate on the Common Market.

A most important Division will take place and your attendance at 9.30 p.m. is essential.

<u>ON FRIDAY</u>, 4th August, the House will meet at 11 a.m.

Adjournment for the Summer Recess.

Your attendance is requested

MARTIN REDMAYNE
(CONSERVATIVE WHIP)
1961

The Assistant Whips are each responsible for a number of MPs from a certain geographical district, and make systematic contact with them, carrying their opinions to the Chief Whip and vice-versa.[1] The collection of information about back-benchers is more formally organized in the Conservative than in the Labour party. Each Conservative Whip is delegated to a different backbench committee, and makes a written report to the Chief Whip on the various criticisms of party policy which occur, especially noting any members who might be rebellious. Moreover, the Tory Whips are responsible to the Chief Whip for any private information they hear in the House. They report this information on a form actually entitled 'Dirts'. One such 'Dirt' shown to the author told of a Tory Member who, while drunk in the Members' Bar, said that the Tory Prime Minister was a 'bloody fool'. These written reports are filed in the Chief Whip's office.

Labour Whips do not attend backbench committees as representatives of the Whips' Office. As one Whip declared: 'We thought about sending Whips to our backbench groups but decided not to. We thought they might be called snoopers.' Special clerks report the proceedings of Labour backbench committees to the secretary of the PLP. Informal soundings by Labour Whips are reported verbally to the Chief Whip, and are undoubtedly as significant as the Conservatives' written reports. Moreover, the Labour Chief Whip gets the minutes of all group meetings so there may be no need to have Whips in attendance.

Since 1964, each Whips' Office has had a Pairing Whip who keeps detailed records of which MPs are paired and which intend to be absent at each division, along with the reasons for their absence. After each division the Pairing Whip and the office assistants analyse how their MPs voted, and whether or not anyone abstained without giving a reason. These records,

[1] The PPSs sometimes perform a role much like that of the Whips, and they often report certain information to the Chief Whip.

which are kept secret, contain detailed information about what each MP did in every division. Both Whips' Offices also scrutinize the national newspapers closely for reports of Members' behaviour and for MPs' letters to editors.

Thus there are four significant methods of collecting information about Members; committee reports, informal soundings, the national press, and division records.[1] The information is kept in the Whips' Office, but except in the case of persistent rebels it is not customary to file the information under the names of individual MPs. However, detailed reports are kept about Members' attitudes to specific contentious issues, and at one time in the Conservative party these papers were filed under the title 'Difficult Customers'. For example, a survey of party attitudes in the Conservative parliamentary party was taken before Alec Douglas-Home was made Foreign Secretary. These records are often kept by Chief Whips when they leave office. Incidentally, after a Conservative Prime Minister retires, some of his strictly party correspondence is often filed in the Whips' Office.

The Whips have a regular weekly meeting and a shorter gathering every day to discuss Members' division records, potential rebellions, and what action should be taken in each case. After some divisions Chief Whips inform the press how their party voted, but they do not feel compelled to provide reasons for the Members who abstained.[2] Sometimes the Whips' Office gives more detailed information to particular journalists who they know will present the facts in a favourable light.

Whips help MPs to find pairs, but extremely troublesome MPs are not treated as well as other Members in this respect.

[1] The central offices of both parties also have newspaper clipping services for the use of party officials and research workers. Records of MPs who have caused trouble for the party are kept by the NEC. In recent years the NEC has retained less detailed records of Members because they almost had to show their files over a libel action.
[2] Interview.

Unpaired absenteeism is very much discouraged, but Whips realize that it is sometimes necessary.[1] The Conservative Whips' Office introduced a novel procedure in the 1959 parliament. They empowered Assistant Whips to allow a certain number of unpaired absences called 'bisques' for each division, and encouraged their use as a device for rewarding party loyalty. When all the 'bisques' were given for a division, the Conservative majority naturally fell proportionately. It was a very temporary arrangement because individual Whips lost this power in the second half of the 1959 parliament when Conservative rebelliousness increased.

Although the two parties have different approaches to the question of formal regulations, their parliamentary organizations for maintaining party discipline are very similar. They each have highly organized and extensive methods of sounding out backbench opinion, and this communication is very important in helping leaders to accommodate the various views in the party in order to maintain cohesion. The following chapters examine how successful each party was in coping with internal dissension from 1945 to 1964.

[1] If a Member is going abroad he must inform the Whips' Office.

Part II

Part II outlines the history of party rebellions from 1945 to 1964. It demonstrates that the Labour party had more revolts than the Conservatives after the Second World War, but that this trend was reversed after the 1955 general election.

Although both parties were extremely cohesive in the division lobbies, more revolts took place than are usually acknowledged, and only on the rarest occasions were sanctions imposed on recalcitrant MPs. It is insufficient to assert that penalties are imposed on Members when they disobey their party Whips because contrary examples can be cited for every case. Moreover, an analysis of party revolts is easily distorted by concentrating on a specific set of rebellions such as the Bevanite controversy, or by focusing on a particular style of rebellion such as floor revolts or Early Day Motions. Members have publicly revolted against their parties in various ways, and it is important to consider all of these.

Each chapter in Part II studies party revolts in a particular parliament, and discusses special factors such as collective responsibility and the size of the majority. This parliament by parliament approach is necessary because there was a significant change in the membership of the House after each election, and because the issues varied in each parliament. The chapters relate the rebelliousness of Members to such factors as sponsorship, education, and their year of first entry to the House. Chapter 8, the concluding chapter in Part II, analyses the pattern of revolts for all the years from 1945 to 1964, and draws general conclusions from the statistics. The evidence produced is used in the first half of Part III (chapters 9, 10) to examine the history of MPs who were disciplined for rebellion or rewarded for loyalty.

45

3 Rebellions and Party Discipline 1945-1950

Neither the Tory Party nor the Liberal Party has a discipline so rigid as that of the Labour Party; and it is difficult not to feel that, when the Labour Party is in office, it would benefit a great deal were it to make the practice of toleration as real as it seeks to persuade the public to believe it is.[1]

The 1945 election gave the Labour party an overwhelming victory, indicating that the government could not seriously be threatened by minor party rebellions. The Conservative defeat on the other hand was so decisive that some pundits predicted that backbench dissension would arise within the opposition. Paradoxically in the 1945 parliament there were extremely few public revolts in the Conservative party and more than three dozen incidents in the Labour party.[2]

The massive Labour majority of 146 was an underlying cause of the large number of intra-party revolts. William Whiteley, Labour Chief Whip 1942–55, had very little trouble handling domestic legislation since most Labour rebellions took place in the field of foreign affairs. The few domestic policy disagreements tended to be restricted to activity in the House of Commons. They occurred over such issues as old age pensions, civil aviation, inflationary pressures, and the nationalization of iron and steel. Their relative insignificance is shown by the fact that in each case the disagreement was not sustained; it was generally expressed only once and then dropped.

[1] Harold J. Laski, *Reflections on the Constitution*, p. 89.
[2] This distinction was also found in the 1950 election addresses. H. G. Nicholas records that there were fewer differences of opinion among Conservatives than among Labour candidates. *The British General Election of 1950*, p. 221.

46

External affairs problems and military issues dominated Labour's dissension. The break-up of the wartime alliance, the new conflict between Russia and NATO, and the increasing reliance of Britain on the United States all contributed to back-bench dissatisfaction with Bevin and Labour foreign policy. This dissension was focused mainly on three major issues which often overlapped. The first was promoted by those Members of the PLP who wanted Britain to lead a third force between the United States and Russia. The second was concerned with the continuation of conscription in peacetime, which had always been an anathema to many Members of the Labour party. The third resulted from some backbenchers' anger at the Labour government's suspicion of communist intentions in Europe. A great deal of the backbench Labour dissatisfaction, particularly in the first and third of these issues, was expressed in the form of telegrams, letters, and other actions outside the House of Commons.

Labour Members also disagreed over Britain's policy in Palestine and Ireland. In both of these cases however Labour criticisms were mainly confined to expression within the House, in speeches and divisions. This was in contrast to the vigorous activity outside parliament on the other foreign policy issues.

Both domestic and foreign policy revolts were very large in size. There was an average of over 30 Members involved in every expression of dissatisfaction. Jean Mann may be correct that when the new MPs arrived in parliament in 1945 they were told to do '. . . exactly nothing! "Keep mum, and let the Bills go through" ',[1] but this advice was not followed. There were at least 39 different incidents when factions within the PLP publicly expressed dissatisfaction with government policy.

Throughout the parliament the Conservative party appeared extremely united. Some general reasons can be suggested for their high degree of cohesion. Although the Conservative parliamentary party was reduced to only 213 MPs, the leadership

[1] Jean Mann, *Woman in Parliament*, p. 13.

was not a source of controversy. Churchill had no strong rival, probably because his wartime greatness was much appreciated and many Conservative MPs felt indebted to his popular appeal. In consequence, Conservative policy was often simply expressed as – follow the lead of Churchill.[1] As Leon D. Epstein remarked, 'Although the disagreements of prewar years had left anti-Churchill resentments among the still devoted friends of Baldwin and Chamberlain, there was hardly any Conservative disposition openly to question Churchill's postwar reputation for sagacity and knowledge in world affairs. It was hard, at any rate, to challenge greatness.'[2]

The Conservative party had the advantage of not needing to present a coherent policy which could be applied to day-to-day administration. Churchill more than once said that he would not commit the Conservatives to a definite policy until they held office and could examine the detailed reports of the civil service. Conservatives were unified mainly by their dislike of socialism, and every Tory MP could respond to a call made by their Chief Whip which was based on that principle.[3]

Conservative leaders were in general agreement with the Labour government about foreign policy, and although this greatly increased factional dispute in the Labour party, it decreased it among Conservatives. The only controversies in the Tory party were minor ones over the lack of a concerted attack on Labour policy, and over the Charters which expounded new Conservative policies. Only on the question of Burmese Independence did any Conservative MPs cross-vote in outright defiance of their party leaders.

[1] *Conservative Party Conference Report (CPCR)*, 1947, p. 38.

[2] Leon Epstein, *Britain – Uneasy Ally*, p. 174.

[3] James Stuart was Chief Whip 1941–48 and then Patrick Buchan-Hepburn held the position until 1955. In 1949 when accepting the *Right Road for Britain*, Churchill said characteristically: 'I have advised you consistently during these last four years not to commit yourselves to detailed rigid programmes...', *CPCR*, 1949, p. 118.

THE LABOUR PARTY

Table 1 : Labour Revolts 1945–50

	Number of Revolts	Main Issues
Domestic	8	Bretton Woods Civil Aviation Incomes, Costs and Prices Old Age Pensions United States Loan
Foreign Affairs and Defence	31	Atlantic Pact Conscription Criticism of British Foreign Policy Ireland Bill Keep Left and Keeping Left Palestine Socialism in Europe

The 1945 parliament opened with a series of minor rifts in the Labour party over domestic issues. The majority of these were a result, mainly, of the critical financial situation which Britain faced in the immediate postwar years and the rising inflation which accompanied her attempts to adjust to economic realities half way through the parliament. The party's Standing Orders were in effect at the time of the first three demonstrations, but then they were suspended, and in spite of threats to re-establish them during the ensuing rebellions, they were not reimposed during the remainder of the parliament.

The first of these backbench demonstrations occurred on 16 October 1945, only a few weeks after the election, when 169 Labour MPs signed an Early Day Motion criticizing James Griffiths' statements on old age pensions.[1] The motion called

[1] Early Day Motions are hereafter referred to as EDMs.

for more consideration of the 'hardship and privation' of old age pensioners, and asked for an increase in their weekly income.[1] The EDM indicated that many Labour backbenchers were concerned that the Labour government would not act quickly to cure social problems. This rebel group included even the most loyal government supporters, some of whom became ministers before 1950. The government told them privately that it hoped to meet their demands by the next year, and that food subsidies would help to alleviate the problem in the meantime.[2] Subsequently, there were no rebellions in the division lobbies on this issue, and there was no mention of party discipline.

The adverse financial situation, which had caused the government's tardiness over old age pensions, produced another revolt in December. The termination of Lend-Lease forced the Labour government to solicit a loan of £4,400,000,000 from the United States. This loan provoked considerable criticism, and resulted in both parties splitting when the bill was introduced in the House of Commons on 13 December 1945. Labour party opposition to the loan was instigated by the strange combination of R. R. Stokes, Norman Smith, and Michael Foot, who put forward the following amendment:

> That this House refuses its assent to a Bill which, irrespective of whether or not the American Congress approves a dollar credit for this country, commits Great Britain to an international monetary system likely to frustrate the effective planning of British industry and trade.[3]

After a PLP meeting, the Prime Minister said there was a small group of Labour MPs who opposed the bill with an 'almost religious fervour'.[4] Attlee asserted however that party

[1] *Notices of Motions*, 16 Oct 1945. The EDM called for the weekly income to be raised for single persons by 7/6d., and for married couples by 12/6d.
[2] *Manchester Guardian*, 24 Oct 1945, and 26 Oct 1945.
[3] *The Times*, 11 Dec 1945. This was the most critical amendment, cf. 417 *H.C. Deb.*, col. 641 ff.
[4] *The Times*, 13 Dec 1945, and *Tribune*, 5 Dec 1947.

discipline would not be enforced because the dissidents felt 'conscientiously bound to vote against the government'.[1] Moreover, some Labour leaders hoped that a small rebellion would show the United States that many people were dissatisfied with the terms of the loan. One of the dissidents, Raymond Blackburn, later wrote that 'Hugh Dalton was not particularly satisfied with the result of his negotiations and even told me privately that a few votes in protest against the bill could do no harm and might do some good'.[2] And Stanley Evans claimed that Herbert Morrison told him that a few cross-votes might actually help the government.[3]

The Speaker decided that there would be a straight vote on the bill, so no amendments were called. The bill passed easily but 23 Labour MPs voted against it and approximately 44 abstained, even though a three-line whip had been issued.[4] The government then set about to repay this loan over a period of 50 years, with the burden of the payments destined to be heaviest in the early years of postwar recovery.

One of the conditions of the loan was that Britain had to ratify the agreements made at Bretton Woods, U.S.A. in July 1944 for the creation of an International Monetary Fund and an International Bank for Reconstruction and Development. Although there was some backbench dislike of this condition being tied to the loan, the Bretton Woods Agreement Bill still received much less opposition than the loan itself. The government obtained a vote of 314 to 50; but four Labour MPs (who had also opposed the loan), Victor Collins, Stanley Evans, Michael Foot, and R. R. Stokes voted with the opposition.[5]

Both of these revolts contained Members from the left and

---

[1] *The Times*, 13 Dec 1947.
[2] Raymond Blackburn, *I Am an Alcoholic*, p. 65.
[3] Stanley Evans, interview.
[4] The number of cross-votes in this study always includes the rebel tellers.
[5] 417 *H.C. Deb.*, col. 745.

right wings of the party.[1] James Callaghan relinquished his position as PPS to John Parker (Under-Secretary for the Dominions) because he voted against the government over the loan, but Barbara Castle did not lose her position as PPS to Stafford Cripps although she had joined the same revolt.[2] The remainder of the Labour rebels were not punished, even though the 1945 Standing Orders were still in effect and remained so until January 1946. This illustrates that the Standing Orders were not automatically imposed in every instance, and subsequent chapters also suggest that the suspension of the Standing Orders had little effect on party discipline.

The first time Labour MPs cross-voted after the suspension of the Standing Orders was in August 1946 over the nationalization of civil aviation. There were cross-votes on three occasions during the committee stages; the most critical of these concerned Ian Mikardo's amendment which opposed the appointment of part-time directors.[3] Some of the trouble was due to backbench dissatisfaction with Lord Winster, Minister of Civil Aviation, and Ivor Bulmer-Thomas, his Parliamentary Secretary. Altogether, 43 different Labour MPs voted against the government in the three divisions, but no sanctions were imposed. The Civil Aviation Bill became law, but the rebels achieved partial success when within two months Lord Winster was removed and Bulmer-Thomas was transferred to another ministry.

The only other revolt over nationalization came during the Iron and Steel Bill in April 1948.[4] Government ownership of

[1] Only one of the rebels, David Grenfell, was sponsored by a trade-union.
[2] *The Times*, 18 Dec 1945.
[3] For more details see 426 *H.C. Deb.*, col. 713 ff.
[4] There were no rebellions over the nationalization of the Bank of England, Cable and Wireless, Coal Industry, Electricity, Transport, or Gas. There was a minor dispute over the Control of Engagement Order, which provided for the direction of labour to essential industries. On the Second Reading, Raymond Blackburn voted against the

Iron and Steel had been proposed by the Labour party for decades and very little dissent was expected from within the party over this primarily ideological issue. However, two right-wing Members, Alfred Edwards and Ivor Bulmer-Thomas violently opposed the bill. They spoke against nationalization to such a degree that they aroused the anger of the whole Labour parliamentary party. One of the critics, Alfred Edwards, was expelled from the party by the NEC in May 1948 and shortly afterwards Bulmer-Thomas resigned the Labour whip. Both of them later accepted the Conservative whip and stayed in parliament until dissolution. The histories of these two Members and the sanctions imposed on them are discussed in detail in chapter 9.

By early 1948 the programme of the Labour government was experiencing serious restrictions because of inflationary pressures. The government was forced to attempt to curb the steady increase of wage demands in order to keep the prices of exports at a bargaining position with the rest of the world. This policy was certain to cause consternation in Labour ranks, and in February 1948 sixty MPs sent Attlee a letter which advocated that if there was to be a policy of restraint on wage claims there should also be a limitation on profits. Following this, on 11 February, Ellis Smith tabled a motion signed by 21 Labour MPs calling on the government '. . . to withdraw the White Paper which is the subject of the debate' because they did not think it provided the most effective methods for handling their economic problems.[1] Before the debate in the House Arthur Deakin met Members of the T & GWU parliamentary group, and advised them not to rock the boat or take precipitate action in view of the current discussions between the TUC and the

bill, and the final vote was opposed by Raymond Blackburn, Rhys Davies, S. O. Davies, Alfred Edwards, and David Grenfell. See 441 *H.C. Deb.*, col. 1885.

[1] *The Times*, 12 Feb 1948. Also see B. C. Roberts, *Trade Union Government and Administration in Great Britain*, pp. 438–9.

government.[1] The rebel threat appeared ominous because W. Dobbie, chairman of the trade-union group, had signed the motion, but the crisis soon subsided when minor compromises were made and Dobbie withdrew his name. The other critics followed Dobbie's lead and the issue was not raised again.

Throughout this parliament Ernest Bevin, the Foreign Secretary, faced continual criticism of his handling of foreign affairs. A large number of backbenchers wanted Britain to help form a third bloc between Russia and the United States. Their ranks were bolstered by the addition of MPs who disliked the economic system of the United States and by pacifists who thought a third force would help to prevent another world conflict. In spite of this opposition Bevin steadfastly aligned Britain with the United States in forming a North Atlantic Treaty Organization in order to counteract Russia's power in Eastern Europe. Prime Minister Attlee backed Bevin's stand that communist aggrandizement in such countries as Poland, Hungary, Czechoslovakia, Yugoslavia, and Eastern Germany should not be allowed to take place in Western Europe.

The first sign of party dissension occurred on 16 October 1946 when a letter, marked 'not for publication', was sent to Attlee by 21 MPs. It called on the government to abandon its misguided foreign policy and to initiate socialist principles in international affairs.[2] This was the beginning of the dispute with Bevin, which was to last until his death in 1951. The backbenchers criticized Bevin's handling of foreign affairs, especially his desire that Britain should remain closely allied with the United States. Even some members of the Cabinet thought Bevin was out of touch with parliamentary opinion. The private letter was published and the criticism exposed. Hugh Dalton in *High Tide and After* complained that:

[1] Martin Harrison, *Trade Unions and the Labour Party since 1945*, p. 296.
[2] Published in *Manchester Guardian*, 16 Nov 1946. For criticism of this letter see F. A. Voigt, 'Twenty-one "Rebels" and a Letter'.

... the thing has been mishandled by the rebels. They have laid themselves open to the charge of not having gone through the proper channels. They had asked to see the Prime Minister, sending him an argumentative letter. He had replied that they should first see Hector McNeil, Bevin's Under Secretary, but that if, after that, they still wanted to see him, he would see them. They had not seen McNeil, but instead had given a copy of their letter to the P.M. to the Press.[1]

Finally, the rebels were told that there would be no changes in foreign policy, and as a result 57 Labour backbenchers tabled an amendment to the Debate on the Address. Again the rebels proposed that Britain should mediate between Russia and the United States, and not be allied with either of them. Before the debate on the amendment the PLP met and strictures were made against the MPs who had signed the amendment. It was 'recommended' by 126–32 that they should withdraw their names.[2] This proposal was reinforced by Herbert Morrison, Leader of the House of Commons, who declared that although the Standing Orders had been suspended, 'Power rests with the Government to recommend the withdrawal of the party from individuals in any event.'[3] What then did the suspension of Standing Orders mean? Morrison also hinted that the leaders could recommend that the NEC take action against the rebels. However, no such recommendation was made, and a motion to that effect was defeated by 126 votes to 38 in the PLP.[4]

The rebels continued with their plans. R. H. S. Crossman moved the amendment and Joe Reeves, a Co-op member of the NEC, seconded it. The amendment asserted that the 57 Labour MPs:

... express the urgent hope that His Majesty's Government will so review and recast its conduct of International Affairs as to afford the utmost encouragement to, and collaboration with,

[1] Hugh Dalton, *High Tide and After, Memoirs 1945–1960*, p. 168.
[2] *Manchester Guardian*, 14 Nov 1946.
[3] *Ibid.*   [4] *News Chronicle*, 14 Nov 1946.

all Nations and Groups striving to secure full Socialist planning and control of the world's resources and thus provide a democratic and constructive Socialist alternative to an otherwise inevitable conflict between American Capitalism and Soviet Communism in which all hope of World Government would be destroyed.[1]

In the debate the critics were somewhat hostile to the United States, but few of them appeared to be Russophiles. Crossman indicated that the rebels would not force the amendment to a division, but a vote was called when John McGovern (ILP) and Campbell Stephen (ILP) acted as tellers.[2] No Labour Members voted for the amendment, and since the Conservatives voted with the government the vote was 0–353, but approximately 70 Labour MPs abstained. The rebels obtained considerable publicity for their opinions, and no sanctions were employed against them. Five PPSs signed the amendment, and at least four of them, Barbara Castle, J. P. W. Mallalieu, John Haire, and George Wigg were among the group who abstained ostentatiously. None of them lost their positions.[3] Since it has always been understood that the division following the King's Speech should command the full support of the government party, inaction against the rebels, especially the PPSs, was strange. But, as one member of the Cabinet explained, '... a hundred is too many to be disciplined and, after the usual excitement and long discussion in National Executive and Party Meeting, it was decided to do nothing, save express regret.'[4] The fact that none of the rebels voted for the amendment must have given the leaders some satisfaction, and it also

[1] 430 *H.C. Deb.*, col. 526; and see col. 591.
[2] John McGovern and Campbell Stephen were elected as ILP members, but both joined the Labour party in 1947.
[3] *Manchester Guardian*, 14 Nov 1946. A new addition to the ranks of the rebellious was Geoffrey Bing, who had resigned his post as a junior Whip only the preceding week.
[4] Dalton, *High Tide and After*, p. 168.

showed that this party rebellion was not intended to overthrow the government.

It was rumoured that the 57 Labour rebels would act as a bloc if any of them were singled out for punishment.[1] Whether or not the press had evidence for such a statement, the announcement must have had a dampening effect on those who wanted to single out the leaders of the recalcitrants for punishment. Some of the 57 MPs were asked by their constituencies to explain their rebellious action. For example, the Coventry Labour party asked R. H. S. Crossman and Maurice Edelman 'to explain at a conference . . . their action in signing the anti-Government foreign policy amendment'.[2] However, no disciplinary action was taken by the PLP, NEC, or constituency parties.

A week later the leaders attacked the rebels during a PLP meeting. Some loyalists had been arguing for new penalties to enforce party discipline, and 44 Labour MPs, largely union sponsored Members, signed a resolution calling for a renewal of the Standing Orders. After R. H. S. Crossman admitted frankly that the rebels' choice of methods had been wrong, the resolution to renew the Standing Orders was withdrawn.[3] However, a letter from the NEC declared that there was to be no repetition of the rebellion because it would have disastrous electoral consequences. Herbert Morrison also reminded Members that all of them required NEC endorsement to stand as Labour candidates in the next election.[4] This illustrates the constitutional control held over Labour MPs by the PLP and the NEC. Even though the Standing Orders were suspended the NEC still controlled the endorsement of candidates.[5]

Parliamentary revolts may either reflect dissension which is already prevalent in the mass party or cause new splits within it. This 1946 controversy over foreign policy provoked considerable trouble among the constituency parties. The Spel-

[1] *News Chronicle*, 5 Dec 1946.
[2] *Daily Herald*, 19 Nov 1946.   [3] *Observer*, 24 Nov. 1946.
[4] *Daily Herald*, 29 Nov. 1946.   [5] See chapter 10.

thorne Labour party, for example, sent a circular to all local parties calling for a change of government policy. The NEC countered this with a letter from Morgan Phillips, and Cabinet ministers visited particular constituencies to convince local members of the correctness of their policy.[1]

Pacifist feelings have been present in the Labour party since its birth, and at times they have been mentioned specifically in the conscience clause in the party's Standing Orders. Throughout its history, the Labour party has found it necessary to accommodate individuals who rebel on issues concerning military affairs.

Labour revolts concerning conscription in peacetime were often interwoven with those on foreign policy. The conscription controversy of 1946–48 provides an excellent example of this accommodation and also illustrates the potential influence of backbenchers.[2] But it is also important in illustrating how Labour leaders maintained party solidarity, and avoided having to employ sanctions.

As early as June 1946, 88 Labour MPs signed an EDM which stated:

> That this House, while welcoming the decision of His Majesty's Government as set forth in Command Paper 6831, gradually to reduce the period of compulsory service in the fighting forces, is of the opinion that military conscription in peacetime is alien to the traditions of this country and should come to an end as soon as is practicable.[3]

This minor criticism of government policy indicates how important the issue of conscription was to a large number of Labour backbenchers; when it became entangled with questions of foreign policy and manpower it threatened to destroy the internal cohesion of the Labour party.

[1] *Daily Herald*, 17 Dec 1946, and *The Times*, 9 Jan 1947.
[2] For R. T. McKenzie's discussion of this revolt see his *British Political Parties*, pp. 451 ff.
[3] *Notices of Motions*, 25, 26, 27 Jun 1946.

On the same day as the bitter debate on foreign policy in November 1946, Victor Yates moved another amendment which regretted the government's intention to embark on peacetime conscription.[1] The amendment was forced to a division, and 45 Labour MPs voted against their party.[2] This did not deter the government and it continued to make plans for compulsory conscription. During March 1947 it introduced a National Service Bill which called for eighteen months' compulsory military service for all youths over the age of 18. The opponents of the bill disapproved for two main reasons. Some were confirmed pacifists and hence maintained a clear pacifist line, and others argued that the economy could not bear the loss of manpower necessitated by the bill. The latter argument was presented by 28 Labour MPs, who urged a review of military commitments in order to improve the manpower situation and reduce financial expenditures.[3]

On 30 March 1947 at a stormy meeting of the PLP, Attlee defended the bill to extend conscription to eighteen months. The next day the Minister of Defence, A. V. Alexander, strongly supported this extension of military service. In the division 72 Labour MPs voted against the Second Reading and approximately 20 abstained publicly. Criticism mounted, and between the Second and Third Readings the government agreed to reduce the maximum conscription period to twelve months. This backbench success was coupled with a resolution passed by the PLP which confirmed that backbenchers should be consulted before the introduction of government legislation. It stated:

That prior to future parliamentary debates upon major issues the party shall, if necessary, hold a special meeting for the

[1] 430 *H.C. Deb.*, col. 594, and col. 639–49.
[2] A third Labour amendment was tabled by 5 MPs. It regretted that the King's Speech failed to mention any government intention to widen the democratic control of publicly owned industries. 430 *H.C. Deb.*, col. 594 ff.
[3] *Manchester Guardian*, 20 Mar 1947.

purpose of discussing such matters and arriving at a decision thereon.[1]

The official government excuse for reducing the period of conscription to twelve months was that the Cabinet had been convinced by the debate that conscription for one year would suffice.[2] It was alleged that Stafford Cripps had led a revolt within the Cabinet, and it appears that R. H. S. Crossman and other critics were approached privately by Attlee and asked what they wanted.[3] The critics demanded that the length of conscription be reduced to twelve months, and Attlee agreed to this proposal. The government's compromise reduced the opposition to 37 Labour MPs on the Third Reading.[4] This number still included Konni Zilliacus and John Platts-Mills, who voted against conscription on the grounds that it was offensive to the Soviet Union.[5]

Many critics were disturbed by this Cabinet reversal,[6] and it was also reported that '. . . members of the trade-union section of the PLP and even a Junior Whip criticized the leadership, in a later PLP meeting, for modifying its proposals in the face of minority opposition'.[7]

The conscription revolt continued. On 20 March 1948 another anti-conscription motion was supported strongly by Labour MPs, and in December of the same year the discord

[1] *The Times,* 21 May 1947.
[2] *The Economist,* 12 Apr 1947, p. 527. For newspaper statements about what happened see the interesting comparison made in the *Report of the Committee of Privileges* (23 Jul 1947), appendix 4.
[3] 437 *H.C. Deb.,* col. 2619. The wording change to '12 months' was accepted by a vote of 368 to 17 during the Committee stage. 437 *H.C. Deb.,* col. 559.
[4] 435 *H.C. Deb.,* col. 1869.
[5] *Manchester Guardian,* 22 May 1947. 437 *H.C. Deb.,* col. 2617.
[6] Henry Pelling, *A Short History of the Labour Party,* p. 100.
[7] Burns, 'The Parliamentary Labor Party in Great Britain', p. 865.

about National Service again attracted public attention. In order to meet the exigencies of international affairs, or what A. V. Alexander called the 'danger of new military commitments', the government again decided to try to lengthen the period of conscription from twelve to eighteen months.[1] This was certain to provoke Labour backbenchers once more. On the Second Reading the Conservatives did not send a whip to their backbenchers; and Labour, anticipating a revolt, sent only a two-line whip.[2] Forty-one Labour MPs opposed the government in this division, and 19 cross-voted on the Third Reading.[3] During the Committee stage the most serious controversy was, of course, concerned with the clause which extended military service for an extra six months.[4] This time the government would not yield to backbench pressure, and the increase in military service took place, and later actually rose to two years. The success of the March 1947 backbench revolt thus endured for only one year.

Continual revolts over foreign policy and conscription provoked Labour leaders into changing their parliamentary organization. Many of the specialized groups had been performing more than their customary role of study and research; they had been steadily transforming into pressure groups, and had often been centres of backbench criticism.[5] Although Hugh

[1] 458 *H.C. Deb.*, col. 2006. *The Times*, 2 Dec 1948.
[2] *The Times*, 2, 3 Dec 1948.
[3] 458 *H.C. Deb.*, col. 2123–6. 459 *H.C. Deb.*, col. 195–8.
[4] In the two divisions 16 and 21 Labour MPs opposed their leaders. 459 *H.C. Deb.*, col. 135 and 138. The army desired National Service to last for eighteen months. Viscount Montgomery 'assembled the Military Members of the Army Council . . . and asked them if they were all prepared to resign in a body, led by me, if anything less than eighteen months National Service with the Colours were decided upon by the Government. They all agreed'. Quoted in Ralph Miliband, *Parliamentary Socialism*, p. 297.
[5] *LPCR*, 1946, p. 56. McKenzie, *British Political Parties*, pp. 446 ff.

Dalton praised his finance group, other ministers concerned with civil aviation, manpower, defence, and foreign policy complained that their groups were too critical of government policy.[1] For example, Ivor Bulmer-Thomas had considerable difficulty with his civil aviation group, and later wrote that it was 'no less troublesome' than Ernest Bevin's foreign affairs group.[2] Hugh Dalton has written that he avoided trouble by choosing his own backbench committee, and that because Bevin did not put his own supporters on the foreign affairs group '. . . in came all the pacifists and fellow-travellers, pro-Russians and anti-Americans, and every sort of freak harboured in our majority'.[3]

At first the leaders tried merely to change the leadership of some of the groups. In March 1946 when the foreign affairs group differed with government policy in Greece, it was decided to call a special meeting of the PLP. A snap motion defending government policy was accepted by a vote of more than 300 to 6, and Seymour Cocks (chairman of the group) resigned his position in disillusionment.[4] The post was then filled by a rather orthodox former minister, John Hynd.

In a short time the specialized groups were changed to a series of regional groups which each contained critics, loyalists, and apathetic followers. Their function was to consider general rather than specific questions, thus making vigorous pressure group tactics more difficult. This move was effective in dampening criticism, but it also encouraged the formation of informal rebel groups which were even more difficult for Labour leaders to disperse.

Keep Left was the most persistent informal group which

---

[1] *The Economist*, 8 May 1948.

[2] Bulmer-Thomas, *Party System in Great Britain*, p. 131.

[3] Dalton, *High Tide and After*, p. 23.

[4] C. R. Rose, 'The Relation of Socialist Principles to British Labour Foreign Policy, 1945–51' (unpublished D.Phil. thesis, Oxford, 1959), pp. 458 ff.; *New Statesman*, 23 Mar 1946.

opposed government foreign policy. It consisted of 15 Members (including seven journalists), who met regularly and privately in the House of Commons.[1] They kept notes of their meetings, and made decisions on a majority basis. Keep Left members criticized the government in the press, at party meetings, and to a lesser extent in the House of Commons. In April 1947, they published a pamphlet which revived the idea that Britain should form a third force between Russia and the United States. This criticism extended into domestic affairs; and on 8 August 1947, 19 Labour MPs sent a letter to the *Daily Herald*. It was based on Keep Left reasoning, and criticized government economic policy.[2]

Keep Left did not remain cohesive throughout the 1945 parliament, but most of its members helped to publish *Keeping Left* on the eve of the 1950 general election.[3] This manifesto criticized party leaders, and the government's large armament expenditure. It advocated more socialist economic planning and an increase in welfare services. Generally, Keep Left attempted to shift party policy to the left, while maintaining enough cohesion to prevent party leaders from punishing individual rebels.

One result of this movement was that some loyal party members formed a group in opposition. In May 1947 a new propaganda campaign was instigated by Hugh Dalton, Morgan Phillips (Party Secretary), and Denis Healey (Secretary of the International Department).[4] In order to combat Keep Left

[1] They were Geoffrey Bing, Donald Bruce, R. H. S. Crossman, Harold Davies, Michael Foot, Leslie Hale, Fred Lee, Benn Levy, Ronald Mackay, J. P. W. Mallalieu, Ian Mikardo, E. R. Millington, Stephen Swingler, George Wigg and Woodrow Wyatt.

[2] *Daily Herald*, 8 Aug 1947.

[3] Little was heard of this critical manifesto, *Keeping Left*, during the 1950 election campaign. Nicholas, *British General Election 1950*, p. 78.

[4] Denis Healey strongly opposed Keep Left, and the Bevanite group. Interview.

propaganda, they published a pamphlet called *Cards on the Table*, which vigorously supported Bevin's foreign policy.[1] Within the next few months many Labour Members joined them in attacking Keep Left, and in the face of this official Labour party opposition, Keep Left had little success in changing party policy.[2]

In spite of this continual fight over 'keeping left', the only attempt to depose the Prime Minister was the curious and little reported AMGO or the 'Attlee must go' movement. According to some authors this revolt was publicly launched by an anonymous letter in the *New Statesman* written by Percy Daines, a junior Whip.[3] Hugh Dalton recorded in his memoirs[4] that the height of the crisis occurred between 24 and 28 July 1947 when Stafford Cripps, leader of the rebels, wanted Ernest Bevin to become Prime Minister and Hugh Dalton to take the position of Foreign Secretary. The revolt failed when Ernest Bevin would not join the *coup*, and Attlee appointed Cripps to be Minister of Economic Affairs. This abortive attempt to depose Attlee is one example of how difficult it is for even senior ministers to overthrow a Prime Minister, and it also shows that the Prime Minister's control of ministerial positions allows him great flexibility in appointing recalcitrants to government office in order to silence criticism.

Throughout this parliament Labour leaders reacted more vigorously against MPs who rebelled outside the House of Commons than against those who rebelled in the House. While no sanctions were imposed on rebels who abstained or cross-voted in divisions over foreign policy and conscription, severe reprisals were taken against some Members who simply acted

[1] It was approved by the NEC.
[2] See, for example, *Daily Herald*, 4 Aug 1947.
[3] Leslie Hunter, *The Road to Brighton Pier*, p. 18; and Emanuel Shinwell, *The Labour Story*, p. 181.
[4] Dalton, *High Tide and After*, pp. 238–40. Attlee has also accepted this account of the crisis: Francis Williams, *A Prime Minister Remembers*, pp. 223–4.

independently in regard to certain communist movements in Europe. The Labour government was continually forced to take stands on European issues and many left-wing Labour MPs were disturbed by what they considered to be the government's opposition to socialism in Europe.

In April 1946 some members of the Labour movement and 27 Labour MPs sent a telegram, later known as the Berlin telegram, to the Social Democratic Congress in Berlin. This Congress was called to register the fusion of the Social Democrats and the communists in the Russian zone of Berlin. The telegram wished the Congress success even though the British, American and French governments regarded it as being controlled by the communists. The significant fact about the telegram was that it had been signed by many members of the Labour movement who were not MPs, and by many individuals who could not be considered fellow-travellers.[1] The PLP met to discuss the Berlin telegram on 8 May 1946. The meeting registered its disapproval of the action taken by the 27 MPs, but took no further measures.[2]

The Labour party was not so lenient with Members who signed the Nenni telegram in April 1948. This rebellion is significant because it illustrates the power that Labour leaders exercised over Members' actions outside the House of Commons, and because it led to the expulsion of John Platts-Mills. On the eve of the Italian election 37 Labour MPs sent a telegram wishing success to Signor Nenni, who was the Left Socialist candidate in alliance with the Italian communists.[3]

---

[1] *Manchester Guardian*, 20 Apr 1946. Another less objective periodical reported that thirteen Labour MPs sent a message of welcome to the People's Congress in Berlin, which was organized by the communist-controlled Socialist Unity party. 'Socialists Rifts and Revolts', p. 12.

[2] *The Times*, 9 May 1946. *Daily Herald*, 9 May 1946.

[3] The Labour party had maintained relations with Signor Nenni's party even after its entry into the Popular

The NEC was disturbed by the telegram, and denounced it publicly. The party had been troubled consistently with the problem of how much freedom to allow Members, and how much to control the actions of the so-called crypto-communists. On this particular issue the major fellow-travellers were isolated from the left-centre of the Labour party, and the leaders were therefore able to react harshly. Sixteen of the MPs declared that they were not responsible for the telegram.[1] The remaining 21 Members received letters from Morgan Phillips demanding that they write to the NEC and pledge renewed loyalty to the party. The NEC stated that it was '. . . seriously disturbed by the activities over a long period of certain members of the party which are considered to be subversive of party policy'.[2] It warned the rebels that unless they each made a pledge of loyalty by 27 April 1948, and undertook '. . . to desist in future from such conduct they are excluded from membership of the Labour party'.[3] The 21 MPs issued a statement that they were equally responsible, and were not to be dealt with individually. The NEC must have been confident that most of the rebels would agree to pledge loyalty to the party since the loss of so many Members would have been an electoral hazard. The gamble was successful because all the rebels gave the pledge, and the NEC thought it had demolished some of the popular suspicion that the Labour party was closely connected with the communists.

Front. Early in 1948 the Labour party transferred its blessing to the Independent Socialists.

[1] According to the *Daily Herald*, 19 Apr 1948, John Baird, Frederick Longden, S. Tiffany, and L. Wilkes denied signing the telegram. W. J. Farthing and Mrs. Edith Wills claimed that their signatures were secured under a misunderstanding, and a large number of MPs wanted to withdraw their names, including G. House, A. J. Irvine, W. McAdam, and Charles Royle.

[2] *Labour Party Press and Publicity Department*, 28 Apr 1948.

[3] Unpublished letter, Morgan Phillips to John Platts-Mills, 22 Apr 1948.

The Members who reaffirmed their loyalty included the four who were expelled from the party before the 1950 election, and the ten MPs who signed both the Berlin and Nenni telegrams. The pledges were not all complimentary to the NEC. For example, William Warbey complained that the NEC sent exactly the same letter to all the signatories of the Nenni telegram. He pointed out that he had not signed the letter to the German Unity Congress, and said that the letter from the NEC had intimated that he had. Warbey asked the NEC to explain this to his constituents. He then went on to object to a phrase in the letter which referred to his 'activities over a long period', and asserted that 'not on any single occasion until this incident of the Nenni telegram has it ever been suggested or even hinted to me, either by any member of the NEC or by any member of the Government, that I have acted in the way alleged.'[1]

In 1945 Warbey had cross-voted on the United States Loan Bill, and in 1947 he had joined the revolt on the amendment to the King's Speech. Therefore, there was some evidence that he had been a rebel, but he was not one of the most persistent Labour recalcitrants in the 1945 parliament.

Konni Zilliacus and Sydney Silverman were even more forthright in their statements. They asserted frankly that they would not undertake to 'agree with whatever the NEC may do'.[2] Silverman went a step further, giving a hint of the complaints which were to arise at the 1949 annual conference. He said, 'We cannot, like the Communist party, ask our members for a blind obedience to a Politburo.'[3]

Several Labour rebels complained to their constituents about the NEC's action, and Konni Zilliacus told his local party that he would not be expelled. Many of the rebels were given votes of confidence by their constituency parties. Percy Barstow was asked to resign by part of the Pontefract Labour party but he refused, and a few weeks later received a vote of confidence from

[1] *The Times*, 3 May 1948.   [2] *Ibid.*, 6 May 1948.   [3] *Ibid.*

the local party.¹ He did not stand in 1950. According to some newspapers he later joined the Communist party.

The Labour party was very jumpy at this time, and criticism was leveled at every type of party dissension.² A constitutional question was raised about the Nenni telegram on 19 April 1948. Raymond Blackburn moved that the Committee of Privileges should investigate the circumstances in which a number of signatures had been added to the Nenni telegram without the consent of the MPs. That same day ten Labour MPs signed a motion calling for a Select Committee to investigate the Nenni telegram. The Speaker ruled that this was not a matter of privilege, and the recommendation was defeated.³ A Select Committee would possibly have discovered some interesting facts, but Labour leaders were wise to avoid an investigation because there was more than one instigator. It appears that the idea of sending the greeting came from a L. W. Caruthers, who was not a MP. He suggested the idea to John Platts-Mills, Konni Zilliacus, and D. N. Pritt.⁴ Tom Braddock was also a key figure, since he acted as chairman of the group, sending out messages about meetings and giving instructions on how the rebels should answer the NEC charge.⁵ William Warbey collected the money, and Geoffrey Bing probably sent the telegram.⁶

¹ *Daily Mail*, 8 May 1948. *The Times*, 31 May 1948.
² For example, a minister, Emanuel Shinwell, was strongly denounced in the PLP for merely suggesting to the Co-operative Productive Federation that there had been little detailed preparation for nationalization. *The Times*, 13 May 1948.
³ 451 *H.C. Deb.*, col. 439–82. Four Labour MPs voted for this Conservative motion. They were Hugh Delargy, P. Asterley Jones, John McGovern, and Reginald Paget.
⁴ Unpublished letter, L. W. Caruthers to John Platts-Mills, 17 Mar 1948; and Platts-Mills to Caruthers, 19 Mar 1948.
⁵ Unpublished letter, Tom Braddock to all members of the group, 30 Apr 1948.
⁶ Unpublished letter, Tom Braddock to all members of the group, 6 Apr 1948; and Tom Braddock, interview.

In order to avoid individual Members being punished, the group agreed not to send the telegram unless 21 Members signed it. Although this number was achieved the NEC picked John Platts-Mills as their scapegoat. Platts-Mills was singled out from the other rebels and expelled for his general rebellious activities. This case is discussed in detail in chapter 9.

Communist purges of socialists in Eastern Europe had an immediate impact on the Labour government, and in March 1948 the Cabinet decided to remove communists and fascists from civil service positions where national security might be involved.[1] Labour MPs tabled two EDMs criticizing this proposal as constituting a departure from principles of democracy and civil liberty. In the debate of 27 March 1948, the Communist MPs, William Gallacher and Phil Piratin, were joined by John Platts-Mills in an attack on Attlee. When the most important motion with 41 signatures was forced to a division only 5 Labour MPs continued to support it.

Two other minor incidents caused anxiety to Labour leaders. After the British government protested about the suppression of democratic rights and liberties in Rumania, Norman Dodds, Leslie Solley, and John Platts-Mills sent messages to the new government praising its constitution. And on 2 March 1948, after the NEC criticized the Czechoslovakia *coup d'état*, Geoffrey Bing, Norman Dodds, and Konni Zilliacus publicly repudiated their party's action.

The accumulation of these criticisms of Labour foreign policy in regard to communism provoked the NEC to react harshly against the left-wing rebels, especially those considered to be crypto-communists. Between 1948 and 1949 three of them joined Platts-Mills in being expelled from the Labour party. Lester Hutchinson, Leslie Solley, and Konni Zilliacus were all expelled for their critical speeches and articles in the press. In none of these cases was rebellion in the House of Commons even

[1] 448 *H.C. Deb.*, col. 1703–9. *The Times*, 16, 18 Mar 1948.

listed as a reason for the expulsion.[1] All four MPs were defeated as Independents in the 1950 General Election, and only Konni Zilliacus was later allowed to be reinstated as an official Labour candidate. A detailed examination of these cases, and those of other expelled Members, is found in chapter 9.

Other similar controversies over European affairs caused no party discipline. In May 1948 the Labour party was invited to send delegates to the conference on European Unity. The NEC refused the invitation and said that no Labour Members should go to the meeting. Forty-two Labour MPs gave notice that they would attend regardless of the NEC's decision, but after further requests by Labour leaders only 26 MPs actually went to the conference. The issue of European Unity did not seriously divide the Labour party until the 1959 parliament, and there was little disapproval of the 1948 rebels. In fact, that June a group of those MPs who went to the conference styled themselves the 'Loyal Order of Labour Rebels' and entertained the government Whips at dinner.[2]

The controversy over Britain's role in world affairs, and especially over her attitude to communism in Europe, reached a climax in May 1949 when the government decided to join the North Atlantic Treaty Organization. A division occurred on 12 May, and although a three-line whip had been issued the extent of disagreement was indicated when more than 100 Labour MPs were absent from the House. Nothing happened to these absentees. Three Labour Members, Tom Braddock, Ronald Chamberlain, and Emrys Hughes voted against the government in the division.[3] They were suspect because the two communists and the expelled Labour MPs, Konni Zilliacus

[1] See chapter 9 for evidence about this idea.
[2] *Daily Mail*, 15 Jun 1948.
[3] Newspapers tended to exaggerate the amount of Labour party discipline employed. For example, the *Daily Graphic*, 13 May 1949, thought that it was certain that these three MPs '. . . would not be accepted as Labour candidates at the next election'.

and John Platts-Mills, also voted against NATO.[1] However no sanctions were imposed even on these three Labour MPs, and all were readopted for the 1950 general election.

Two remaining foreign policy issues split the Labour party. The longest lasting affair concerned British policy toward what was to be the new state of Israel and the difficulties plaguing the setting up of a Jewish state in a hostile environment. The second issue was much closer to home. The partition of Ireland left hard feelings among many partisans in both Northern Ireland and England and a change in the law regarding Northern Ireland again raised the issue of partition in the minds of certain MPs.

From 1946 to 1948 the Labour government tried unsuccessfully to solve its difficulties in the mandated territory of Palestine. The first sign of trouble in the Labour party over Palestine appeared in July 1946 when Sydney Silverman challenged the Labour government's action in arresting leading Zionists in an attempt to curb terrorism after the King David Hotel tragedy. Michael Foot and R. H. S. Crossman took up the criticism during the debate on the adjournment of the House. Crossman complained that 'the British Government were pursuing a dangerous policy that might lead to disaster'.[2] Only these three MPs could be isolated as being openly rebellious at this stage, although undoubtedly many others agreed with them. Much later, in March 1948, the Labour government's decision to end the British mandate in Palestine, without providing for either partition or a bi-national state composed of Arabs and Jews, drew considerable criticism. The crisis provoked the tabling of two critical motions. The first, signed by 12 Labour MPs, criticized the Palestine Bill for not giving independence to both Jewish and Arab states in Palestine; the second, signed by 11, complained that the bill was not in accord with the

---

[1] 464 *H.C. Deb.*, col. 2127.
[2] *The Times*, 2 Jul 1946. The general reasons for this dislike of Bevin's Palestine policy can be found in R. H. S. Crossman, *Palestine Mission*.

policy of the United Nations.[1] The Second Reading of the Palestine Bill was held on 10 March 1948. The official opposition abstained and therefore the government easily won by 240 votes to 30. These 32 rebels were joined by several more Labour Members during the Committee stages of the bill.[2] The Conservatives abstained every time there were Labour rebellions, but they divided the House twice in the Committee stage, and on these occasions not one Labour MP voted against his party.[3]

On 29 January 1949 another controversy arose when Britain at last recognized the state of Israel. The Conservatives accused the government of mishandling the whole Middle East problem, and tabled a motion for the adjournment of the House. The Conservatives circulated a three-line whip, but Labour issued only a two-line whip as was usual on motions for adjournment.[4] The motion was defeated 283 to 193, but 50 to 60 Labour MPs abstained, and S. Segal voted against the government. It was reasonable to expect that some of the rebels would be disciplined, but none were. The *Manchester Guardian* commented 'Such action might offend a substantial body of Labour supporters'.[5] Moreover, the abstainers were not the only Labour MPs who opposed the government's action, because a number of MPs who voted with the government wrote to Attlee criticizing his Palestine policy.[6] Thus in the Palestine revolts from 1946 to 1949, many MPs criticized the government and several cross-voted, but no disciplinary action was taken on any occasion.

As parliament neared the end of its five-year duration a new issue faced the government front bench. During April and May

---

[1] *Daily Herald*, 10 Mar 1948.
[2] 448 *H.C. Deb.*, col. 1363–6; col. 2499–500; and col. 2935–8.
[3] 448 *H.C. Deb.*, col. 2861–4; and 2933–5.
[4] *The Times*, 28 Jan 1949.
[5] *Manchester Guardian*, 28 Jan 1949.
[6] *Daily Telegraph*, 28 Jan 1949.

1949 there were several rebellions on the Ireland Bill.[1] On the Second Reading ten Labour MPs voted against the government, and this number increased to 63 during the Committee stages. This made a total of 66 different Labour MPs who voted against the government on three-line whips.[2] Most of the rebels opposed a clause in the bill which said that Northern Ireland would remain part of the United Kingdom until a parliament of Northern Ireland decided otherwise. The dissidents declared this statement to be a deplorable reinforcement of partition. There was also considerable personal criticism of Attlee because he had not consulted the PLP about the vital clause.[3]

Maurice Webb, chairman of the PLP, sent a letter to the 67 MPs who revolted on either the Ireland Bill or the Atlantic Pact (discussed earlier). The letter asserted that further rebellion would result in a request to the NEC that these rebels be refused endorsement for the next election.[4] It reaffirmed that Members could abstain, but since the Standing Orders were still suspended one would not have thought this was necessary. The rebels were required to acknowledge the letter with their signatures.

Five PPSs were removed from their positions because of their revolt on the Ireland Bill.[5] This uncommon disciplinary

---

[1] According to one Labour leader, at the time, the cross-votes were mainly intended as a demonstration, and it was known that the government would not be forced to resign. He thought it also helped the Labour cause among the Irish. Interview.

[2] 464 *H.C. Deb.*, col. 1961, and 465 *H.C. Deb.*, col. 119, 123, and 164.

[3] *Manchester Guardian*, 26 May 1949.

[4] One week prior to this revolt the Liaison Committee asked Wilfred Burke and Edwin Gooch to explain why they voted against the government on a Liberal amendment to set up a Royal Commission on war pensions. *The Times*, 19 May 1949.

[5] They were Frank Beswick (Uxbridge), PPS to Under-Secretary of State for Air; J. P. W. Mallalieu (Hudders-

measure was enforced shortly before an election, and may have been an attempt to tighten Labour ranks before parliament was dissolved. The action was coupled with an appeal for party loyalty which declared that slackness of party discipline on one issue could lead to the defeat of the party's other policies.[1]

The decision to remove the PPSs from their positions took place the same evening that Leslie Solley and Konni Zilliacus were expelled. The emotional situation undoubtedly contributed to the enforcement of such harsh measures. Many commentators thought that the five PPSs were punished merely as an example to other MPs. There was also much concern because on past occasions rebellious PPSs had not lost their positions, but this time five PPSs, who were normally faithful supporters of party policy, were dismissed. Of the five PPSs only J. P. W. Mallalieu had been involved in several other rebellions during these five years. More typical was George Rogers who had cross-voted on only one amendment to the Ireland Bill, and had joined no other revolts. The disciplinary measures employed in this situation did not prevent any of the PPSs from receiving future promotions or from being elected in 1950. A detailed examination of the role of PPSs is found in chapters 8 and 9.

Some of the Labour rebels on the Ireland Bill had no doubt been influenced slightly by constituency pressures. Since the end of the Second World War there had been no widespread concern with the 'Irish question', but partition was an issue in a few constituencies during the 1950 general election. The Irish had usually been loyal to the Labour party, but as H. G. Nicholas related, the common feature of the Anti-Partition

---

field), PPS Minister of Food; Robert Mellish (Rother-hithe), PPS Admiralty; George Rogers (Kensington N.), PPS Minister of Supply; and William Blyton (Houghton-le-Spring), PPS Civil Aviation. Blyton anticipated the wrath of leaders and resigned.

[1] *Daily Mail*, 26 May 1949.

candidates was that all their Labour opponents had failed to vote against the ' "iniquitous Ireland Bill" '.[1]

CONSERVATIVES IN OPPOSITION

Although the Conservative party received its most severe defeat since 1906 in the 1945 general election, it survived the parliament with no major and few minor rebellions. This cohesion endured until the Conservatives formed the government in 1951. One author has concluded that: 'Although the party had had notable rebels in the recent past and appeared to have some minor ones again in 1953, the postwar years were characterized by a general inhibition against *public* revolts in opposition to policies of the established leadership.'[2]

The 1945 defeat caused many Conservatives to advocate a reformulation of party principles and to suggest the development of a new programme on which the next general election could be fought. The party organization set out to construct a new platform immediately after the election. Much of the inspiration for the new *Charters* came from R. A. Butler and his Research Department. The organizational leadership required for putting these ideas into practice came from Ralph Assheton and Lord Woolton, Chairmen of the Party Organization, 1944–46 and 1946–55 respectively.

Their efforts resulted in the publication of the *Industrial Charter* in May 1947, followed within a year and a half by several other policy statements.[3] The *Industrial Charter* was criticized

---

[1] Nicholas, *British General Election 1950*, p. 258; and see J. A. Jackson, *The Irish in Britain*, p. 127. Irish Anti-Partition candidates stood in three Scottish constituencies and at Bootle in Lancashire, but they polled a total of only 5,045 votes.

[2] Epstein, *Britain – Uneasy Ally*, p. 173.

[3] For an examination of the background to the formulation of the Charters see J. D. Hoffman, *The Conservative*

very mildly in most newspapers, but the left-wing periodical *Tribune* prophesied that the Charter would force a major split in the Conservative party. This conjecture proved false. At the 1947 Conference when Sir Waldron Smithers called the Charter 'milk and water Socialism', his attack was supported by only three votes.[1] Similarly, the *Agricultural Charter* was opposed by few speakers and only one vote at the 1948 Conservative conference.[2] Lord Woolton declared, 'Our ranks are closed. . . . The press must have found us perhaps a little dull, but in the face of the enemy it is wise that we should be united.[3] Later the Conservatives published *The Right Road for Britain*, and only eight votes were cast against it at the 1949 conference.[4] When parliament was dissolved *This is the Road* was published, and although no MPs objected publicly to the policies, some important proposals from it were omitted from most Conservative election addresses.[5]

There was very little general criticism within the Conservative parliamentary party during these five years. There were no revolts from the 15 Conservative backbench committees, and even the Tory Reform Committee ceased its concerted group action after 1945.[6] The latter group did not disband, but continued to have dinner meetings for discussing Conservative policy.[7] However, not until the One Nation group emerged in 1950 did a reformist faction arise within the party.

Party in Opposition, 1945–1951, especially chapter 8 where he concludes that the extent of the revolution in party doctrine has been exaggerated. And see R. A. Butler, *Fundamental Issues* (C.P.C. 1946), p. 2.

[1] *CPCR*, 1947, p. 49. *Tribune*, 16 May 1947. Harold Macmillan, 'Forces of Reaction', *Observer*, 15 Jun 1947.

[2] *CPCR*, 1948, p. 53.

[3] *Ibid.*, 1948, p. 145, and see McKenzie, *British Political Parties*, pp. 188–99.

[4] *CPCR*, 1949, p. 98.

[5] Nicholas, *British General Election 1950*, p. 222.

[6] *Conservative Party Committees, 1946–51*, pp. 1–2.

[7] The Tory Reform Committee had been formed in 1943

The absence of public revolts in the Conservative party was partially due to the fact that the Tories were more secretive about their internal affairs than the Labour party. Furthermore, the Conservatives used a different technique than Labour did for controlling minor criticisms while they were in opposition. Between 1951 and 1964 when Labour formed the opposition her leaders often forced backbenchers to abstain on contentious issues. In contrast, the Conservative party in opposition declared bills non-controversial or called for free votes when there was much dissension. A thorough study has shown that the Labour whips were put on for every division, but that the Conservatives did so on only about three out of four occasions.[1] The first example of this tactic occurred in 1945 when the Bank of England was nationalized. Early in the parliament Churchill declared that this legislation raised no party principle, but that he had given his opinion and 'anybody else may give his own'.[2] Churchill, Butler, and many other Conservatives abstained on both the Second Reading of 29 October 1945 and the Third Reading of 19 December 1945. Nevertheless, a large number of Conservatives voted against the bill, and Robert Boothby voted with the Labour government in both divisions.[3] The whipping arrangements had not been violated, and there was no talk about party discipline.

The Conservatives faced another potential split in December 1945 when, during the debate on the United States loan, their party was more divided than at any other time in six years of opposition. Rather than risk a rebellion, Churchill called for a free vote. He advised his followers to abstain, and then at the last moment tried to force abstention in order to avert a crisis

---

to promote domestic reform, and especially the Beveridge Report. The officials of this group were Viscount Hinchingbrooke, Hugh Molson, Peter Thorneycroft, and Frederick Hooper. Viscount Hinchingbrooke, interview.

[1] Beer, *British Politics*, p. 263.

[2] 413 *H.C. Deb.*, col. 94.

[3] 415 *H.C. Deb.*, col. 162. 417 *H.C. Deb.*, col. 1403.

in the House of Lords.[1] His fear proved to be unfounded because the government proposal was accepted by a vote of 90 to eight in the Lords. The upshot of the Conservative free vote was that 71 Conservatives voted against the loan and eight favoured it.[2] Later the Conservatives called for another free vote on the Bretton Woods agreement. There was therefore no talk about party discipline when the party split.[3]

Over a year later, in January 1947, the Conservatives vacillated on what approach to take toward the government's Statistics of Trade Bill. Some Conservative backbenchers did not think there was any need for further enquiries into the public consumption of products. Churchill found the new legislation uncontroversial, but a large number of his backbenchers forced it to a division. The Whips' Office, therefore, called for a free vote, and 48 Conservatives voted against the new law.[4]

The Independence Bills for India and Burma nearly caused a cleavage in the Conservative party. By agreeing to self-determination for India and Burma, the Labour government placed the Tories in a difficult position; they either had to agree to independence and take the wrath of British Empire stalwarts, or to vote against independence and appear to lack any feelings for the wishes of what was to be the new Commonwealth. Churchill did not force a division over Indian independence until the Labour government set a specific date for the independence to be granted.[5] The argument therefore took place over the date of independence and not independence itself. There were no cross-votes in the division, and only a few known ab-

---

[1] *New Statesman and Nation*, 22 Dec 1945, p. 419.

[2] 417 *H.C. Deb.*, col. 641 ff.

[3] 417 *H.C. Deb.*, col. 745, *Daily Telegraph*, 14 Dec 1945.

[4] 432 *H.C. Deb.*, col. 155, *Daily Telegraph*, 22 Jan 1947. *Star*, 22 Jan 1947.

[5] Churchill said earlier that although he would dissociate himself from the government's Indian policy, he would not cause a division. 431 *H.C. Deb.*, col. 1360, and 434 *H.C. Deb.*, col. 772–6.

stentions. On 5 November 1947, the Second Reading of the Burma Independence Bill was forced to a division. Three Conservatives, led by Sir Stanley Reed's vigorous speech in favour of the bill, voted with the Labour government.[1] There was no talk about party discipline, and when the Conservatives divided the House again in the Committee stage no Conservatives voted with the Labour party.[2] Although the break-up of the Empire caused strong feelings in the Tory party, no sanctions were imposed on MPs who defied the party over these issues.

The whip was not withdrawn from any Conservative MPs during this parliament. Only A. L. Gandar Dower withdrew from the Tory whip, and this was because his local party chose Sir David Robertson as their prospective candidate for the 1950 general election. A more detailed study of his readoption problem is found in chapter 10.

During this period there were 434 different Labour MPs, 428 of whom were in parliament when at least one of the rebellions occurred. This total of 428 consisted of 340 backbenchers, and 88 MPs who held ministerial office at some time during this parliament. As would be expected no minister joined any of the rebellions, not even those minor incidents which occurred outside parliament. About three out of every four backbenchers, however, were associated with at least one revolt.

Six MPs took part in almost half of the public rebellions. The four so-called crypto-communists each joined a high per-

[1] 443 *H.C. Deb.*, col. 1957–60. The three were A. R. Low, G. Nicholson, and Sir Stanley Reed (Editor of *The Times of India.*), *Daily Telegraph*, 6 Nov 1947.
[2] 444 *H.C. Deb.*, col. 702–4.

centage of them; Konni Zilliacus 41%, Leslie Solley 37%, John Platts-Mills 38% and Lester Hutchinson 21%. Ivor Bulmer-Thomas and Alfred Edwards, on the other hand, joined almost no rebellions; and of the six PPSs who lost their positions, only one had been very rebellious.

The following Tables correlate certain factors about MPs with the number of rebellions which they joined. Percentages are used in the Tables rather than numbers because of the large turnover of MPs due to deaths, resignations, and consequent by-elections. The extremely small number of Conservative revolts in this period makes a statistical analysis for that party of little value, and consequently only the Labour party is studied here.

Table 2: Labour Party Discipline and
Collective Responsibility 1945–50

Rebellious % out of number of revolts (Total 39)	0%	1–10%	11–30%	31% Plus	
Ministers (88)[1]	100%	0%	0%	0%	(100%)
Backbenchers (340)[2]	27%	42%	24%	7%	(100%)

The fact that backbenchers had been actively associated with rebellions did not always prevent them from being made junior ministers. For example, James Callaghan and John Freeman both cross-voted shortly before they were given office in the government. Furthermore, the termination of ministers' careers

[1] There were 434 Labour MPs altogether during this period, but 6 (including two ministers) were not in parliament at the time that any rebellions occurred. Note that many MPs were not ministers for the whole period. This rank includes the rebellions of MPs only while they actually were ministers.
[2] All MPs who did not hold ministerial rank are included as backbenchers. This includes unpaid Whips and PPSs.

did not prevent them from joining revolts after they left office. Ellis Smith and W. Foster both joined a number of revolts after they were relieved of their positions.

During this parliament at least 43 MPs were Parliamentary Private Secretaries. It is impossible to obtain the exact dates for which they held these positions. Therefore, Table 3 correlated MPs who were PPSs sometime between 1945 and 1950 with the total number of rebellions which they joined. None of the PPSs appears in the highest category of rebellion, which suggests that a greater degree of loyalty was required from PPSs than from ordinary backbenchers. An examination of the role of PPSs is found in chapters 8 and 9.

*Table 3: Labour Party Discipline and
Parliamentary Private Secretaries 1945–50*

Rebellious % out of number of revolts (Total 39)	0%	1–10%	11–30%	31% Plus
PPSs (43)	26%	58%	16%	0% (100%)
Backbenchers (340)[1]	27%	42%	24%	7% (100%)

Controversy over Palestine and conscription caused two important rebellions in this period. The social character of the MPs who rebelled on each of these issues varied greatly. The Palestine revolts were almost completely dominated by non-sponsored MPs who had been elected first in 1945. Furthermore, most of them had been educated at a university. The conscription revolts were joined by 125 different MPs, which was slightly over a third of all Labour backbenchers. The composition of the 125 rebels indicates that some belief in pacifism existed throughout the party. Approximately one-third of both union-sponsored MPs and non-sponsored MPs were included.

[1] Includes the PPSs.

Only the Co-op-sponsored MPs were more highly represented. Nearly all the Labour MPs involved in the conscription revolts were rebellious on other occasions. Party cohesion did break down over conscription issues, and on at least one occasion the government was forced to change its policy.

Many analyses have been made of the rebelliousness of parliamentary groups. The most consistent argument has been that union-sponsored MPs are less rebellious, and more in favour of party discipline than other MPs. In this period union-sponsored MPs joined fewer rebellions than other Members. Table 4 shows that the number of union-sponsored MPs who rebelled in more than 31% of the overt rebellions was very low. However, one of them, S. O. Davies (NUM), was one of the most frequent rebels in the Labour party. The most rebellious MPs were those sponsored by the Co-op, and much of their dissension was concerned with foreign policy, especially the conscription issue.[1]

Table 4: Labour Party Discipline and Sponsorship 1945–50[2]

Rebellious % out of number of revolts (Total 39)	0%	1–10%	11–30%	31% Plus
Co-op-sponsored MPs (22)	14%	41%	37%	9% (101%)
Trade-union-sponsored MPs (96)	32%	50%	17%	1% (100%)
Non-sponsored MPs (222)	26%	39%	27%	9% (101%)[3]

[1] It is important to note that the 1947 Co-op conference passed a resolution which called for Britain to form a third force between the United States and the Soviet Union. *The Times*, 7 Apr 1947.

[2] Backbenchers only.   [3] Caused by rounding.

It is sometimes suggested that certain unions sponsor more rebellious MPs than others. Between 1945 and 1950, the number of MPs sponsored by most unions was so small that no positive statement can be made about them. Furthermore, a pilot study indicated that no particular union rebelled consistently during these years.

There was only a slight difference between the number of rebellions joined by Members elected prior to 1945 and those elected later. In this period, at least, date of entry to the House had little effect on Members' rebelliousness. But Table 6 illus-

Table 5: Labour Party Discipline and
Date of Entry to the House 1945–50[1]

Rebellious % out of number of revolts (Total 39)	0%	1–10%	11–30%	31% Plus	
Pre-1945 MPs (52)	31%	40%	19%	10%	(100%)
Post-1945 MPs (192)	23%	39%	29%	9%	(100%)

Table 6: Labour Party Discipline and
Formal Education 1945–50[2]

Rebellious % out of number of revolts (Total 39)	0%	1–10%	11–30%	31% Plus	
Non-university-educated MPs (135)	30%	39%	25%	7%	(101%)
University-educated MPs (109)	19%	39%	30%	11%	(99%)[3]

[1] Trade-union-sponsored MPs have been eliminated.
[2] *Ibid.*   [3] Caused by rounding.

trates that Members who had been educated at a university were more rebellious than those who had not. This was partially due to the Palestine crisis which caused large numbers of university-educated MPs to rebel.

From 1945 to 1950 there was no consistent general opposition to Labour leadership. Of course, if the cases are limited to inherently 'right' or 'left' or 'foreign policy' issues a more consistent grouping appears. After 1951 a consistent general opposition to Labour leadership did develop, and this is discussed in chapter 5. However, in the first post-war parliament, rebellion did come more often from university-educated MPs who were not sponsored by a trade union and who had not been given a paid position in the party.

The Labour party used its severest form of party discipline five times during these years. Four crypto-communists were expelled for their attitudes to Labour foreign policy, especially their activities outside the House of Commons. They were all well known for their articles and speeches attacking Bevin's foreign policy, had all signed the Berlin and Nenni telegrams, and had made themselves generally obnoxious to party leaders. Alfred Edwards was the fifth person to be expelled. He voted against the government on the Civil Aviation Bill and on the Direction of Labour Bill, but no punishments were enforced until after he publicly criticized nationalization, and made a direct attack on the principle of strike action.

The whip was not withdrawn from any Labour backbenchers during these years. This was not due to the suspension of the Standing Orders because Herbert Morrison had made it clear that the whip could still have been withdrawn from Members. James Callaghan relinquished his position as PPS because he voted against the United States loan, and five other PPSs were dismissed for voting against the government on various stages of the Ireland Bill.

Thus, many Labour MPs cross-voted, abstained, tabled hostile motions, signed critical letters, and made speeches condemning government policy in both domestic and foreign affairs. Some rebels were warned by the leaders of the PLP, and others were called before the NEC, but sanctions were imposed on only an exceedingly small number of them. The Conservative party, on the other hand, had almost no overt rebellions during its years in opposition, and therefore had no reason to employ disciplinary measures.

4 Rebellions and Party Discipline 1950-1951

Some degree of stupidity and docility is vital to our affairs, as I am sure the Patronage Secretary would agree.[1]

The 1950 general election left the Labour party with an absolute majority of only five. This altered the circumstances for whipping; pairing was greatly curtailed, and the government faced the threat of defeat almost every day. Conservative policy vacillated between using parliamentary procedures to obstruct Labour policies, and waiting for the government to make its own electoral blunders. Disagreements, particularly in the field of foreign affairs, continued to flourish within the Labour party, but the size of the rebel group and the method of expressing the discontent was carefully chosen to avoid destroying the government's small majority.

The small government majority overshadowed all other factors in this parliament. Conservatives were united in the hope that they would soon have control of the reins of government, but, in spite of considerable dissension, the Labour party maintained enough cohesion to allow Attlee to determine the date of dissolution. Early in the new parliament Herbert Morrison told the PLP that because of the small majority no revolts could be tolerated.[2] Even the left-wing *Tribune* declared the need for a new 'self-discipline'; an announcement which implied that some of the most rebellious elements in the party did not intend to cause a government defeat.[3] It was therefore not an exaggeration when J. M. Burns concluded that 'Any formal

[1] R. A. Butler, quoted in Young, *British Parliament*, pp. 109–10.
[2] 1 Mar 1950.   [3] *Tribune*, 24 Mar 1950.

control of members has been rendered unnecessary by the ready and spontaneous acceptance of a new self-discipline'.[1] Although many of the earlier controversies recurred in 1950, the critics contented themselves with expressing hostile opinions and signing EDMs. Even persistent rebels were concerned with the survival of the party, and therefore did not force a dissolution on the government by rebelling in the division lobbies.

Most of the Labour rebellions during these two years were again in the field of foreign affairs. Two of the most contentious issues, conscription and the role of Britain as a third force in world affairs, were continuations of unresolved problems which had arisen during the previous parliament. The other foreign policy revolts were over policies toward Bechuanaland, the Korean War, and German rearmament. Only the last of these issues was to remain important in future parliaments, but the economic pressures associated with the Korean War substantially increased the bitterness in the sole domestic revolt over charges on the health services. The financial situation led to the first open rift in the Labour Cabinet when Aneurin Bevan resigned his position as Minister of Health.

The Conservative party greatly enlarged its membership and brought some excellent new Members into the House of Commons in the 1950 general election. This improved Conservative morale and helped to perpetuate a high degree of cohesion in the parliamentary party. The united front was disturbed more in foreign policy issues than in domestic affairs. Arguments arose over the Schuman Plan and Seretse Khama while minor incidents over corporal punishments also split the party.

THE LABOUR PARTY

The trepidation of this parliament with its small majority

[1] Burns, 'The Parliamentary Labor Party in Great Britain', p. 870.

may possibly be best illustrated by recalling the incident when R. R. Stokes caused a re-count because he pushed the Serjeant-at-Arms out of the way when he was locking the door for a division.[1] The crisis mood was heightened when Labour Whips had to manoeuvre every man into the lobbies and especially on those occasions when they were forced to rush Members from their hospital beds to the grounds of the Westminster Palace in order to save the government from defeat.

Besides helping to produce a colourful parliament, the slender majority caused the government to be defeated on five occasions and to have its advice rejected on two Private Members' Bills. Once, the government was defeated because of backbench abstentions. This occurred on 29 March 1950, when an adjournment motion was carried against the government by a vote of 283 to 257.[2] The opposition, indignant about the inferior quality of coal supplies, called for a snap division and caught the Labour party with twenty-one MPs absent and unpaired.[3] On another occasion, concerned with a change in the rules for private members' bills, the government ordered only a two-line whip and accepted the will of the House when they were defeated.[4] The remainder of the government defeats were on relatively minor items such as the reduction of the cheese ration and the price of plaster-board.[5]

These defeats naturally caused a certain degree of consternation within the Labour party, and when illness and death further reduced the government's majority, Morrison asked for

---

[1] 486 *H.C. Deb.*, col. 2133 ff.   [2] 473 *H.C. Deb.*, col. 527.
[3] There were not twenty-six cross-votes as the *Observer* maintained on 15 Mar 1964. See 473 *H.C. Deb.*, col. 527–32.
[4] *The Times*, 9 Nov 1950. The amendment was concerned with restoring the ten minute rule.
[5] The defeats are recorded in 473 *H.C. Deb.*, col. 527; 480 *H.C. Deb.*, col. 976; 486 *H.C. Deb.*, col. 777; 489 *H.C. Deb.*, col. 2655; 490 *H.C. Deb.*, col. 939. The government was also defeated on two Private Members' Bills. 484 *H.C. Deb.*, col. 1703, and col. 2516–618.

'a tightening of the ranks'. The minor defeats not only embarrassed the government, but occasionally caused small administrative problems. For example, a prayer was tabled against an Order to decrease the cheese ration from three ounces per person to two ounces, and it passed. The government later had to reverse the defeat.[1] The limited majority also caused difficulties in the standing committees where the government had to accept an occasional defeat.[2]

None of the revolts in the Labour party over foreign or domestic policy issues ever caused the government to be defeated in the division lobbies. Foreign policy controversies began in March 1950 when the government was confronted with a backbench revolt over the recognition of Seretse Khama as Chief of the Bamangwato tribe. In order to prevent trouble in the Bechuanaland Protectorate, the government, led by Patrick Gordon Walker, decided to withdraw recognition from Seretse Khama. The African chieftain had married a white English girl, and when recognition was withdrawn the Labour government was accused of furthering racial discrimination. The government published a White Paper to justify its position, but would not report the details of the Harrigan Inquiry.[3]

> R. W. SORENSEN asked: Does my right hon. Friend's answer mean that even Members of this House will not at any time be able to read the details of the report?
>
> PRIME MINISTER: Yes, Sir.[4]

Herbert Morrison tried to avoid a PLP debate on the subject, but there were so many complaints that a meeting was called. The government would not reverse its decision at the meeting, and many backbenchers accused Attlee and Gordon Walker of instigating a colour bar. However, the most vociferous complaint

[1] There was so much of this type of obstruction that an 11.30 p.m. deadline on filibustering against delegated legislation was introduced.
[2] For an example see the *Report of House of Commons Standing Committee C* (1950–51), col. 1021–2.
[3] 477 *H.C. Deb.*, col. 1535.   [4] *Ibid.*

was made against the premature attempts of Herbert Morrison and William Whiteley to terminate the debate. Before the meeting ended Attlee warned the dissidents that they might precipitate an early election if they did not vote with the government.[1]

The debate in the House of Commons was very emotional. Reader Harris later described it in the following words:

> Members of the Labour Party went into the Lobby with tears running down their cheeks when they had to vote for their own Government's motion in relation to Mr. Seretse Khama. Mr. Seretse Khama was sitting at the back of the Chamber, and I saw Labour Members go to apologize to him because, on the whips' orders, they had to vote against him.[2]

Many Labour MPs thought that a free vote should have been allowed, but on 28 March 1950 the government issued a three-line whip for the closure motion. Seven Labour rebels, therefore, disregarded the Whips' instructions and voted against the government.[3]

All seven rebels were reported to the Liaison Committee. At the next meeting of the PLP some union sponsored MPs complained about the 21 Members whose absence had caused the government's defeat on 29 March 1950, and about the seven who revolted during the Seretse Khama debate. Although the seven MPs had been consistently rebellious since 1945, no further action was taken.[4] The rebellion in the Labour party over Seretse Khama did not continue into 1951.[5] Moreover,

[1] Interview.   [2] 536 *H.C. Deb.*, col. 843.
[3] 473 *H.C. Deb.*, col. 357 ff. Ian Mikardo acted as a teller, and the following 6 cross-voted: Sir Richard Acland, R. H. S. Crossman, Tom Driberg, Michael Foot, Jennie Lee, and Woodrow Wyatt.
[4] *Daily Express*, 3, 29 Mar 1950, and 17 May 1950.
[5] After their defeat in the 1951 election, the Labour party suggested that new negotiations should take place about Khama, and the Conservatives put forward a plan to this effect at their 1955 conference. In late 1955 Khama was allowed to return home, and new democratic councils

no Labour MPs voted against the government on a similar case when the Liberals put down a motion condemning the continued banishment of Tshekedi Khama from the Bamangwato Territory.[1]

The PLP contained many critics of the Korean War. But, although the dissatisfied MPs expressed their views openly, they did not at any time vote against their party in the division lobbies. Their discontent was shown mainly through critical motions. On 18 July 1950 one of these motions was signed by Sydney Silverman and 22 other Labour MPs calling for the pacification of Korea by negotiation instead of arms. The Prime Minister asked the signatories to take their names off the motion. Six assented but Emrys Hughes added his name.[2] In November, 40 Labour Members tabled another critical motion. The rebels, mainly pacifists and Keep Left advocates, suggested that a line be drawn in Korea beyond which UN troops would not pass.[3] The size of this group increased considerably when President Truman announced that atomic bombs might be used in Korea. One hundred MPs immediately sent a letter to the *Daily Herald* objecting to the use of atomic bombs in Korea, and stating that if they were used British troops should be withdrawn.[4] This letter was never published nor were the names ever disclosed, and no evidence of these complaints reached the division lobbies. Although the Korean

were set up. Much later he became leader of the Bechuanaland Democratic party, and finally Prime Minister. *Labour Party Talking Points*, no. 19 (1956), and *The Times*, 16 Mar 1964.

[1] 489 *H.C. Deb.*, col. 1312–18. Tshekedi Khama had been chief of the tribe while Seretse Khama was young. Tshekedi was also involved in the complicated problem of who should be Chief after 1951.

[2] There was a confusion over Leslie Hale's name, but on 17 July the *Notices of Motions* reported that he had not signed the EDM. See also *The Times*, 20 Jul 1950, 21 Jul 1950. *LPCR*, 1950, p. 141, and *Tribune*, 28 Jul 1950.

[3] *Notices of Motions*, 20 Nov 1950.

[4] *Daily Herald*, 1 Dec 1950.

conflict disturbed Labour Members, they were not willing to defeat the government, and Labour Whips could do nothing to punish the large number of critics.

One Labour MP, Tom Driberg, went as a reporter to Korea and the Far East during the height of the crisis. He was absent from debates and divisions in the House of Commons, and did not even respond to a cable from the Whips' Office asking him to return.[1] The NEC eventually censured him for 'gross neglect' of his parliamentary duties. There was also an attempt to expel him from the Labour party, and Driberg has claimed that this was initiated by 'a few Right-wing extremists [who] overreached themselves by trying to use the natural resentment at my absence from important divisions as a means of getting me actually expelled from the party'.[2] The attempt failed, but Driberg apologized, expressing 'deep regret' for his action. He had considerable support in his constituency, and the Maldon Labour party gave him a vote of confidence.[3]

Another Labour MP, S. O. Davies, was criticized in November of the same year because he sent a message of support to the left-wing Peace Congress. It was suggested that Davies might be expelled from the Labour party because many local parties had expelled members for attending the Congress.[4] Although Davies was not expelled, his wife was! The Merthyr Tydfil party explained that they expelled her because of left-wing activity, but S. O. Davies claimed that the expulsion was 'the result of a directive from the National Executive of the Labour Party insisting that it be done'.[5] Davies was one of the most rebellious Labour MPs, but he neither lost the whip for supporting the Peace Congress, nor received any other punishment.

[1] *The Times*, 16 Nov 1950.
[2] Tom Driberg, *The Best of Both Worlds: A Personal Diary*, p. 27.
[3] *The Times*, 17 Nov 1950.
[4] *Sunday Empire News*, 19 Nov 1950, and *Daily Express*, 11 Nov 1950.
[5] *The Times*, 21 Dec 1951, and *Manchester Guardian*, 28 Dec 1951.

It was also during this parliament that Raymond Blackburn resigned from the Labour party. He advocated the formation of a coalition government led by Churchill because he thought that it would be the only government capable of solving Britain's domestic problems and the crisis caused by the Korean War. Blackburn was already in grave difficulty with his constituency party in King's Norton because of personal affairs, and might not have been readopted in any case.[1] His resignation lowered the Labour majority even further; and Blackburn, realizing the usual fate of Independents, did not contest the 1951 general election.

In early February 1951 a Conservative censure motion was tabled criticizing the government's defence policy.[2] This unsuccessful Conservative manœuvre was an attempt to split the Labour party, as the playful debate in the House clearly indicated.

> CHURCHILL: It is very likely, and I fully recognise it, that the terms of our Amendment will have the effect of inducing the pacifists and other dissentients on the benches opposite –.
>
> EMRYS HUGHES: Nothing doing.[3]

Nevertheless, Labour was not completely united in its defence programme, and in March there was a revolt on the Reserve and Auxiliary Forces Bill. During the Committee stage a number of Labour backbenchers objected to a clause which called for total conscription, and demanded exemption for 'persons serving in agriculture and fishing, mining, building or the textile industry, or any other industry which the Minister of Labour shall certify is of urgent importance to the national interest'.[4] Thirty-four Labour and two Liberal MPs voted

---

[1] See Blackburn, *I Am an Alcoholic.*
[2] 484 *H.C. Deb.*, col. 743.
[3] *Ibid.*, col. 624. The censure motion was defeated by 308 votes to 287. 484 *H.C. Deb.*, col. 739–44. *New Statesman*, 24 Feb 1951.
[4] 484 *H.C. Deb.*, col. 2306.

against the government. The revolt was partially due to the fact that the government would not accept backbenchers' views on conscientious objectors. Later, the Conservatives tried to take advantage of the Labour disagreement over defence, and divided the House twice at the Committee stage and once at the Report stage. On none of these occasions did any of the rebellious Labour MPs vote against the government.[1] The Labour dissidents wanted their views publicized, but had no intention of causing a government defeat.

The most important revolt of this period, which was also the only major trouble over domestic issues, took place in April 1951 when Aneurin Bevan resigned from the Labour Cabinet. The rising cost of armaments, due to the escalation of the Korean conflict, had caused much uneasiness in the Labour Cabinet and had begun to affect Labour's socialist programme. The first sign of a dispute against these rising costs broke into the open when the former Minister of Health, Bevan, asserted that he would 'never be a member of a Government which makes charges on the Health Service for the patient'.[2] Then when Attlee accepted Hugh Gaitskell's Budget of £3,600 million, which included a proposal for charges on dentures and spectacles, Bevan reacted by resigning his position as Minister of Labour. He was accompanied by Harold Wilson (President of the Board of Trade), and John Freeman (Parliamentary Secretary in the Ministry of Supply).

In a personal statement to the House, Bevan asserted that the

[1] 484 *H.C. Deb.*, col. 2497, and col. 2501–4. In the second division on the Committee stage, 19 Labour MPs, who had earlier cross-voted, abstained. 485 *H.C. Deb.*, col. 87–90.

[2] Quoted in Hunter, *Road to Brighton Pier*, p. 32. Bevan had agreed with Gaitskell on the need to cut the housing programme from 200,000 to 175,000. Douglas Jay, 'Civil Servant and Minister' in *Hugh Gaitskell, 1906–1963*, ed. W. T. Rodgers, p. 96. The economics of this period are discussed in chapters 6 and 7 of Joan Mitchell's *Crisis in Britain 1951*.

new charges in the National Health Scheme were not the only reasons for his resignation.[1] His friends attributed his resignation to policy differences, but others complained that Bevan was disappointed at not having received either the position of Secretary of State for Foreign Affairs or Chancellor of the Exchequer.[2] Another more balanced view has been given by Douglas Jay:

> This news [that there would be charges] . . . unhappily if understandably provoked in Bevan a state of mind in which any change in his treasured Health Service appeared the last straw. It was one of those unfortunate issues where, in all reality, not much was at stake, but where it had become hard for either protagonist to retreat.[3]

After his resignation, Bevan said he would not try to defeat the government and would leave Attlee free to choose the date of the next election.[4]

Immediately after resigning, Bevan, Wilson, and Freeman received votes of confidence from their constituency parties. However, the leaders of the parliamentary party would not accept the resignations as final. In fact, Hugh Dalton made a rather blunt but futile attempt to reconcile one of the former ministers.

[1] 487 *H.C. Deb.*, col. 34–43.
[2] Bevan and Freeman allowed their letters of resignation to be published, but Wilson declined. Bevan's letter was worded as follows: 'In previous conversations with you, and in my statements to the Cabinet, I have explained my objections to many features of the Budget. Having endeavoured in vain to secure modifications of these features I feel I must ask you to accept my resignation.' *The Times*, 23, 24, 25 Apr 1951. See also Williams, *A Prime Minister Remembers*, p. 247; and Dalton, *High Tide and After*, p. 359.
[3] Douglas Jay, 'Civil Servant and Minister', pp. 99–100.
[4] *Manchester Guardian*, 24 Apr 1951. *The Times*, 26 Apr 1951.

> Next day I [Hugh Dalton] walked with Freeman on Hampstead Heath and, with Attlee's authority, told him this: Attlee had for some time been planning a further rearrangement of the Government. . . . If Freeman stayed in the Government, Attlee had in mind the possibility of promoting him to be either Secretary of State for War or President of the Board of Trade.[1]

When the controversial health charges came before the House, five Labour Members cross-voted, and several abstained. The five rebels were James Carmichael, S. O. Davies, Emrys Hughes, John McGovern, and Archibald Manuel. Of the three ministers who had resigned, Bevan and Freeman abstained, and Wilson voted with the government. There was little that Labour leaders could do to discipline either the three ministers or the five backbenchers without causing a defeat of the government. The Cabinet, therefore, chose to take no public actions against either group. Later, the Conservatives put down a motion expressing anxiety that the government's rearmament programme was based on a financial policy which some ministers were unable to accept. The motion stated that:

> This House learns with anxiety that the rearmament programme which it approved in February was based on estimates of defence production which were not accepted by the Ministers principally concerned.[2]

This attempt to exploit the differences in the Labour party met with absolutely no success; the Labour dissidents all voted with the government.[3]

After resigning, Bevan joined the former Keep Left Members in a new cabal. The new group met privately, and although the rebels supported the government in the division lobbies, they promoted their controversial opinions among local Labour parties. In July 1951 they published *One Way Only*. This pamphlet revived the idea that the United States might be as

---

[1] Dalton, *High Tide and After*, p. 368.
[2] 487 *H.C. Deb.*, col. 1015.   [3] *Ibid.*, col. 1137–42.

much a threat to world peace as the Soviet Union, and advocated that Britain should form a third force between the two great powers.[1] The next month the NEC published a pamphlet entitled *Our First Duty – Peace*, which was largely an attack on the proposals propounded in *One Way Only*. Then, only 36 hours after Attlee announced the date of the election, the rebels issued another controversial pamphlet, entitled *Going our Way?*, which attacked trade-union members of the NEC and criticized the party leadership. The pamphlet was published anonymously, but contained a foreword signed by Bevan, Freeman, and Wilson.

Not all former members of Keep Left joined the new Bevanite group. Of those who did not, Woodrow Wyatt was the most outspoken. He criticized the left-wing rebels soon after he severed connections with them. One Labour MP declared cynically that: 'Attlee rewarded Wyatt for attacking Bevan by giving him a post as Under-Secretary for War. Such are the rewards for those who place party loyalty before personal loyalties.'[2]

The Bevanite group did not actively oppose Labour leaders in the House until after the Labour party was defeated in 1951, even though the issue of German rearmament had begun to disturb the party as early as February 1951. There were at least two PLP meetings on German rearmament, and the dissension in the Labour party reached the House when two critical motions were tabled. The first was signed by 8 Labour backbenchers, and it explicitly demanded that the government reconsider the question of German rearmament. Secondly, 12 Labour MPs signed a motion which opposed branding China an aggressor, and implied opposition to the arming of Germany.[3]

[1] See Bevan's resignation speech, 487 *H.C. Deb.*, col. 38. *Tribune*, 5 Jun 1951, and *The Statist*, 14 Jul 1951.
[2] Blackburn, *I Am an Alcoholic*, p. 53. George Wigg also refrained from joining the new rebel group. See *Daily Express*, 11 May 1951.
[3] *Notices of Motions*, 8 Feb 1951. A few MPs later added their names.

Most of the MPs who signed these two motions joined the more significant rebellions on German rearmament between 1952 and 1954. Moreover, most of them had rebelled over the King's Speech in 1946, and had been members of Keep Left.

On 24 August the NEC called on the party to stand united for the general election.[1] All factions within the Labour party yielded to this appeal, and even the Bevanites made little reference to their particular views during the election.[2] The conflict had been a two-edged sword. If Bevan had continued to criticize the government many votes might have been lost through purposive abstentions or by Labour supporters voting Conservative. Conversely, if Bevan had been punished Bevanite candidates might have emerged in some constituencies and caused loss of morale and vote-splitting.[3] Moreover, Bevan agreed that the most important objective was to defeat the Conservatives.[4] Regardless of this appearance of party unity Conservative newspapers declared that a vote for Labour was an 'electoral gamble', because no one knew whose policies would be accepted, those of Attlee and Gaitskell or those of Bevan.

CONSERVATIVES IN OPPOSITION

Early in the new parliament there were rumours that Conservative party leaders could not agree about what tactics to employ against the government. It was reported that Anthony Eden favoured a soft line toward the government, but that Churchill preferred to force the Prime Minister to call an

[1] *Daily Herald*, 5 Sep 1951.
[2] D. E. Butler, *The British General Election of 1951*, p. 54.
[3] Emanuel Shinwell reports that Labour leaders feared electoral repercussions if Bevan was expelled. *The Labour Story*, pp. 191–3.
[4] *Reynolds News*, 23 Oct 1951.

early election by a series of snap divisions and all-night debates. As would be expected, Churchill publicly denied that there was any difference of opinion over parliamentary strategy.[1] This terminated the rumours about Conservative dissension, and the speculation about a leadership contest died away.

The aspiration of some Members to reintroduce corporal punishment for criminals has been a difficult and persistent problem for the Conservative party. Early in 1950 several Conservative backbenchers sponsored two EDMs calling for a change in the penal system; the first was signed by twelve Members, and the second by nineteen.[2] There has always been some support for corporal punishment among the Conservative rank and file and, of course, the leaders showed little concern over these small demonstrations while they were in opposition. They were not to be so complacent about this type of dissension later when they formed the government.

In June 1950 the Labour government declared that Britain would not participate in the Schuman Plan, but resolved to continue negotiations about future possibilities for association with Europe. Conservative leaders were adamant in their demand that Britain join the new Europe, but in spite of this six fairly right-wing Conservatives abstained ostentatiously on a three-line whip when the issue was forced to a vote in the House.[3] This inauspicious revolt was joined by Air Commodore Arthur Vere Harvey, Sir Harry Legge-Bourke, Stephen McAdden, Sir John Mellor, Gerald Nabarro, and Enoch Powell.[4] Some of these rebels were later to lead a movement which helped to prevent Britain from joining the Common Market.

The last dispute in this parliament concerned the continued banishment of Tshekedi Khama from the Bamangwato Territory.

[1] *Western Mail*, 8 May 1950.
[2] *Notices of Motions*, 14 Mar 1950.
[3] *The Times*, 27 Jun 1950.
[4] 476 *H.C. Deb.*, col. 2171 ff. *Manchester Guardian*, 28 Jun 1950.

On 25 June 1951, a Liberal motion was tabled deploring the banishment, and over a dozen Conservatives quietly abstained when their party voted against the government.[1] As usual, nothing was said about party discipline on such a minor issue, and the parliament ended with the Conservative party having experienced no serious rebellions.[2] No permanent dissident movements had formed, and the Tories approached the election with high morale and with united ranks.

During this period the Whips had to expend considerable energy to ensure a constant government majority, but no formal disciplinary measures such as expulsion or withdrawal of the whip were used in either party. The need for unity and compromise was evident in the Labour party and, as there was very little overt rebellion in the division lobbies, corrective measures were not necessary. The Conservative party had even less rebellion, and its most serious problem was over how much to harass the Labour government.[3]

The fact that three ministers resigned did not increase rebellion or the use of harsh disciplinary devices in the Labour party. Bevan was forced to realize some of the implications of being out of party favour when, shortly after his resignation,

[1] 489 *H.C. Deb.*, col. 1313–18. *Yorkshire Post*, 7 Jul 1951, and see above in this chapter.

[2] Of course, a classic rebellion had taken place within the mass party at the 1950 conference when a floor revolt occurred over housing, and Lord Woolton finally accepted a goal of 300,000 houses a year. It was a qualified acceptance however, because it was not given priority over defence expenditure. See McKenzie, *British Political Parties*, p. 197.

[3] The composition of rebel groups in this period has not been analysed because of the small number of rebellions.

the Scottish Trade Union Congress repudiated an invitation to him to speak at their conference, and asked Gaitskell instead.[1] However this rebellion clearly illustrates that some members may revolt and yet become more important in subsequent years. Bevan became Shadow Foreign Secretary, Freeman eventually became British High Commissioner in India, and Harold Wilson rose to be Leader of the Opposition and finally Prime Minister. Even as early as 1951 the resignations gave rise to the Bevanite cabal which was to disturb Labour leaders until at least 1956.

In this period the size of the government majority played a major part. None of the forms of rebellion which were used would have defeated the government, nor were they so intended. The Labour dissidents knew that they could not rebel in the division lobbies without causing the downfall of the Attlee government. Rebellion was forced underground, and it was not until after the general election that the Bevanite faction was able to show its strength in the division lobbies.

The small majority and its consequent hardships could not be tolerated, and after only eighteen months in office Attlee dissolved parliament. Although Labour received more total votes than the Conservatives did in the 1951 general election, they were defeated and this ended Labour rule until 1964.

[1] *The Times*, 25 Apr 1966.

5 Rebellions and Party Discipline 1951-1955

The Conservative party has, save at rare intervals,
maintained its cohesion with little formal machinery for
penalizing open disagreements: the Labour party,
however, has been unable to preserve its unity, despite
the existence of elaborate procedures for discovering and
enforcing the will of the party.[1]

The Conservative party returned to power in 1951 with a small but workable majority of seventeen, and this success began the longest continuous period of one-party dominance in modern British history. As an opposition party the Conservatives had been extremely cohesive, and this pattern did not radically change now that they were in power. However, there were six overt Conservative revolts during this period, a slightly higher number than when they were in opposition, but this increase in Conservative rebellions was greatly overshadowed by numerous arguments and revolts in the Labour party. Disagreements which had divided their ranks while they formed the government reached a new height, and Aneurin Bevan became the focal point of rebellion within the party.

Although the Labour party won more votes than the Conservatives in the 1951 election, it held only 295 seats, and this set-back, coupled with the deaths of Ernest Bevin and Stafford Cripps, had a crippling effect on the party. Furthermore, although the 1950 parliament had witnessed the emergence of the Bevanite movement, it was not until after 1951 that this rebel group openly opposed their party in the division lobbies. Labour leaders were often bound by decisions which had been made by the Labour governments of 1945 and 1950, and Churchill constantly reminded them that in foreign affairs he was simply

[1] Iain Macleod, *The Future of the Welfare State.*

following the policies of former Labour governments. The Bevanites were mainly concerned with the issue of German rearmament, and consequently nearly all Labour revolts occurred in the field of foreign affairs. In practice this meant that the Labour leaders were opposed by a fairly cohesive group in most of the fifteen major revolts.

German rearmament was the dominant controversial issue, recurring in several forms throughout the parliament, but the Japanese Treaty Bill, Defence, Central African Federation, British Guiana, SEATO, hydrogen bombs, and the Atomic Energy Bill were also sources of bitter conflict within the party. Domestic issues on the other hand presented very little dissension at all.

The few Conservative revolts were almost entirely over domestic issues. Such topics as denationalization, corporal punishment, pensions, the National Coal Board inquiry and the reshaping of electoral boundaries aroused backbench ire, but in most cases their grievances were recognized and the government proposals were either compromised or changed. The Suez controversy, which began in this parliament and did not come to a head until succeeding years, provided the only revolt in foreign affairs, and it initiated the only large-scale cross-voting by Conservatives during this parliament.

In these revolts the Conservative dissidents came mainly from the right-wing whereas the Labour rebels were nearly all from the left-wing of their party. Moreover, not only were Labour rebellions more frequent than Conservative revolts in this parliament, but whereas Labour backbenchers commonly showed their disagreements in publications and cross-votes in the House of Commons, Conservatives very rarely resorted to such methods to make their opinions known. Generally, they expressed their disagreement by tabling motions, but often they did not have to go that far to have their views acknowledged. For example, on three different occasions when the party was divided on policies over commercial television, judges' salaries and MPs' salaries, private negotiations behind the scenes prevented open splits in the party. In view of these compromises, Patrick Buchan-Hepburn, the government Chief Whip, did not have to employ harsh methods to keep his party cohesive.

There was no widespread criticism of Churchill's leadership, and this eliminated one possible source of trouble in the Conservative party. The Labour rebels, on the other hand, formed a relatively unified group of individuals who followed the leadership of Aneurin Bevan and were often heard to say privately that fundamental changes were needed in their party's leadership.

THE CONSERVATIVE PARTY

Table 7 : Conservative Revolts 1951–55

	Number of Revolts	Main Issues
Domestic	4	Corporal Punishment National Coal Board Inquiry Service Officers' Pension
Foreign Affairs	2	Suez

The first backbench complaint of the parliament over domestic issues came from a group of Tory MPs who thought the government was too slow in securing denationalization. Although the Conservatives had always been against nationalization, it was well known that Churchill was not very much in favour of repealing such former Acts as the nationalization of steel and road haulage,[1] and some backbenchers resented his slowness to act. On 3 April 1952, 39 Conservative Members signed an EDM castigating the government for its inaction. Almost immediately Churchill announced at a 1922 Com-

[1] Earl of Woolton, *Memoirs*, pp. 378–9.

mittee meeting that steel and road haulage would be denationalized as soon as possible.[1] Thus, the first minor dispute ended with the dissident backbenchers achieving satisfaction, and receiving no rebuke for their action. They were not so successful later in 1952 when they advocated the restoration of birching. Although 17 Conservative Members signed one motion and 69 another, the government would not reinstate corporal punishment or even take much notice of these motions.[2] Several months later, Conservative backbenchers applied this type of pressure to government leaders again. In April 1953, a 1922 Committee meeting was held to discuss the Conservative Fuel and Power Committee's demand for an inquiry into the functioning of the National Coal Board.[3] Geoffrey Lloyd, Minister of Fuel and Power, explained the government's reasons for refusing this demand, and the 1922 Committee appeared to be satisfied. However, several backbenchers would not accept their decision, and in May, Victor Raikes, chairman of the Fuel and Power Committee, and six other Conservative Members tabled a motion calling for an inquiry into the National Coal Board.[4] After a few months the National Coal Board itself asked the Fleck Committee to investigate its organization.[5]

In November 1953, Conservative backbenchers criticized the Prime Minister's statement that the government would not be able to restore the $9\frac{1}{2}\%$ cut in the 1919 value of the retirement pensions of service officers and civil servants.[6] The 1922

---

[1] *Daily Telegraph*, 10 Apr 1952. *Guardian*, 10 Apr 1952.
[2] *Notices of Motions*, 28 Oct 1952, and 4 Nov 1952.
[3] *The Times*, 21 Apr 1953. *Daily Telegraph*, 22 Apr 1953.
[4] *Notices of Motions*, 18 May 1953. It was signed by Cuthbert Alport, Col. Ralph Clarke, Col. Oliver Crosthwaite-Eyre, Capt. John Crowder, Col. Claude Lancaster, Gerald Nabarro, and Victor Raikes.
[5] *The Times*, 9 May 1955.
[6] Although the Conservative government had a majority of 17, it was nevertheless defeated in the House. On 11 Nov 1953 the opposition refused leave for the withdrawal

Committee was not able to resolve the difficulty, and by 7 November 1953, 55 Conservative backbenchers led by Anthony Marlowe and Sir Edward Keeling had signed a motion proposing that 'this House views with concern the refusal of Her Majesty's Government to recommend an increase in the retired pay of officers of Her Majesty's armed forces. . . .'[1] The campaign eventually succeeded in forcing the government to increase pensions by two shillings in the pound.[2]

In December 1954 the government decided to change certain electoral boundaries for the ensuing election, a decision which often causes internal troubles in parties.[3] This particular decision affected the narrow constituency interests of a number of Tory MPs, and its controversial nature was illustrated by the fact that there had to be 15 divisions and two all-night sittings. Many Conservative backbenchers criticized the government's action and some abstained, but only four of them voted against the boundary changes, and one Labour MP voted in favour of the redistribution.[4] There were many complaints because the

of a rather insignificant motion on the importation of glass, and this was carried against the government by a vote of 145 to 141, with no Conservative cross-votes. As is usual when the government is defeated in a division, an opposition spokesman, in this case Herbert Morrison, demanded that the government either make a statement or resign. Churchill responded that the government would not resign, and that the defeat was not caused by the opposition Whips, but by members of the Bevanite faction who 'emerged suddenly from cellars and other hiding places'. 520 *H.C. Deb.*, col. 1099–144. *The Times*, 12 Nov 1953.

[1] *Notices of Motions*, 24 Nov 1953.

[2] *News Chronicle*, 3 Mar 1954: The official opposition was not opposed to these measures, and there were no divisions. 524 *H.C. Deb.*, col. 2246; and 525 *H.C. Deb.*, col. 342.

[3] D. E. Butler, *The Electoral System in Britain Since 1918*, pp. 131 ff.

[4] See Harold Lever's comments in the House, 535 *H.C. Deb.*, col. 1867-71. The Conservative rebels were Ralph Assheton, J. J. Astor, Mrs. Eveline Hill, and Miss

whips were put on for these divisions, but a free vote would not have been more successful.[1] The main complaint was that if a government used its whips on a division involving the re-distribution of seats, it would be possible for the government party to remain in power forever. Christopher Hollis declared that, '. . . who wins or loses an Election depends enormously on the way in which redistribution takes place, it is obviously going to be very undesirable indeed to allow a custom to grow up of settling the boundaries of constituencies by party divisions in this House. . . .'[2] The debate illustrated several problems about party cohesion. Harold Lever, who did not want the government to abide by the dictates of the Boundary Com-mission, asked 'How can it be that although not a soul has spoken in favour of this Measure except its formal supporters on the Front Bench, it is a moral certainty that it will be carried in the Division Lobbies tonight?'[3] The debate also provided a clarification of the degree of loyalty expected from a PPS even when the division affected a boundary revision in his own constituency. When F. M. Bennett was asked why he did not speak against the proposed boundary changes in his con-stituency of Reading North, he answered, '. . . the only reason that I have not spoken today is that I happen to be in the position of a Parliamentary Private Secretary to a Minister in the Department concerned. The right hon. Gentleman is aware of the convention attached to that position.'[4] This illustrates the well-known fact that a PPS is prevented from speaking against his ministry's legislation, even when it affects his own constituency.

Florence Horsbrugh; and the lone Labour dissident was Clifford Kenyon. 535 *H.C. Deb.*, col. 2055–8, 2125–8, 2177–80, 2125–8. It was actually debated in the House whether or not the Conservatives had called for a two- or three-line whip. 535 *H.C. Deb.*, col. 2216–17.

[1] See D. E. Butler, 'The Redistribution of Seats', pp. 125–47, especially p. 140.

[2] 535 *H.C. Deb.*, col. 1824.   [3] 535 *H.C. Deb.*, col. 1868–9.

[4] 528 *H.C. Deb.*, col. 149–58.

There were at least three other occasions when the Conservative party faced the possibility of serious splits in the party, but through private negotiation and compromise it avoided this completely. The first of these disputes occurred when a number of Conservative backbenchers sponsored the introduction of commercial television in opposition to official party policy. According to Lord Woolton, chairman of the Conservative party organization from 1946 to 1955, this issue 'might well have split the Conservative Party'.[1] Negotiations about ITV were held privately, and although there were no overt rebellions, the government finally accepted the introduction of commercial television as its own policy. When the bill was brought before the House no Conservative MPs voted against it in any of the divisions.[2] H. H. Wilson concludes in his book on this event that the most curious and remarkable aspect of the introduction of ITV was the '... defeat of the Conservative Party leadership by a very small group of nominally insignificant backbenchers'.[3] In this dispute, as in others, Conservative backbenchers were able to influence government policies without joining in open rebellion.

A similar situation occurred when backbench uneasiness was incited by the government's bill to raise judges' salaries by a tax-free allowance of £1,000. The government introduced this bill on 13 March 1953, and promised to have the Second Reading in a few days.[4] Conservative dissentients joined Labour MPs in opposing the principle that anyone should receive a tax-free salary, and on 24 March Harry Crookshank, Leader of the House, announced that the bill would be postponed because the government did not want it to be a subject for dispute.[5] The government solved its difficulties on 4 November 1953 by introducing a bill which increased judges'

---

[1] Woolton, *Memoirs*, p. 392. Also see *The Economist*, 3 Apr 1954.

[2] 525 *H.C. Deb.*, col. 1553–60; 529 *H.C. Deb.*, col. 375–80.

[3] H. H. Wilson, *Pressure Group*, p. 14.

[4] 512 *H.C. Deb.*, col. 1695.   [5] 513 *H.C. Deb.*, col. 655.

salaries by £3,000, but actually left an increase of only £734 after taxes. The Labour Party did not attack the new policy; and the dissident Conservative backbenchers, although critical of any increase in judges' salaries, did not force a division.[1]

A third such event occurred near the end of the parliament when a Select Committee recommended an increase in MPs' pay. On 24 May 1954, the result of free votes in the House determined that there should be an increase, and the Prime Minister implied that he would act on this decision.[2] This caused considerable trouble in the Conservative party, and Robert Boothby, who favoured the increase, has since reported that:

> Oddly enough, the roughest treatment I ever got from the Tory Party was when I advocated an increase in the salaries of Members. . . . There was a moment when I hardly dared face the party Committee, and addressed it with my hand on the door, in case immediate escape became necessary.[3]

Because of Churchill's tacit acceptance of the free votes, Sir John Mellor resigned the Conservative whip. He said he could not accept the leadership of a Prime Minister who was 'prepared to override the objections of a majority of Conservatives towards an increase in MPs' salaries.'[4] Sir John also suggested that the Prime Minister should be guided by the views of the majority of the Tory party, and not by the Socialists combined with a small minority of Conservative Members. The officers of Mellor's constituency association met him *in camera*, and afterwards announced that a unanimous vote had been passed in his favour. Soon after this vote of confidence he asked for the whip to be returned, and it was given to him on 14 July.[5]

[1] 520 *H.C. Deb.*, col. 151, and 525 *H.C. Deb.*, col. 1057–1103.
[2] 528 *H.C. Deb.*, col. 149–58.
[3] Lord Boothby, *My Yesterday, Your Tomorrow*, p. 38.
[4] *The Times*, 23 Jun 1954.
[5] See chapter 9 for a more detailed discussion of Members who resigned the whip. *The Times*, 15 Jul 1954.

Ultimately there was enough pressure against the reform to force the government to drop the idea of a direct increase in salaries, and to accept an alternative system involving a sessional allowance. Churchill then argued that although a free vote represented the opinion of the House, all money bills had to be initiated by the government, and that in this case the Cabinet had decided against the proposal.[1] The opposition retorted that free votes should be put into effect, and listed three incidents when a government had thought a free vote was binding: the expulsion of Garry Allighan, capital punishment, and the Coalition's vote on amusements for soldiers at theatres. Churchill repudiated this claim on the principle that these matters were not financial and did not require further action by the government.[2] The free vote was not accepted, and hence the revolts by Mellor and the other critics were somewhat responsible for preventing a direct increase in MPs' salaries.

One exceptional case of the period was that of Captain Peter Baker. He disagreed with the Conservative party many times during this parliament, and according to his own account he wrote repeatedly to the Whips suggesting that he should resign. He was told not to do so, even though his personal life had become embarrassing for the Conservative party.[3] Baker's candid reasons for accepting his party's advice on German rearmament are instructive:

'I shall vote with you', I told Patrick Buchan-Hepburn [Conservative Chief Whip], 'for three reasons. Firstly, because I believe that a rearmed Germany, with a European Defence Community is just the least of four possible evils. Secondly,

[1] *The Times*, 25 Jun 1954.
[2] 529 *H.C. Deb.*, col. 595–600.
[3] A combination of overwork and drink made Baker so ill that he could not even remember whether or not he had been in the House. Subsequently he was sent to gaol for fraud, had a mental breakdown, and was expelled from the House.

because I want my summer holidays. And thirdly because without a German Army, you would be the last survival of Prussianism in Europe.'[1]

Most backbench criticism was over domestic issues, but the most significant split in the Conservative party occurred in the field of foreign affairs. Government policy aroused a series of backbench complaints which extended into, and came to a climax in, the next period of Conservative rule.

The trouble began when a significant number of Conservative backbenchers became dissatisfied with both the government's policy of Home Rule for the Sudan and its handling of Egyptian affairs.[2] These critics formed a secret cabal within the party. They made their biggest show of strength when Ralph Assheton and Captain Charles Waterhouse tabled an EDM which called for the government to withdraw from the Cairo talks on the future of the Canal Zone. Altogether 41 Conservative backbenchers signed this motion urging:

> ... Her Majesty's Government in these circumstances for the time being to suspend negotiations for a revision of the Anglo-Egyptian Treaty forthwith, to withdraw such terms as may already have been offered, and for the present to retain in the Canal Zone sufficient armed forces to discharge our responsibilities for the defence of the Canal.[3]

The government took little notice of this motion, and to show their dissatisfaction with this continued intransigence on Middle Eastern policy Harry Legge-Bourke resigned the Conservative whip, and Captain Charles Waterhouse relinquished his position as chairman of the Conservative Defence Committee. Legge-Bourke's attitude to colonial affairs is best summarized in his own words:

> All too often in the last few years we have been given racial, economic, or military reasons for taking the line of least resis-

[1] Captain Peter Baker, *My Testament*, p. 254.
[2] Background information about the Suez crisis can be found in Leon D. Epstein, *British Politics in the Suez Crisis.*
[3] *Notices of Motions*, 15 Dec 1953.

tance, All too often have Conservatives supported this line. From Palestine, Burma, India, Persia, the Sudan, and now Egypt the ignominious retreat has gone on.[1]

He said that resignation of the whip was the strongest step left open to him and asserted that in the last two election campaigns he had 'reserved the right to disagree with the Conservative party on matters such as foreign affairs, which ought to transcend party consideration'.[2] Later, when Legge-Bourke asked for the whip to be returned, the Chief Whip did not hesitate in complying with his request, even though Churchill had been very angry with Legge-Bourke's public opposition to Conservative policies.[3]

Concurrently with Legge-Bourke's resignation in July 1954, the Suez rebels informed the government that they would vote against any agreement with Egypt which involved removing all fighting troops from the Suez Canal area.[4] The next day Captain Waterhouse publicly explained the attitude of the Suez group to the House of Commons, but the government proceeded with their plans to remove all British bases from the zone. Thereupon, 28 Conservatives voted against the Agreement, but the government won easily when the Labour party abstained.[5] At the annual conference there was very little talk about the Suez Agreement, and the most serious split within the Conservative party on this issue did not arise until after the 1955 general election.

When the 1951 parliament ended, the Conservative party had had only six noteworthy rebellions, and no sanctions had

---

[1] *The Times*, 19 Jul 1954. *Evening Standard*, 14 Jul 1954.
[2] *The Times*, 20 Jul 1954, and 19 Oct 1954.
[3] *The Times*, 19 Oct 1954. Interviews.
[4] 530 *H.C. Deb.*, col. 510 ff.
[5] 531 *H.C. Deb.*, col. 819–22. In spite of the Labour decision to abstain six Labour MPs voted for the Suez Agreement: Fenner Brockway, James Carmichael, Desmond Donnelly, John Forman, Emrys Hughes, and John McGovern.

been imposed on any of the rebels. This was a larger number of revolts than had been experienced between 1945 and 1950, but the rebellions which occurred during the 1951 parliament were less significant and fewer in number than those which took place after 1955. Two of the six open rebellions were successful in changing the direction of government policy. Furthermore, there were many examples in this parliament of the government changing its policy in response to backbench pressure without the discord reaching the stage of open rebellion. The most obvious backbench successes were over the introduction of commercial television and the adjustments in judges' and MPs' salaries, but the government was also influenced by backbench pressure to terminate the Supplies and Services Acts, and to prevent the introduction of the Industrial Organization and Teachers' Superannuation Bills.[1] Backbench pressure was also important in causing the resignations of John Maclay (Minister of Transport) in May 1952, and Sir Thomas Dugdale (Minister of Agriculture and Fisheries) in July 1954.[2]

The fact that the government accepted these backbench proposals lends support to the proposition that backbenchers are more likely to succeed in changing government policy when there is a small majority. However, the 1950 Labour government had a much smaller majority, and there were very few backbench triumphs in that parliament. More evidence is needed before a conclusive statement can be made about this problem.

LABOUR IN OPPOSITION

Labour revolts were almost exclusively in the general field of foreign affairs. Throughout these years a cohesive rebel group

[1] 525 *H.C. Deb.*, col. 2213.
[2] 530 *H.C. Deb.*, col. 1294–8. See R. Douglas Brown, *The Battle of Crichel Down*.

Table 8: Labour Revolts 1951–55

	Number of Revolts	Main Issues
Domestic	1	Membership on Select Committee on Estimates
Foreign Affairs and Defence	14	Atomic Energy Bill Bevanite Group Abandonment Defence Policy German Rearmament Japanese Treaty Bill National Service Nuclear Weapons

within the PLP, often led by Aneurin Bevan, challenged the official Labour leaders on foreign affairs, and caused most of the fifteen major public rebellions. Because of this unusual circumstance one can perhaps see the pattern of revolts more clearly by examining the breakdowns in cohesion in chronological order. The revolts were all interwoven and dominated by one outstanding individual who was often more significant in provoking the revolts than were the issues themselves.

Throughout this explosive parliament Bevanites claimed that what they wanted was loyalty to the ideals and philosophy of the party and that Bevan was adhering to these principles. Bevan's opponents, however, claimed that he did not want changes in party policy as much as publicity. Attlee later reflected, 'In my experience a good deal of so-called independence owes more to desire for notoriety than to conscience.'[1] And, in an explicit statement about his views on party discipline, Attlee declared, 'For myself, I have seldom, if ever, had such a high opinion of my own judgement as to esteem it above that of the consensus of the views of my colleagues. The majority are more likely to be right than I am. As a democrat I accept the position.'[2]

[1] Attlee, 'Party Discipline is Paramount', p. 16.
[2] Attlee, 'The Role of the Member of Parliament', p. 8.

Bevan was a major figure in the Labour revolts from the beginning of the parliament. The first overt rebellion took place on 26 November 1951 during the Second Reading of the Japanese Treaty Bill. Bevan disliked the Treaty because he believed that it showed that the United States was overriding British policy in the Far East. When it came to a vote, he and 34 Labour MPs cross-voted and 83 abstained. Several of the rebel Members who supported Bevan on this issue were already declared Bevanites, but the group also contained a very high percentage of Members from cotton and pottery constituencies who wanted to protect local interests. The latter argued that the bill provided no adequate safeguards against unbridled and unfair competition from Japan.[1]

The Conservative party and Labour leaders combined to defeat the dissidents, and Japan was allowed to export to Britain. But the rebellious action still constituted a significant attack on Labour leadership because the treaty had been negotiated by Herbert Morrison for the Labour government.

Although this rebellion did not result in any sanctions being imposed, it did shed some light on the British party system.[2] After analysing the speakers and the division lists, P. M. Williams came to the following conclusions. Half of the 35 Labour opponents were Bevanites, and most of the remainder were pacifists or former recalcitrants. Although 4 of the 5 MPs from North Staffordshire voted against the treaty they had all been rebels before; and out of 27 Labour backbenchers from Lancashire, 15 failed to vote, only 7 voted for the treaty, and 3 of the latter came from constituencies which were not affected. Williams concluded that:

> It seems that the ordinary Labour member will not vote against his party over a constituency grievance; he leaves that to the perennial rebels. Probably he will silently abstain. But

[1] 494 *H.C. Deb.*, col. 879–1008. Also see Epstein, *Britain – Uneasy Ally*, pp. 70–80.
[2] P. M. Williams, letter to the editor, *Economist*, vol. 161 (8 Dec 1951), p. 1395.

he may prefer the combination favoured by many Conservatives – a critical speech to impress his constituents, followed by an obedient vote to satisfy the Whips.[1]

This revolt in the division lobbies was not the end of the complaints, and on 29 January nine Labour dissidents tabled a motion criticizing the Treaty.

Bevan and his followers were involved almost immediately in another dispute. In March 1952 the PLP defeated a Bevanite resolution which declared that the Conservative government's defence programme was beyond the capacity of the country. Approximately three out of every four Labour MPs accepted the Shadow Cabinet's plan to abstain in the division lobbies, and a motion was passed binding the PLP members to abstain.[2] The Whips' Office circulated a three-line whip, and a letter signed by Attlee, Morrison, and Whiteley, was sent to all Labour Members to remind them of the PLP's decision. Nevertheless, 57 Labour MPs voted against the government's defence programme. They maintained that defence policy involved conscientious convictions, and argued that if the Labour party had decided to vote in the division, Members would have been allowed to abstain to demonstrate their beliefs. However, since the party had decided to abstain, the rebels were forced to vote against the White Paper in order to indicate their views. In this division the so-called '57 varieties' were easily defeated by a vote of 313 to 55.[3] Later, when the official opposition motion of censure came to a vote, approximately 60 Labour MPs abstained, and only four of the earlier 57 rebels voted with the Labour party.[4] Of the MPs who had signed the Nenni telegram, 17 were still in the House, and 14 were among the Members who voted against the government's defence policy. The 57 rebels included ten union-sponsored Members, one of whom was Walter Padley, president of the

---

[1] *Ibid.*   [2] Most newspapers gave the count as 120–41.
[3] 497 *H.C. Deb.*, col. 559–60.
[4] They were David Grenfell, Cecil Poole, Ellis Smith, and Barnett Stross.

USDAW. Over a third of the 57 rebels had also revolted on the Ireland Bill in 1949.

The Labour Chief Whip, William Whiteley, announced that he favoured withdrawing the whip from all 57 rebels, but this was much too extreme. There were at least three reasons why none of them lost the whip. The Standing Orders were still suspended, the rebel group was very large, and the dissidents had considerable support in the constituencies.[1] One rebel Member, Hugh Delargy, resigned his position as a junior Whip on the night of the first division.[2]

The local Ebbw Vale party passed a resolution in complete support of Aneurin Bevan, and many national newspapers published letters congratulating the Labour rebel and his followers. However, the *Daily Herald* violently attacked Bevan under the title 'This is a time for frankness'. The article declared, 'We must tell Mr. Aneurin Bevan and his supporters that they have set out a course which will harm the country and imperil the future of the Labour Movement'.[3] Newspaper comments became so bitter that Labour supporters finally said that the Tory press was trying to discredit the Labour party by writing about non-existent 'splits', 'feuds' and 'intrigues'. The truth was that Labour newspapers and Labour partisans had been using the same vocabulary.[4]

During the height of the Bevanite controversy the Parliamentary Committee recommended that the whip should be withdrawn from any of the 57 rebels who would not give an undertaking for better conduct in the future.[5] This proposal was unacceptable to a majority of the PLP, but they did accept

[1] *Daily Telegraph*, 3 Mar 1952. *Manchester Guardian*, 3 Mar 1952. For a general discussion see chapters 9 and 10.
[2] Unpublished letter, Hugh Delargy to author, 21 May 1965.
[3] *Daily Herald*, 6 Mar 1952.
[4] Emrys Hughes even complained that the *Daily Herald* suppressed parliamentary news in favour of news about official party policy. See *Forward*, 15 Mar 1952.
[5] Morrison, *Government and Parliament*, p. 130.

I

a compromise proposal by George Strauss that the Standing Orders should be reimposed.[1] The NEC noted this decision 'with approval'.

The Bevanites extended their rebellion to the issue of German rearmament in May 1952. They put down a motion which declared that before the Federal Republic was rearmed there ought to be a Four Power Conference to discuss the possibility of free elections for Germany.[2] Party leaders were indignant about this EDM, and criticized the rebels for acting without permission from the Whips' Office. Bevan replied that since the motion was practically identical with a NEC statement, no permission was needed to place it in the Order Paper.[3] This disagreement prompted some Labour Members to assert that they had signed under a misapprehension and to withdraw their names from the motion. But three left-wing Members added their names.[4]

Since the new Standing Orders did not prevent the Bevanites from publicly criticizing party policy, charges were raised that the Labour party was becoming two parties. Employing an analogy with Communist infiltration, Attlee said that there was 'a party within' the Labour party, and demanded that the Bevanite group be disbanded. On 23 October the PLP carried the following resolution by 188 votes to 51:[5]

> This PLP accepts and endorses the statement of the leader of the party, calls for the immediate abandonment of all group organizations within the party other than those officially recognized; it further calls upon all members to refrain from making

[1] The vote was 162–73. *News Chronicle*, 6 Mar 1952.
[2] *Notices of Motions*, 26 May 1952.
[3] *Daily Telegraph*, 30 May 1952.
[4] Those who removed their names were: S. O. Davies, Wilfred Fienburgh, Charles Gray, and James Johnson. James Carmichael, Horace King, and David Weitzman then signed the EDM.
[5] *Oldham Chronicle*, 12 Oct 1952. Approximately 50 Members abstained.

attacks on one another either in the House, the press, or the platform.[1]

On 28 October the Bevanites agreed not to hold any more meetings in the House of Commons, and with their formal organization discontinued, the group soon became less cohesive. However, the rebels defiantly announced that they would attempt to reverse the PLP's decision and would continue their Brains Trusts' meetings in the constituencies.

According to the Gallup poll, Bevan lost 11% of his support with the Labour rank and file between September and October 1952.[2] Nevertheless, his group received extensive newspaper coverage because of the activity of their Brains Trusts. They had access to *Reynolds News* (Tom Driberg's column), the *Sunday Pictorial* (R. H. S. Crossman's articles), and especially to *Tribune*. They also made use of the *New Statesman* and radio broadcasts. All of these channels of information were used in order to gain more support for Bevanite policies in the constituencies.

In November 1952 Bevan was unsuccessful in his contest for the deputy leadership, and was the last member to be elected to the PLP Committee.[3] This did not deter his followers. Through *Tribune* they criticized the role of unions in the party,

[1] *The Times*, 24 Oct 1952. *Manchester Guardian*, 24 Mar 1955.

[2] The Gallup polls asked 'Which are you more likely to support, Bevan and his views or those of the other Labour leaders?' *News Chronicle*, 23 Oct 1952.

All	Sept 1952	Oct 1952
Bevan	34	22
Other Labour Leaders	53	51
Don't Know	13	27
Party Members		
Bevan	51	40
Others	44	48
Don't Know	5	12

[3] Herbert Morrison became deputy leader by a vote of 194 to 82. Morrison defeated Bevan for this position again on 28 Oct 1953, by a vote of 181 to 76.

and even attacked Lincoln Evans for accepting a knighthood from the Conservative government. This provoked the NEC to investigate *Tribune* and its various activities, and on 25 February, it ruled that the Brains Trusts were 'contrary to the spirit and intention of the recent decisions of the PLP'.[1] The *Manchester Guardian* retorted that the Bevanites were being systematically disarmed, and claimed that Labour leaders had first prevented group activity within the party, and then tried to thwart all press criticism.[2] *The Economist* complained that 'Mr. Bevan has been weakened only by imposing on Labour MPs a far more rigid discipline than has ever been experienced before in British politics'.[3] And it pointed out that 'In fighting Bevanism the Labour Party has adopted methods that could be exploited, if power ever fell into illiberal hands, on dangerous authoritarian lines'.[4] *Tribune* declared that it would not stop its activities, and stated that the Brains Trusts were held at the request of either constituency parties or Fabian societies, and did not require permission from the NEC or the PLP. Moreover, *Tribune* claimed that the action of disbanding group activity within the PLP was a breach of parliamentary privilege, and they asked party leaders to explain the difference between the Bevanites and other parliamentary groups.[5]

The Bevanite revolt reached its zenith at the Morecambe conference in October 1952 when Harold Wilson and R. H. S. Crossman were elected to the NEC.[6] This success gave the Bevanites six of the seven constituency places on the executive,

---

[1] *Daily Herald*, 26 Feb 1953. The NEC also criticized Sir William Lawther and the *Daily Herald* for attacking the Bevanites. *Tribune* had been founded in 1937 by Stafford Cripps, Aneurin Bevan, George Strauss, and others.
[2] *Manchester Guardian*, 26 Feb 1953.
[3] *The Economist*, 1 Nov 1952.   [4] *Ibid*.
[5] There were, for example, groups in the PLP concerned with Africa, Temperance, World Government, and a Parliamentary Socialist Christian group.
[6] Herbert Morrison, who had been a member of the NEC since 1922, was defeated along with Hugh Dalton.

and they were able to hold them again in 1953 at Margate. The rebel group was suspected of having sent secret letters to constituency parties asking them to support Bevan's adherents at the conference. In order to counteract this suspected move Herbert Morrison sent a letter to every local party repudiating Bevan and his followers. An anti-Bevanite group had also been formed,[1] and three powerful trade-union leaders, Arthur Deakin, Sir William Lawther, and Sir Thomas Williamson had made public their opposition to Bevan. Of course, not all unions opposed Bevan, and some were split internally over whether or not to support him.[2] Two such unions were the USDAW and the NUR. Although USDAW supported Bevan, its sponsored MPs were split on the question of German re-armament. The editor of the *Railway Review* asked NUR MPs how long they intended to support policies which were condemned by both the NUR and the vast majority of constituency parties. The NUR executive repudiated the editor's opinion, and '. . . the NUR MPs retorted that they were bound by the "higher law" of the decisions of the PLP, not by the Annual General Meeting of the NUR'.[3]

After the Margate conference, the Bevanite controversy persisted in a variety of minor forms. On 13 November 1953, J. P. W. Mallalieu wrote an article which attacked the principle of secret voting in the PLP. It ended with the caustic remark: 'It looks as though some of these chaps [Labour MPs] say one thing in public in the country and another thing behind closed doors at the party meetings.'[4] The PLP Committee warned

---

[1] This was really only an extension in the activities of the so-called XYZ Group which had been formed in the 1930s.
[2] According to the *Sunday Times*, 5 Oct 1952, the AEU, USDAW, ETU, NUPE, and possibly the NUR supported Bevan. Throughout the entire period the *Daily Worker* listed all of the organizations, large or small which supported Bevan.
[3] Harrison, *Trade Unions and the Labour Party*, p. 294.
[4] *Tribune*, 27 Nov 1953.

Mallalieu about writing such articles,[1] but no more was said about this offence.[2] On 10 December the NEC censured Ian Mikardo for writing a *Tribune* article attacking the TUC. Mikardo had opposed a TUC statement on British Guiana and had spoken at a meeting for Dr. Jagan, who was leader of the People's Progressive party. Labour leaders showed that they were just as concerned with the bad publicity brought by Mikardo's actions as they were with preventing every deviation; when Donald Chapman abstained in a division over British Guiana there was little criticism of his revolt.

Labour backbenchers had protested against German rearmament since 1951, and a number of them still disagreed with the official party policy on Germany. On 9 February 1954, the critics placed an EDM in the Order Paper welcoming Ollenhauer's promotion of elections for a unified Germany, and congratulating him for his efforts to prohibit a military alliance between Germany and the Four Powers. A second motion advocating the same solution was tabled almost a year later on 25 January 1955.[3] The Labour Whips did not demur at either of these EDMs even though the motions publicized the extent of party dissension over Germany.

Bevan personally did not sign either of the motions; but on 14 April 1954 when he resigned from the PLP Committee, ostensibly because of Labour policy on SEATO, he declared his dissatisfaction with German rearmament. This resignation had two immediate results; Harold Wilson replaced Bevan on the PLP Committee, and public attention was focused more sharply on the troubles within the Labour party. Shortly after Bevan's resignation, a Gallup poll suggested that only 29% of Labour supporters in the country accepted his views.[4]

[1] Dalton, *High Tide and After*, pp. 394–6.
[2] *News Chronicle*, 27 Nov 1953. *Daily Telegraph*, 27 Dec 1953.
[3] *Notices of Motions*, 9 Feb 1954, and 25 Jan 1955.
[4] The April 1954 Gallup poll asked: 'Which are you more likely to support, Bevan and his views, or those of the other Labour leaders?' The results were:

At the end of April, Bevanites and pacifists joined to support Frank Beswick's amendment on the Third Reading of the Atomic Energy Bill. Beswick's amendment would have required the government to obtain approval from both Houses before manufacturing hydrogen bombs. The amendment stated: 'Nothing in this Act shall be deemed to authorize the Authority to produce a thermonuclear (or hydrogen) bomb unless a Resolution to that effect shall have been passed by each House of Parliament.'[1] George Strauss appealed to Labour Members to abstain, but 65 of them voted in favour of the amendment. Among the rebels were three Labour Whips, Kenneth Robinson, Charles Royle, and John Taylor.[2] Two of them were forced to resign their positions, but Taylor was reprieved after writing a letter of apology to the Labour Chief Whip. (An examination of Members who lost party positions because of their rebelliousness is included in chapter 9.)

In May the NEC reaffirmed that its decisions were to be obeyed on all issues. But after considerable pressure the NEC amended this statement, and declared that 'the issue of German rearmament shall be declared to be exempt as regards individual expression of opinion from the implications imposed by the resolution passed by the NEC on May 18'.[3] In the mean-

	Labour supporters
Bevan	29%
Others	54%
Don't Know	17%

News Chronicle, 30 Apr 1954.

[1] 526 *H.C. Deb.*, col. 1795.

[2] 526 *H.C. Deb.*, col. 1843 ff. Twelve of the signatories were ex-ministers: Aneurin Bevan, Frank Beswick, Geoffrey Bing, Arthur Blenkinsop, Ernest Davies, Hugh Delargy, William Paling, John Parker, Kenneth Robinson, Charles Royle, Julian Snow, Frederick Willey. Another significant vote took place in July 1954 on the Army and Air Expenditures. The Labour party abstained, but George Wigg and Geoffrey Bing acted as tellers and forced a division. 530 *H.C. Deb.*, col. 643–4.

[3] *Manchester Guardian*, 24 Mar 1955.

time the dispute continued on a personal level. Bevan questioned Attlee in the House about Labour's attitude to SEATO. Herbert Morrison attacked Bevan in *Socialist Commentary*, claiming that there were no real policy differences between Bevan and the Labour leaders, and that Bevan's tactics were aiding the Tories.[1] The leaders of the Bevanite group published a controversial pamphlet entitled *It need not happen. The alternative to German rearmament,* and organized regional conferences to familiarize the rank and file with the 'disastrous' policies of Transport House. Morgan Phillips replied with another warning.[2] This type of threat and counter-threat continued throughout this period, and although no rebels were punished the threats portended a more significant crisis in the party.

The 1954 annual conference was the scene of further conflicts over German rearmament. Bevan withdrew from the contest for a constituency seat on the NEC and stood against Gaitskell for the position of Treasurer. He undoubtedly hoped this tactic would lead to the defeat of Gaitskell and that this would mean he would have one more supporter on the NEC. When Gaitskell won the election, Bevan was left without a place on the NEC, and this may have contributed to the final break-down of relations between Bevan and Attlee. After considerable controversy the Scarborough conference accepted the NEC's policy on German rearmament. Although the decision could have gone either way, at the last minute the Woodworkers supported the official policy, and the NEC was victorious by the narrow vote of 3,270,000 to 3,022,000.[3]

In November 1954 the Conservative government proposed to accept the principle of German rearmament. In view of the close decision at Scarborough, the PLP decided to abstain in

---

[1] *Socialist Commentary*, 5 May 1954.
[2] *Daily Mail*, 16 Jul 1954. The editors of *Tribune* and the members of the NEC continued to attack each other throughout this period. See *Daily Herald*, 28 Oct 1954, and *News Chronicle*, 1 Oct 1954.
[3] *LPCR*, 1954, p. 108.

the division, and the usual instructions from the Whips' Office were reinforced by a letter from Attlee.[1] Nevertheless, six Labour Members voted against the government and one voted for it.[2] John McGovern claimed that he voted with the Conservatives because both the annual Labour conference and the PLP had decided in favour of German rearmament. The other six, George Craddock, S. O. Davies, Ernest Fernyhough, Emrys Hughes, Sydney Silverman, and Victor Yates, asserted that this issue involved moral convictions, and that therefore they were allowed freedom of action. But the PLP adhered to the exact wording of the Standing Orders, and said that Members only had the right to abstain.

At the next PLP meeting the Parliamentary Committee asked that the whip be withdrawn from the rebels because they had voted against the instructions from the Whips' Office.[3] The seven Members were allowed to present their views to the PLP, but the whip was withdrawn from all of them.[4] Many Members complained that the PLP Committee should not have recommended the withdrawal of the whip until after the rebels had been heard in the meeting. They argued that when the Committee recommended that the whip be withdrawn from a Member the vote was more an expression of confidence in the leaders than a decision on the merits of withdrawing the whip. The seven recalcitrants applied to receive the Labour whip before the 1955 general election, and after providing assurances about future loyalty, they were received back into the parlia-

[1] A majority of Labour's backbench committee on Foreign Affairs opposed German rearmament. See *Daily Mail*, 15 Nov 1954.
[2] 533 *H.C. Deb.*, col. 693–6.
[3] Carol Johnson, Secretary of the PLP, wrote to Emrys Hughes that: '. . . in accordance with the Standing Orders, you have the right, if you so desire, to be heard at the party meeting when this recommendation is submitted.' Recorded in *Tribune*, 3 Dec 1954.
[4] *Daily Herald*, 24 Nov 1954. The vote was 131 to 93.

mentary party. (A study of Members who lost the whip is found in chapter 9.)

This disciplinary action led to another parliamentary revolt. When the Whips' proposals for membership on the Estimates Committee was published, it was evident that Victor Yates's name had been left off because he had lost the whip. This angered a number of Labour MPs and they forced a debate and division on the membership of the committee. The debate was conducted in a lighthearted fashion, but the whips were applied by both parties. Although the government and opposition frontbenches agreed that all committee nominations should go through the Whips' Offices, 35 Labour MPs cross-voted in the division lobbies.[1] The dissidents had made their point, but the leadership carried the day.

In February 1955 the PLP rejected a Bevanite resolution that it should declare itself in favour of immediate Four Power talks. Thereupon, Bevan and 113 Labour MPs tabled a motion calling for these talks, and condemned the government for not having had discussions before the ratification of the London and Paris treaties. There was little that could be done to punish this many MPs, but the PLP later passed a resolution regretting the tabling of such an EDM in defiance of a PLP decision.[2] Labour leaders argued that Bevan's motion was unacceptable because it was linked with the question of German rearmament, and later they tabled their own motion censuring the Conservative government for delay.[3] One Labour MP, Edwin Gooch, was so convinced by this tactic that he took his name off the rebel EDM, and signed the official Labour motion.

The Labour party's first major rebellion on the issue of hydrogen bombs took place in early 1955 when Emanuel Shinwell moved an amendment on the Defence White Paper.[4]

---

[1] 536 *H.C. Deb.*, col. 804 ff.   [2] *Observer*, 20 Feb 1955.
[3] *Daily Telegraph*, 11 Mar 1955.
[4] An EDM critical of the government's testing of nuclear weapons had been tabled as early as March 1954, but it

Since the amendment implied support for the use of hydrogen bombs, Aneurin Bevan and 61 Labour MPs abstained even though a three-line whip had been issued.[1] The rebel group did not include all of Bevan's allies, but there were still too many rebels for the leaders to punish, and moreover the Standing Orders allowed Members to abstain.[2] Some Labour leaders thought the circumstances were different in the case of Bevan, and alleged that he had insulted Attlee when he asked him to state precisely how and when Labour would employ nuclear weapons. Bevan had turned to Attlee and asserted: 'The Amendment which has been moved by the opposition speaks about the deterrent effect upon aggression of the threat of using thermo-nuclear weapons . . . it does not say "nuclear aggression", but merely "aggression" of any sort.'[3]

The thought that a general election was impending magnified the difficulties in the Labour party. The *Evening Standard* explained that: 'Not for the first time, Mr. Bevan has proved one of the Tory party's greatest electoral assets',[4] and the *Daily Mail* declared that: 'It is well known that the Socialists are split on foreign policy, defence, NATO, SEATO, German rearmament, National Service, Nationalization, House of Lords reform, and on Colonial policy.'[5] With frightened MPs and a vocal press all talking about Bevan's disloyalty, Labour leaders were inclined to punish him.

had been withdrawn at the request of Labour leaders. *Notices of Motions*, 30 Mar 1954.

[1] There were two divisions, but most of the dissidents voted with their leaders on the defence statement. 537 *H.C. Deb.*, col. 2176 and 2191. See also *The Times*, 4 Mar 1955, and *Manchester Guardian*, 4 Mar 1955.

[2] The following allies of Bevan did not join the rebellion; R. H. S. Crossman, Hugh Delargy, John Freeman, Leslie Hale, A. J. Irvine, and Stephen Swingler.

[3] 537 *H.C. Deb.*, col. 2176. Attlee replied that he was speaking only 'in the most general terms'.

[4] *Evening Standard*, 3 Mar 1955.

[5] *Daily Mail*, 7 Mar 1955.

On 8 March Bevan received a letter which said that because of his recent action and his earlier challenge over SEATO, the Parliamentary Committee had decided to ask the PLP to withdraw the whip from him. It was rumoured that the only Members of the Shadow Cabinet who opposed the decision were Hugh Dalton, Chuter Ede, and Harold Wilson. Apparently the Whips had decided to resign *en masse* if the whip was not withdrawn from Bevan.[1] In private Herbert Morrison had argued with Attlee that withdrawal of the whip was of no value without expulsion, but Attlee had disagreed.[2]

At the PLP meeting a compromise resolution to chastise Bevan without withdrawing the whip from him was defeated by only 14 votes, and the final decision to withdraw the whip was won by only 29 votes.[3] This narrow success cannot be considered a victory for Attlee, especially since Labour MPs had been told that if they voted for the motion to censure Bevan without withdrawing the whip, it would be 'a vote of no confidence in Mr. Attlee.'[4] Bevan said that he had not broken the Standing Orders because he had only abstained, but party leaders argued that the whip ought to be withdrawn because of his 'conduct over a period.'

Before the PLP met to discuss Bevan's action, a Gallup poll was issued which indicated that twice as many people wanted Bevan to retain the whip as wanted it withdrawn from him.[5] And some local parties demanded that their Members vote against any punishments. The Coventry Labour party, for example, told Miss Elaine Burton, R. H. S. Crossman, and Maurice Edelman that the whip should not be withdrawn from Bevan.[6] Therefore during the PLP debate, Elaine Burton

[1] *Birmingham Evening Dispatch*, 18 Mar 1955. See also *Coventry Evening Telegraph*, 17 Mar 1955.
[2] Morrison, interview.
[3] The vote was 141 to 112. *Economist*, 19 Mar 1955.
[4] *New Statesman*, 2 Apr 1955, p. 461.
[5] *News Chronicle*, 17 Mar 1955.
[6] *Daily Express*, 10 Mar 1955; Dalton, *High Tide and After*, p. 409.

asked Attlee if he considered the vote a question of confidence in his leadership. He replied in the affirmative.[1] Thus, when the Coventry Labour party met to discuss Miss Burton's vote against Bevan, she replied that the vote had been an expression of confidence in Attlee. The Coventry party reacted by passing a vote of no confidence in her.[2] Other local parties asked their Members to explain why they had voted for withdrawal of the whip, and the Darlington Labour party, which had condemned the disciplinary measures used against Bevan, was not deterred from getting rid of its own rebel councillors.[3]

Rumours were circulated that if Bevan were expelled he might lose the £150 he received from the National Union of Mineworkers. The Secretary of the NUM, Arthur Horner, stated publicly that the rumours were false and that Bevan would not lose his stipend.[4] Nevertheless, Bevan claimed that if the NUM took away his allowance, the House of Commons would consider it a breach of privilege. It is doubtful that this would have happened because of the precedent which had been set in the cases of W. A. Robinson in 1944 and W. J. Brown in 1947. In the latter case the Civil Service Clerical Association proposed to discontinue the appointment of W. J. Brown as their parliamentary secretary because he opposed their desire to repeal the 1926 Act on the affiliation of civil service unions to the TUC. The Committee of Privileges ruled that no breach of privilege had taken place, and declared that:

> It is a breach of privilege to take or threaten action which is not merely calculated to affect the Member's course of action in Parliament but is of a kind against which it is absolutely necessary that Members should be protected if they are to discharge their duties as such independently, without fear of punishment or hope of reward.[5]

[1] *Daily Herald*, 17 Mar 1955.
[2] *Ibid.*, 23 Mar 1955. Discussed in chapter 10.
[3] *Northern Dispatch*, 18 Mar 1955.
[4] *Daily Mirror*, 17 Mar 1955, and *Daily Sketch*, 17 Mar 1955.
[5] *Report of the Committee of Privileges*, H.M.S.O. (17 June,

Bevan's situation was even more similar to the 1944 case of W. A. Robinson. Robinson was General Secretary of the NUDAW when he was asked by his union to vacate his parliamentary seat because of his personal conduct and his handling of constituency duties. When Robinson refused to resign the NUDAW withdrew his retainer, but this was not held to be a breach of privilege.

Bevan's supporters applied pressure in the form of publicity and appeals to Transport House in an attempt to prevent his expulsion. The Margate Labour party sent 1,000 letters to constituency parties inviting them to a conference where the rank and file could make known their opinions about Bevan.[1] Morgan Phillips announced that the NEC might take action against any parties which attended such a conference, but this proved unnecessary when the NEC solved the difficulties.

At the NEC meeting Attlee proposed a compromise resolution to prevent Bevan from being expelled. He suggested that Bevan should meet a sub-committee, and offer a pledge of party loyalty. Attlee probably feared that an expulsion would widen the split in the party, and have serious electoral consequences. The NEC accepted their leader's proposal by a vote of only 14 to 13.[2] Bevan's following statement of loyalty proved acceptable to the NEC sub-committee:

1947), p. xii. W. J. Brown had been General Secretary of the CSCA from 1919 to 1942, a Labour MP for West Wolverhampton from 1929 to 1931, and an Independent MP for Rugby from 1942 to 1950. Also see chapter 7 of Geoffrey Marshall and Graeme C. Moodie, *Some Problems of the Constitution*.

[1] *The Times*, 22 Mar 1955. A Gallup poll at the time showed that $53\frac{1}{2}\%$ of Labour voters opposed Bevan's expulsion.

[2] The chairman, Edith Summerskill, did not vote. A resolution to expel Bevan was proposed by Jack Cooper and Percy Knight. One member who voted for this proposal, Wilfred Burke, was later criticized and was reported to the executive of his union. *Northern Echo*, 26 Mar 1955. In 1939 both Attlee and Morrison had voted

The charge is that in what I have done and also in the way I have done it I have created difficulties for Mr. Attlee and caused him embarrassment in his position as the leader of the party.

This was certainly never my intention, but if my action or speech could lend themselves to the interpretation that such was my motive then I am sincerely sorry, and apologize to Mr. Attlee for any pain I may have caused him.

I ask for nothing more than the opportunity to serve our party under his leadership. In doing so, I claim no more privilege than, and accept all the obligations shared by, other members of the party.[1]

In a few weeks Bevan applied for the Labour whip, and after only 44 days as an Independent it was restored to him.[2] The left-wing claimed this as a victory for their cause, but Labour leaders had both maintained their former policies and kept the party united before an imminent general election.

Bevan's expulsion completely overshadowed the resignation of another Labour backbencher which also took place in the last months of the parliament. Sir Richard Acland resigned from the House and the Labour party, and sought re-election as an Independent in order to make known his opposition to the manufacturing of hydrogen bombs in Britain.[3] A sub-committee of the NEC met immediately and decided that Acland was automatically deprived of party membership since he was standing as an Independent candidate. The sub-committee also decided that an official candidate would stand if there was a by-election in Gravesend.[4] However, the 1955 general election eliminated the need for a by-election, and Acland was defeated in a contest where the special issue of

to expel Bevan from the party. See Mark Krug, *Aneurin Bevan: Cautious Rebel*, p. 12.

[1] *Birmingham Mail*, 25 Mar 1955.
[2] *Daily Express*, 29 Apr 1955.
[3] Acland was financially independent, and this may have enabled him to rebel. See *New Statesman*, 2 Apr 1955.
[4] *Daily Mail*, 15 Mar 1955.

hydrogen bombs was obscured. Whereas he had received 55% of the vote as an official Labour candidate in 1951, he obtained only 13·7% when he stood as an Independent in 1955. This small percentage of the vote was enough to cause the Labour candidate to be defeated by a Conservative, Peter Kirk, by a majority of 6·1% of the total vote.

The only Labour revolts during this parliament in which Bevan was not somewhat involved were over the proposals for a Central African Federation and the National Service Act. The first of these controversies began within the PLP in March 1953 when a so-called Keep Right group met privately, and decided that they would abstain in the division if a specified number of Members declared their intention to rebel.[1] They made their views known to the PLP Committee, and hence were called to a special meeting with James Griffiths and Sir Frank Soskice before the debate. This had little effect since party leaders asserted that they could not compromise because the Tory policy for the Central African Federation was initiated while Labour was in office. At the end of the debate 16 Labour MPs abstained, even though a three-line whip had been issued. The rebels did not abstain publicly, and this made their offence less conspicuous, and hence less serious for Labour leaders. The Bevanites were delighted with this revolt because some of these Keep Right rebels had been their most severe critics. Much attention was also given to the fact that Patrick Gordon Walker was a member of the group which abstained. Since Gordon Walker had been the minister responsible for the dispute over Seretse Khama, many Members wanted to know why it was possible to invoke the conscience clause in one case but not the other.[2] The difference was simply that if the Labour government had allowed the conscience clause to be invoked in 1951 the government would have been defeated. None of the Members who abstained over Central Africa were punished, and the emotion quickly subsided.

[1] Stanley Evans, interview.   [2] *Observer*, 29 Mar 1953.

The conscience clause was invoked again over the National Service Act. In November 1953 a motion was proposed to approve an Order-in-Council which would have extended the Act from 1954 to 1959. An official spokesman said that the Labour party agreed to the continuation of conscription, but that the executive should not be given this power for five years. Therefore the Labour party abstained in the division, but 40 of its backbenchers voted against the proposal.[1] Labour leaders announced that these 40 Members had acted on moral convictions, and that none of them would be punished.

There were only six significant public rebellions in the Conservative party during these four years, and this paucity makes the following statistical conclusions for the Conservatives more tentative than those for the Labour party. The Conservatives had a total of 79 ministers and 256 backbenchers who were Members of the House during at least one rebellion. No ministers joined any of the overt rebellions, which again indicates the effect of collective responsibility. One Member, Fitzroy Maclean, became a minister after joining one small

Table 9: Conservative Party Discipline and
Parliamentary Private Secretaries 1951–55

Rebellious % out of number of revolts (Total 6)	0%	1–33%	34% plus	
PPSs (32)	63%	37%	0%	(100%)
Backbenchers (including PPSs) (256)	48%	44%	9%	(101%)[2]

[1] 520 *H.C. Deb.*, col. 1648.   [2] Caused by rounding.

K

rebellion over the Suez canal. Over half the Conservative backbenchers joined at least one rebellion, and approximately one out of every ten backbenchers was connected with two or more. PPSs again proved to be less rebellious than other backbenchers.

The date of a Member's first entry to the House was not an important factor in the rebellious groupings of this period, but Conservative Members educated at a university did join slightly fewer rebellions than those not educated at a university.

Table 10: Conservative Party Discipline and
Formal Education 1951–55

Rebellious % out of number of revolts (Total 6)	0%	1–33%	34% Plus	
University-educated MPs (148)	53%	39%	7%	(99%)[1]
Non-university-educated MPs (108)	40%	50%	10%	(100%)

Although the Conservative party was in office for four years with a majority of only 17, it did not employ any disciplinary measures. Two Conservative MPs withdrew from the Conservative whip, but neither of them had any difficulties in having it returned. Sir Harry Legge-Bourke chose to stand again as a Conservative in 1955, but Sir John Mellor retired.

There is no indication that the 1952 reintroduction of Standing Orders prevented rebellion in the Labour party; in fact many of the most significant revolts occurred after the new regulations were brought into force. In all, there were still twice as many Labour revolts as Conservative, and three out of every five Labour Members joined at least one rebellion.

[1] Caused by rounding.

Because the Bevanite revolts dominated this period, many Members joined a very large number of the total revolts. More than one out of every ten Labour MPs was involved in over half the revolts, and a few Members joined almost every rebellion.[1]

Union-sponsored MPs continued to be less rebellious than non-sponsored MPs, and Co-op-sponsored Members were in the middle category. Almost three times as many unsponsored MPs as compared to those sponsored by a union appear in the highest category of rebellion. Some individual trade-union-sponsored MPs did however join a large number of rebellions.

Table 11 : Labour Party Discipline and Sponsorship 1951–55[2]

Rebellious % out of number of revolts (Total 15)	0%	1–20%	21–50%	51% Plus
Non-sponsored MPs (185)	38%	29%	18%	14% (99%)
Trade-union-sponsored MPs (108)	46%	39%	9%	6% (100%)
Co-op-sponsored MPs (20)	20%	35%	35%	10% (100%)
All backbenchers (313)	40%	34%	16%	11% (101%)[3]

The most rebellious Labour MPs of this period were those who first entered the House in 1945. The pre-1945 and post-

[1] The following MPs joined at least 12 of the 15 rebellions: John Baird, Cyril Bence, George Craddock, Ernest Fernyhough, Julius Silverman, Sydney Silverman and Stephen Swingler.
[2] All 313 Members were in parliament when at least one rebellion occurred.
[3] Caused by rounding.

1950 MPs appear to have been more content with Labour leadership.

Table 12: Labour Party Discipline and
Formal Education 1951–55[1]

Rebellious % out of number of revolts (Total 15)	0%	1–20%	21–50%	51% Plus	
Non-university-educated MPs (91)	36%	26%	21%	16%	(99%)
University-educated MPs (114)	37%	33%	18%	11%	(99%)[2]

Table 13: Labour Party Discipline and
Date of Entry to the House 1951–55[3]

Rebellious % out of number of revolts (Total 15)	0%	1–20%	21–50%	51%	
Pre-1945 MPs (49)	53%	20%	16%	10%	(99%)[4]
Post-1945 MPs (121)	33%	26%	21%	19%	(99%)
Post-1950 MPs (17)	24%	65%	11%	0%	(100%)
Post-1951 MPs (18)	22%	44%	28%	6%	(100%)

During this period no Labour MPs were expelled, but after the reintroduction of the Standing Orders eight rebels had the whip withdrawn. These eight rebels each had joined a very

[1] Trade-union-sponsored Members have been eliminated.
[2] Caused by rounding.
[3] Trade-union-sponsored Members have been eliminated.
[4] Caused by rounding.

large number of the rebellions of the period: Aneurin Bevan 53%, George Craddock 93%, S. O. Davies 60%, Ernest Fernyhough 80%, Emrys Hughes 73%, John McGovern 33%, Sydney Silverman 87%, and Victor Yates 73%. Despite the fact that these eight Members had been involved in many rebellions they were still allowed to renew their membership in the PLP. The three Whips who lost their positions because of a particular rebellion differed considerably in the number of total revolts which they joined: Kenneth Robinson 40%, Charles Royle 27%, and John Taylor 7%.

Party discipline during this period was not as harsh, as frequently applied, or as much associated with action in the House as is usually alleged. Moreover, there was more public rebellion than political treatises usually acknowledge.

6 Rebellions and Party Discipline 1955-1959

All men have agreed that in the conduct of public affairs
there is nothing more precious than discipline and it is
a great mistake that discipline is incompatible with the
deepest convictions . . . .[1]

The Conservative party again enlarged its share of the electoral
votes, and its absolute majority rose to 58 in the 1955 general
election. This success was accompanied by a significant increase
in the number of public backbench rebellions. The Suez crisis
dominated the twenty-one major disputes, and caused a
significant amount of constituency pressure to be brought
against dissident Tory MPs. Labour's second successive defeat
brought a sharp decline in the number of open revolts in the
party. Although they were still not completely united on a
policy for Germany or nuclear weapons, their nine open
rebellions did not include any cross-votes or abstentions.
Throughout the period Labour's new Chief Whip, Herbert
Bowden, did not have to contend with any significant rebellions
on domestic policy, or any revolts from the right-wing of the
party. Labour Members appear to have decided that their
first priority was to oppose the Conservative government.

During the first few weeks of the 1955 parliament Labour
leaders made a series of statements about the reasons for their
defeat. Gaitskell declared that public quarrels between Labour
Members had undermined public confidence in the party,[2] and
a special committee under the chairmanship of Harold Wilson
concluded that internal dissension was one of the main causes

[1] Disraeli in *The Times*, 7 Aug 1878. Quoted in W. L.
Guttsman, *The British Political Elite*, p. 284.
[2] *The Times*, 3 Jun 1955, and 21 Jun 1955. And see
Shinwell, *The Labour Story*, p. 198.

of Labour's defeat. *Man and Metal*, the journal of the Iron and Steel Trades Confederation, correctly summarized the attitude of many Labour leaders:

> Labour supporters in the country were so confused by attacks within the party on constitutionally-arrived-at decisions that thousands of them did not vote. We lost the general election because of internecine strife, personal vilification, and journalistic ebullience concerned more with its own than party advancement.[1]

Naturally, a few Labour Members would not ascribe the 1955 defeat to party dissension. At the Margate Labour conference Victor Yates maintained that a 'spirit of intolerance' was permeating the party, and said this was proved by the fact that six Labour Members had lost the whip in the last parliament. Attlee retorted with his now famous phrase that conscience should be 'a still, small voice and not a loud-speaker'.[2] The conference agreed with Attlee, and there were so few public revolts in the Labour party between 1955 and 1959 that it appears the PLP also accepted their leader's opinion. The reconciliation of Aneurin Bevan with Hugh Gaitskell, the new party leader, was obviously one of the principal reasons for the decrease in Labour rebellions. The Labour party no longer had to contend with a rebel group as significant as the Bevanites: Victory for Socialism was vociferous, but powerless. In foreign affairs, where backbench rebels had been so clamorous in the preceding parliament, the only policies which caused serious dispute were over Suez, Germany, and especially unilateralism, but none of these proved to be threatening to the leadership.

The new Conservative Chief Whip, Edward Heath, on the other hand, had to control group agitation over many diverse topics. For the first time in their long period in office Conservative backbenchers asserted their opinions aggressively in

---

[1] Oct 1955.
[2] *LPCR*, 1955, p. 210. *The Times*, 15 Oct 1955.

the form of Early Day Motions, abstentions, and even cross-votes. With the salient exception of Suez and one rather minor revolt over NATO, all of the Conservative rebellions were in domestic affairs. Capital punishment caused continual dissension from late 1955 until 1958, but the problems of purchase tax, licensing, coal industry, rent, the economic situation and government expenditures were also hotly contested. There were, as well, three constituency issues which caused revolts – white fish subsidy, local government, and cotton policy.

THE CONSERVATIVE PARTY

Table 14: Conservative Revolts 1955–59

	Number of Revolts	Main Issues
Domestic	13	Capital and Corporal Punishment
		Coal Industry Bill
		Cotton Policy
		Economic Situation
		Licensing Bill
		Local Government Act
		Purchase Tax
		Rent Bill
		White Fish Subsidy
Foreign Affairs and Defence	8	NATO
		Suez

The most troublesome domestic issue for the Conservative government during these years was capital punishment. Criticism began early in the parliament, and by 1958 the Conservative government had dealt with four contentious EDMs over penal reform and capital punishment. Two of them indicated strong support for abolition of the death penalty;

one advocated that for a period of five years no person should be sentenced to death for murder, and the other said that the House would welcome an 'opportunity to consider a Motion that the Death Penalty (Abolition) Bill be read a second time'.[1] These reform proposals were countered by three other motions suggesting that the courts should be allowed to award capital punishment for all murders, and corporal punishment for all crimes against the person.[2] The abolitionists and the diehards had each formed informal groups inside and outside the House to promote their causes. The dissident Members were not punished by the Whips, and in fact party leaders were in a dilemma as to what to do about them. According to one of the diehard leaders, Sir Thomas Moore, 'the Whips never said a word' to him about his activities.[3] Conservative leaders finally allowed a free vote on the capital punishment question.[4]

Conservative leaders were forced to seek compromise solutions for several other domestic revolts. For example, early in the new parliament the Conservative government encountered difficulties over the Road Traffic Bill.[5] Although more than 20 amendments were tabled, changes were finally made, and in spite of some difficulty at the Committee stage there were no floor revolts.[6] Throughout much of the first year there was also backbench agitation for purchase tax reform. Gerald Nabarro persistently questioned the government, Viscount

[1] *Notices of Motions*, 15 Nov 1955, and 16 Nov 1955.
[2] *Notices of Motions*, 28 Feb 1956, 4 Feb 1958, and 3 Feb 1958.
[3] Sir Thomas Moore, interview.
[4] See Christoph, *Capital Punishment and British Politics.*
[5] In July 1955 Gerald Nabarro and Terence Clarke opposed the increase in the price of coal which had been introduced by Geoffrey Lloyd, the Minister of Fuel and Power. As a protest Nabarro resigned his position as joint Secretary of the backbench Fuel and Power Committee, and although there were no divisions on the issue, Lloyd relinquished his position in December 1955. *The Times*, 12, 13 Jul 1955, and see 543 *H.C. Deb.*, col. 944.
[6] 553 *H.C. Deb.*, col. 396. *The Times*, 12 Jul 1955.

Hinchingbrooke voted twice against government motions to increase purchase tax, and Sir Harry Legge-Bourke joined him on 26 October 1955.[1] In the cases of the Road Traffic Bill and purchase tax reform, compromises between the government and backbenchers made it possible to avoid serious splits in the party.

Compromise was also necessary over the White Fish Subsidy Bill. The first government proposal received vehement complaints from Conservative and Labour backbenchers who represented constituencies which were affected by the scheme. Derek Heathcoat Amory, Minister of Agriculture, attended a meeting of Conservative MPs from fishery regions on 14 December 1955, and about 30 of them threatened to disobey the whip if changes were not made in the proposals.[2] A few days later, the Minister introduced a White Fish subsidy scheme which restored half of the cut originally proposed for smaller vessels. In spite of this compromise Robert Boothby and 10 Ulster Unionist MPs abstained.[3] Since this was obviously a matter involving local interests there was no reference to party discipline.

In the same month the NUT opposed the government's new Teachers' Superannuation Bill because it increased teachers' contributions by 1%. The teachers indicated their dissatisfaction with the bill by declining to collect school savings, and on 6 December when the Second Reading was forced to a division, J. C. Jennings, a NUT representative, described to the House the clash of loyalty he felt being both a member of the Conservative party and a representative of the NUT. He did not comply with the instructions from the Whips' Office, but

---

[1] 545 *H.C. Deb.*, col. 231. On 16 Nov Hinchingbrooke cross-voted alone. 546 *H.C. Deb.*, col. 655.

[2] S. E. Finer, *Anonymous Empire*, p. 64. *The Times*, 15 Dec 1955.

[3] During this parliament the Ulster Unionists also agitated for improved pensions for the Royal Ulster Constabulary, and demanded more aid for Northern Ireland's unemployment problems.

voted against the bill.[1] Pressure for change continued after the Second Reading, and some Conservative backbenchers tabled an amendment calling for the increase in teachers' contributions to be delayed. As a result of this criticism the Minister, Sir David Eccles, introduced his own amendment which postponed the bill for six months.[2] This slowing down of the implementation of the measure completely stopped all public criticism of the bill. Although this compromise was a rather weak one, it did again indicate the sensitivity of the Conservative party in solving internal disputes.

Most domestic rebellions during 1956 and 1957 were completely overshadowed by the Suez Crisis, but although they attracted comparatively little attention, there were four occasions during these years when at least two Conservative backbenchers revolted in the division lobbies. On 7 February 1956, Cyril Black and Peter Remnant voted against the Second Reading of the Licensing (Airports) Bill.[3] The aim of this bill was to enable passengers on international flights in or out of Britain to purchase alcoholic beverages at any hour. Remnant felt that the matter should be left to the licensing justices, and Black wanted a free vote. In May of the same year 22 Conservatives led by Gerald Nabarro cross-voted on the Second Reading of the Coal Industry Bill because they opposed increasing the borrowing power of the National Coal Board.[4] However the House negated by 143 votes to 23 Nabarro's amendment for the rejection of the bill. The opposition did not vote in the division, although they supported the government, and enjoyed the opportunity to taunt Conservative leaders about trouble with their backbenchers. On neither occasion was there any public mention of party discipline or sanctions.

The Rent Act also caused considerable animosity in the Conservative party. When dissident Tory Members failed to

<hr />

[1] 547 *H.C. Deb.*, col. 246.   [2] *The Times*, 7 Dec 1955.
[3] The Labour party called for a free vote, but the Conservative party did not.
[4] 552 *H.C. Deb.*, col. 1537.

change the Act by sending delegations to the Minister, they made their discontent public. During the Committee stage in February 1951 they objected to clause 9 which sought to de-control the rent of 800,000 tenants within six months, and finally the Minister amended the bill so that the houses did not become decontrolled for 15 months.[1] This second use of the weapon of delay did not satisfy every objection. At the Report stage, W. R. Rees-Davies and Robert Jenkins moved a motion which placed a limitation on excessive rents by initiating a rental ceiling for three years.[2] The government issued only a two-line whip and 11 Conservatives abstained ostentatiously.[3] Again there was no public mention of party discipline or sanc-tions. The Rent Act dissension continued into 1958, but although two amendments were tabled, there were no Con-servative cross-votes or public abstentions.[4]

In July 1957 three of a small group of seven Independent Conservatives (who are discussed in detail in the foreign affairs section following) joined Martin Lindsay and Col. Claude Lancaster in abstaining during a division concerned with the economic situation. Lindsay said that he and his friends would not support the government's policies because they were leading to a serious inflation.[5] The next year there was a serious split

[1] This applied to tenants whose rent was over £30 per year (in London and Scotland £40). Finer, *Anonymous Empire*, p. 70.

[2] 567 *H.C. Deb.*, col. 989 and 996. One of the dissidents, Robert Price, objected to a clause in the bill, but said he could not lead a major revolt against it because he favoured the rest of the bill. *Ibid.*, col. 1427.

[3] 567 *H.C. Deb.*, col. 1005. *The Times*, 27 Mar 1957.

[4] The amendments are found in 581 *H.C. Deb.*, col. 1199 and 582 *H.C. Deb.*, col. 223. The dissatisfied MPs also sent a special delegation to see the Prime Minister and Henry Brooke, the Minister of Housing and Local Government. See *The Times*, 27 Feb and 1 Mar 1958.

[5] Viscount Hinchingbrooke, Angus Maude, and Lawrence Turner abstained. 574 *H.C. Deb.*, col. 726–7. *The Times*, 26 Jul 1957.

in the Cabinet over government expenditure, but at no time did the government come close to being defeated in the division lobbies over economic policy.[1] When Macmillan refused to authorize a cut in government expenditure Peter Thorneycroft, Chancellor of the Exchequer, and two other Treasury ministers, Nigel Birch and Enoch Powell, resigned. On the day of Thorneycroft's resignation, the Prime Minister, leaving London airport on a tour, announced that he had settled his 'little local difficulties' and was now turning to the wider vision of the Commonwealth. The three former ministers said that they did not intend to extend the revolt, and on 23 January 1958 they all voted for the government's economic policy.[2]

The last two domestic revolts in this parliament, like the White Fish Subsidy Bill of 1955, were concerned with constituency interests. In 1958 a minor demonstration occurred in the division lobbies over the Local Government Bill. Conservative MPs who represented seaside towns and spas opposed the system of giving grants to local authorities because the system of weighting meant that some towns had to pay more than their fair share of rates. On an amendment to extend the transitional period of the bill 14 Conservatives and one Labour MP voted against the government.[3] Since this matter directly affected local interests it is not surprising to learn that there was no discussion of party discipline. In fact, Nigel Nicolson later asked his local association why they applauded him

---

[1] Even with a majority of 58 the government was defeated once by a vote of 158 to 155 on the Maintenance Orders Bill, when 43 Conservatives were absent without pairs. 584 *H.C. Deb.*, col. 515 ff. and col. 551. *Daily Mirror*, 14 Mar 1958, and *The Times*, 13 Mar 1958.

[2] 580 *H.C. Deb.*, col. 1267 and 1381. *The Times*, 9 Jan 1958. When the ministers resigned Geoffrey Hirst said he was considering resigning the whip, and he received support from the Shipley association for his criticism of the government. He did not resign the whip, and nothing more was made public about the incident.

[3] 587 *H.C. Deb.*, col. 1121.

when he voted against the Conservative government on this occasion, yet refused to readopt him when he simply abstained over Suez.

The second of these revolts occurred on 30 June 1958 when seven Conservative MPs ignored a three-line whip and publicly abstained in a division on cotton policy. Since they represented constituencies with important cotton industries no action was taken against them.[1]

The Suez crisis caused the most significant revolts in the Conservative party not only in this parliament, but at any time since the Second World War.[2] The background to these revolts was, briefly, as follows. In 1954 the Conservative government decided to evacuate its last military base in the Suez Canal zone by early 1956. Between this event and the major Suez rebellions the United States withdrew its offer of aid for the Aswan Dam, and Nasser decided to nationalize the canal. Britain and France then attacked Egypt ostensibly to prevent a major war between Israel and Egypt.[3]

There were no Conservative cross-votes in any of the five divisions over Suez.[4] The first vote was called on 30 October 1956 because of Eden's 12-hour ultimatum to Egypt, and since there were no purposive abstentions on the Conservative side, the government won easily by 270 to 218. There also were no

[1] 590 *H.C. Deb.*, col. 1007–12. *The Times*, 1 Jul 1958. There was also considerable criticism of the circumstances which led to the death of 11 Mau Mau at the Hola detention camp, and over the Devlin Report, but there were no public rebellions on either of these issues.

[2] See also Leon D. Epstein, 'British M.P.s and their Local Parties: The Suez Cases'; 'Partisan Foreign Policy; Britain in the Suez Crisis'; and *British Politics in the Suez Crisis*.

[3] 531 *H.C. Deb.*, col. 738–9. This was discussed in chapter 5.

[4] They can be found in 558 *H.C. Deb.*, col. 377–82; 558 *H.C. Deb.*, col. 1729–44; 560 *H.C. Deb.*, col. 403–8; 561 *H.C. Deb.*, col. 1577–86; and 570 *H.C. Deb.*, col. 697–704.

ostentatious Conservative abstentions on the Labour censure motion of 1 November. William Yates, however, chose a rather strange method of expressing his dissatisfaction with government policy: he asked the Speaker if it would be proper to bring down the government.[1] Four days later Anthony Nutting, Minister of State for Foreign Affairs, resigned, and was immediately followed to the backbenches by Sir Edward Boyle, Economic Secretary to the Treasury.[2] The resignations had an immediate effect because they showed beyond any doubt that there was a division within the government over the attack on Egypt. On 8 November 1956, eight Conservatives abstained in a division on Suez; they were J. J. Astor, Colonel Cyril Banks, Sir Robert Boothby, Sir Edward Boyle, Sir Frank Medlicott, Nigel Nicolson, Anthony Nutting, and William Yates. Later, two French authors alleged that Eden had halted the Suez operation because of a private revolt of 40 backbenchers led by R. A. Butler. There is little certain evidence for this assertion, but there is no doubt that there were more than eight MPs in the Conservative party who opposed the Suez venture. Two Conservatives were publicly recognized as opponents of the government's Suez campaign; Alex Spearman because of a speech in the House, and Peter Kirk because of various semi-public statements.[3]

The largest Conservative demonstration against Eden's policy in Egypt took place on 28 November 1956 when 24 left-

[1] 558 *H.C. Deb.*, col. 1716–17.

[2] *The Times*, 5 Nov 1956. For the various arguments about whether or not there was dissension within the Cabinet see the following: Anthony Eden, *Full Circle*, Paul Johnson, *The Suez War*, Randolph Churchill, *The Rise and Fall of Sir Anthony Eden*, and Epstein, *British Politics in the Suez Crisis*.

[3] For an interesting press comment on those Conservatives who opposed the war against Egypt, but did not rebel in the division lobbies, see the *Observer*, 18 Nov 1956. Also see the journalistic book by Merry and Serge Bromberger, *Secrets of Suez*.

wing Conservative MPs signed an EDM which criticized the government's policy.[1] None of these backbench critics lost the Conservative whip or resigned from it, but the ten most rebellious Members experienced some disapproval from their constituency associations, and this is discussed in chapter 10.

After protests from the United States and the Soviet Union forced Britain to withdraw her troops from the Canal Zone, Anthony Eden had to withstand storms of criticism from Conservative backbenchers. A right-wing cabal, which had opposed the British withdrawal from Egypt since 1952, had continued to meet and prepare strategy to convince the government to defend British interests in the Middle East.[2] On 6 December 1956, 15 of these Conservative backbenchers ostentatiously abstained in the division on the withdrawal of British troops.[3] Within a month Eden had retired as Prime Minister, and although he was replaced on 10 January 1957 by Harold Macmillan, party dissension over Suez continued.

The Suez diehards continued to have private meetings with the Prime Minister to complain about government policy,[4] and they tabled three rebellious EDMs between 30 January and 9 May 1957.[5] Although 37 different Conservatives signed these motions, the dissident Members soon realized that a more significant form of rebellion was needed if they were to change government policy.

> We have put down motions upon the order paper. We have held debates in the House . . . We have indulged in single abstentions and mass abstentions, and it has not had a single effect whatever on Government policy and thinking.[6]

[1] *Notices of Motions*, 28 Nov 1956.
[2] Its strength had been shown at the 1956 annual conference when it added a pro-Suez amendment to an official resolution. *CPCR*, 1956, pp. 22, 33–4.
[3] *The Times*, 7 Dec 1956. 561 *H.C. Deb.*, col. 1577–86.
[4] Hinchingbrooke, interview.
[5] *Notices of Motions*, 30 Jan, 17 Apr, and 9 May 1957.
[6] *The Times*, 18 May 1957.

The next division occurred on 16 May 1957 after the government advised shipowners to proceed through the Suez Canal. A number of Conservatives thought that the government decision was simply a capitulation to Nasser, and therefore 14 of them abstained and eight of these also resigned the Conservative whip.[1] The eight newly independent Members were John Biggs-Davison, Anthony Fell, Viscount Hinchingbrooke, Patrick Maitland, Angus Maude, Sir Victor Raikes, Lawrence Turner, and Paul Williams.

Another right-wing critic, Lord Lambton, retained the Conservative whip but resigned as PPS to the Foreign Secretary. According to Lord Poole, this action was decidedly different from that of MPs who resigned from the Conservative parliamentary party.[2] When asked what the party would do to those who resigned the whip, Poole said that: '. . . it is a matter for each association, which is entirely autonomous, to deal with, and for each of these particular members to decide whether to remain outside the party or rejoin.'[3] In most of these cases the constituency parties did not react harshly against their Members, and this is discussed more fully in chapter 10. Two of the right-wing rebels, Angus Maude and Sir Victor Raikes, left parliament when they received lucrative employment outside Britain. The other six Independents continued to rebel for a few months before asking the Chief Whip to allow them to return to the party. Patrick Maitland accepted the whip in December 1957, and the others (Biggs-Davison, Fell, Hinchingbrooke, Turner, and Williams) received it in July 1958.[4]

These right-wing rebels were all members of a cabal called the Expanding Commonwealth group which had been meeting

[1] *The Times*, 17 May 1957. Arthur Butler, '1951–1959: The Conservatives in Power', pp. 328–31. Harry Legge-Bourke said that the resignations should have taken place in 1954 when something could have been done, but that in 1957 they were futile. 570 *H.C. Deb.*, col. 633.
[2] *The Times*, 20 May 1957.
[3] *Ibid.*
[4] *The Times*, 24 Dec 1957, 25 Jun 1958, and 12 Jul 1958.

L

weekly to discuss how to exert right-wing influence in foreign policy. Their aim was to change foreign policy in the Middle East without overthrowing the government. As one MP who had abstained in an earlier division said: '. . . if I thought that by my abstention there was any chance of putting the party opposite in power, I should no more think of abstaining than I should think of singing a song instead of making a speech in this House.'[1] Also instructive was William Teeling's statement that the number of abstentions (15) was calculated to be about the right number to show how serious the rebels were without any real fear of damaging the government.[2]

The Suez debate prompted many statements about the iniquities of Whips and their role in parliament. On 10 December 1956, George Wigg drew attention to Patrick Maitland's statement that 'In view of the extraordinary and unexampled pressures – some of them altogether underhand – which had been used to force Tories into line, I think we did pretty well to have 15 of our members daring to show themselves.'[3]

Wigg asserted that this was clearly improper and claimed a breach of parliamentary privilege against the Patronage Secretary. The next day the Speaker declared that there was no *prima facie* case, and said that in the past the work of the Whips had never been thought to be a matter of privilege. He also pointed to the salient fact that only Maitland himself could show that there had been a breach. When Wigg said that Maitland had told the story to a newspaper, Maitland reminded him that he did not need the protection of George Wigg.

Later in the parliament two other foreign affairs issues were disputed, both of which revolts were joined by the Independent

---

[1] 561 *H.C. Deb.*, col. 1302.
[2] Epstein, *British Politics in the Suez Crisis*, p. 92.
[3] 562 *H.C. Deb.*, col. 32–4, and col. 227–30. Discussed in A. H. Hanson and H. V. Wiseman, *Parliament at Work*, pp. 1–3. *Daily Herald*, 8 Dec 1956.

Conservatives. On 20 December 1957, after a foreign affairs debate on NATO and western policy, six of the seven Suez diehards abstained to show their dislike of the NATO Communiqué, and their dissatisfaction with the speeches of the Prime Minister and the Foreign Secretary over defence matters. The last time the Independents rebelled was over the government's Cyprus policy. On 30 March 1957, Lord Salisbury resigned his positions as Leader in the House of Lords and Lord President of the Council because the government released Archbishop Makarios from detention in the Seychelles without requiring him to give a specific and unqualified denunciation of Eoka.[1] The six Independent Conservatives agreed with Salisbury, and on 5 February they issued a statement that the government should rule out as completely unacceptable either the partition of Cyprus or the fixing of a date for self-determination.[2] Significantly, this continued opposition to the Conservative government did not make it more difficult at a later stage for the rebels to be readmitted to the party.[3]

Although there were a significant number of rebellions in the Conservative party during this parliament, only the Suez crisis caused any serious considerations about party discipline. Eight MPs resigned the whip over Suez, and Sir David Robertson left the Conservative parliamentary party because of its policy for the Scottish Highlands. Of the Independent Conservatives who stayed in parliament only Robertson did not rejoin the party, and in the 1959 general election he was elected as an Independent. The local Conservative association in Caithness and Sutherland did not adopt a candidate to oppose Robertson, and some local members even gave him

---

[1] The letters of Salisbury and Macmillan can be found in *The Times*, 30 Mar 1957. Also see 568 *H.C. Deb.*, col. 37 ff., and Butler, '1951–59: The Conservatives in Power', p. 331.

[2] *The Times*, 6 Feb 1958. They were John Biggs-Davison, Anthony Fell, Viscount Hinchingbrooke, Angus Maude, Lawrence Turner, and Paul Williams.

[3] More details about this case are given above.

informal help.[1] One Conservative MP, Howard Johnson (Kemptown, Brighton) resigned from the Conservative party in 1958.[2] His local association knew about the resignation but Johnson sat with the Conservatives until the 1959 general election and then did not stand. He violently opposed fox-hunting, and this was resented by some Conservative voters. However, he declared that he was leaving politics because his parliamentary duties were causing him to neglect his wife, and he was very busy re-arranging his law business.

LABOUR IN OPPOSITION

Table 15: Labour Revolts 1955–59

	Number of Revolts	Main Issues
Domestic	1	Nationalization
Foreign Affairs	8	German Reunification
and Defence		Unilateralism

The last Bevanite dispute which took place was a straight-forward leadership quarrel. When Attlee decided to retire, Bevan proposed that neither he nor Gaitskell should oppose Morrison.[3] Gaitskell would not accept this compromise, and a three-cornered contest developed in which Gaitskell received 170 votes, Bevan 70, and Morrison only 40.[4] Only two days

[1] Discussed in chapter 9.
[2] *Daily Mail*, 1 May 1962. In 1962 he failed in a bid to become a candidate for the Liberals, and he later re-joined the Conservative party and made another abortive attempt to be their candidate in Kemptown.
[3] *The Times*, 9 Dec 1955. Also see *Tribune*, 16 Dec 1955.
[4] Bevan also lost the contest for deputy leader to James Griffiths by 141 votes to 111.

after Gaitskell's election, Bevan made an extremely critical speech which gave the impression that he intended to maintain the split in the party. He said that when Labour MPs made speeches which were not in accord with caucus decisions, the PLP threatened them with expulsion. He then exclaimed that to enforce policies which had been arrived at secretly was 'basically antagonistic to democratic principles of any sort whatsoever'.[1] In spite of this last flourish of independence the Bevanite split did not recur in either domestic or foreign affairs.

The only Labour revolt that could be classed as domestic was the controversy over nationalization which, although it did not reach either the division lobbies or the Order Paper, did cause a minor revolt in 1957. That spring, the government published a policy statement, *Industry and Society*, which committed the government to renationalization of the steel industry and long distance road transport, but did not contain firm proposals about other nationalization projects. Many Labour MPs felt that the pamphlet was a retreat from socialism, and 32 of them sent a letter to the *Reynolds News* criticizing the policy statements and demanding definite proposals based on nationalization and other forms of public ownership. The signatories included MPs from all branches of the party; there were prominent trade unionists, others who had never been associated with left-wing policies, and still others who were recognized as right-wing. This was a relatively minor demonstration against party policy but it portended a more significant revolt in the 1959 parliament.

Labour revolts in foreign affairs followed the same pattern as in earlier parliaments. None of the issues under criticism were new, and many of the revolts were led by a vociferous group, Victory for Socialism. Aneurin Bevan was more constructively occupied. Shortly after Gaitskell's election as leader of the Party, Bevan accepted the position of Shadow Colonial Secretary. In October 1956 after a minor dispute with the right-wing led by George Brown, he was elected party Treasurer.

[1] Quoted at length in Hunter, *Road to Brighton Pier*, p. 181.

And, finally, Bevan was completely integrated into the party hierarchy as Shadow Foreign Secretary.[1] This reconciliation of Bevan and Gaitskell ended any major disputes in this parliament, and culminated in Bevan's famous speech at the 1957 conference in which he concluded that Britain should retain her nuclear weapons so that a Foreign Secretary would not be sent 'naked into the conference chamber'.[2]

The Suez crisis provoked little public rebellion in the Labour party. Except for some initial doubt Jewish Labour MPs supported Labour policy throughout the affair.[3] On the other hand, Stanley Evans supported the Conservative government during the crisis by abstaining ostentatiously on 30 October, 1 November, and 8 November 1956. The PLP did not even consider withdrawing the whip from him because of these actions, but the Wednesbury local party asked him to resign. Evans complied with this request declaring that: '. . . a General without any army, and what is worse, living on borrowed time, seldom wields much influence and lacks all dignity.'[4] This case is discussed in detail in chapter 10.

[1] It has often been argued that if Bevan had been made Foreign Secretary in 1951 none of the Bevanite rebellions would have taken place. This may have depended on what policies the party was willing to accept since Bevan had already resigned once from the Cabinet over a policy issue at an earlier date. A backbencher's opinion about this may be found in Mann, *Woman in Parliament*, p. 95.

[2] *LPCR*, 1957, pp. 179–83.

[3] On 30 October Harold Lever and Emanuel Shinwell publicly abstained. Lever spoke for both of them when he said 'I deliberately abstained because I could not, by a vote, unequivocally support some of the statements made by my own side of the House.' 558 *H.C. Deb.*, col. 1377–1382. *Daily Telegraph*, 31 Oct 1956, and *The Times*, 12 Jan 1957. The most complete study of the activity of Jewish Labour MPs during the Suez affair is contained in chapter 8 of Epstein, *British Politics in the Suez Crisis*.

[4] *Daily Telegraph*, 21 Nov 1956.

The left-wing of the Labour party, especially those MPs who supported Victory for Socialism, continued to engage in minor rebellions on Germany and nuclear weapons. VFS had begun in 1944, but it was dormant during the successive Labour governments. From 1951 to 1955 it combined in fact, if not in name, with the Bevanite cabal, but when Bevan accepted a position in Gaitskell's Shadow Cabinet, VFS began to agitate on its own. In March 1956 its members published a pamphlet *Tho' Cowards Flinch* in preparation for a conference on democracy within the Labour party. This pamphlet was disliked by Labour leaders because it stated that: 'The structure of the Labour party may appear democratic to the casual observer; in fact its oligarchical tendencies are nearly as strong as those of the Conservative Party. Democracy is preached, not practised.'[1] On 21 March Morgan Phillips told the NEC that he had written to all local parties and MPs associated with VFS and advised them not to attend the conference.[2] This warning did not prevent 13 MPs from attending, and the NEC did not take any steps to punish them.

By 1958 VFS had become so troublesome that the NEC found it necessary to state that it might have to declare the group in conflict with the regulations which prohibited development of 'a party within the party'.[3] In February 1958 the NEC sent letters to every local party warning them about VFS, and received assurances from the group that they did not intend to set up their own branches in the constituencies.[4]

The Labour left-wing did not revolt in the division lobbies over German policy, but some of their Members did place two

---

[1] *The Times*, 2 Apr 1956.   [2] *The Times*, 22 Mar 1956.
[3] *The Times*, 28 Feb 1958, and 7 Mar 1958. In 1958 VFS was reorganized with Stephen Swingler as its chairman. Many Co-op Members held prominent positions in the group. Sir Frederick Messer (President) and A. Oram (Deputy Chairman) had both been Co-op-sponsored MPs, and Ted Bedford (another major figure) was Secretary of the London Co-op political committee.
[4] *The Times*, 1 Mar 1958.

critical motions in the Order Paper. On 21 July 1955, nine Labour MPs signed an EDM which prescribed a radical disengagement policy for Germany even though this suggestion was contrary to official party policy.[1] Later when the doctrine of disengagement became part of Labour policy the most heated argument was concerned with the recognition of East Germany.[2] On 2 February 1959, Sydney Silverman tabled an EDM which called for the *de facto* recognition of the German Democratic Republic.[3] Originally 48 Labour Members signed this EDM, but six later removed their names and signed a moderate motion which requested Four Power talks without advocating recognition of East Germany. The Whips were disturbed by both these EDMs, but no disciplinary measures were even considered.

The unilateralist controversy also originated in this parliament. Official Labour policy until April 1957 proposed that Britain should continue to manufacture and test hydrogen bombs, and work for multilateral nuclear disarmament. Before the 1957 conference the PLP compromised and said that Britain should suspend her tests even if the two major powers would not stop their testing. In March 1958 the NEC and TUC issued a joint statement which confirmed a policy of temporary suspension of hydrogen bomb tests without including a doctrine of unilateral disarmament. The 1958 Scarborough conference accepted this policy, but there was a small increase in the unilateralist vote.[4]

On 29 November 1955, 25 unilateralist MPs demonstrated their views by signing a motion which criticized the continual testing of atomic and hydrogen weapons, and requested that

---

[1] *Notices of Motions*, 21 Jul 1955.
[2] The doctrine of disengagement became part of official policy in the statement *Disengagement in Europe. LPCR*, 1958, pp. 7–8.
[3] *Notices of Motions*, 2 Feb 1959.
[4] *LPCR*, 1958, pp. 5–6. Also see Christopher Driver, *The Disarmers*, pp. 90 ff.

the British government '. . . undertake not to proceed with these tests and to ask the Governments of the United States of America and the Union of Soviet Socialist Republics to act in a like manner'.[1] On 25 June 1956 another critical EDM was placed in the Order Paper. The 15 signatories demanded that the government cease testing immediately.[2]

Militant backbenchers also used other public methods in an attempt to change party policy. In January 1957, 85 Labour MPs publicly demanded fundamental changes and economies in Britain's military policy.[3] And a year later, on 26 February, 69 Labour MPs wrote to the *Daily Herald* asking constituency parties to support a policy of unilateral disarmament. The *Daily Herald*, which had been released from the day-to-day control of the TUC only in 1957, expressed sympathy with the unilateralists. It was evident that Labour leaders were becoming worried about this unrest when Morgan Phillips attacked the *Daily Herald*'s lack of loyalty.

> I have been profoundly disturbed by the tone of the articles on the hydrogen bomb in your issues of Tuesday and yesterday. Tuesday's leading article can only be described as an ill-considered attempt, supported by misleading information, to interfere in current private discussion between the Labour Party and the T.U.C.[4]

In March the new official policy was published in the pamphlet *Disarmament and Nuclear War*, and within a few days 27 Labour backbenchers tabled an EDM attacking this policy in a manner which was considered a 'deliberate effrontery' to party leaders.[5]

None of the Members who signed these critical EDMs or made public protests were punished. As usual the main

---

[1] *Notices of Motions*, 29 Nov 1955.
[2] *Notices of Motions*, 25 Jun 1956.
[3] Finer *et al.*, *Backbench Opinion in the House of Commons 1955–59*, p. 55.
[4] Quoted in *The Times*, 28 Feb 1958, and *Daily Herald*, 27 Feb 1958.
[5] *Notices of Motions*, 12 Mar 1958.

occupation of the Whips' Office was to prevent as many MPs as possible from signing very rebellious EDMs, and the Whips made doubly certain that motions which corresponded to official policy were also placed in the Order Paper.

During this parliament the whip was not withdrawn from any Labour MPs, but two Members are known to have been criticized by party officials. Sir Hartley Shawcross was reproached for his poor attendance record in the House, and for his speech which supported the payment of retirement benefits to self-employed people. Before the end of the parliament he resigned from parliament and in May 1959 he took his seat as a Life Peer in the House of Lords. Another Labour MP, R. H. S. Crossman, was criticized because of an article he wrote for the *Daily Mirror* in 1957 attacking the low calibre of trade-union-sponsored MPs. He stated that the only ones who deserved key positions in the party were Aneurin Bevan, George Brown, James Griffiths, and Alfred Robens. The trade-union group in the PLP unanimously passed a resolution asking the NEC to note Crossman's misconduct in criticizing Labour MPs. Crossman retracted his statement, but the union group would not accept the form of his apology. Then on 25 July it was simply announced that all criticism of Crossman was to be stopped.[1]

There were 373 Conservative MPs during the four years of this parliament, but only 365 of them were in parliament when at least one revolt took place. As usual no ministers rebelled while holding office, but four were associated with a rebellion before they took office, and two after they had relinquished their positions. Half the Conservative backbenchers joined at least one revolt, and the most rebellious MP, Montgomery

[1] *The Times*, 25 Jul 1957.

Hyde, joined nine. PPSs again were more loyal than the average backbencher, but less so than ministers.[1]

Table 16: Conservative Party Discipline and Parliamentary Private Secretaries 1955–59

Rebellious % out of number of revolts (Total 21)	0%	1–10%	11–20%	21% Plus
PPSs (31)	68%	29%	3%	0% (100%)
Backbenchers (268) (including PPSs)	50%	38%	7%	5% (100%)

The least rebellious Conservative MPs were those who had been elected before 1945; only 3% of them joined more than four rebellions. Post-1955 MPs rebelled almost exactly the same amount as those elected after 1945. University-educated MPs were only slightly more rebellious than those not educated at a university.

Table 17: Conservative Party Discipline and Date of Entry to the House 1955–59

Rebellious % out of number of revolts (Total 21)	0%	1–10%	11–20%	21% Plus
Pre-1945 MPs (66)	59%	38%	0%	3% (100%)
Post-1945 MPs (137)	46%	40%	7%	7% (100%)
Post-1955 MPs (65)	51%	35%	12%	2% (100%)

During this period the Labour party had 290 MPs who were Members when at least one revolt occurred, and two out of

[1] There were 275 backbenchers but 7 were not in parliament when any of the revolts occurred.

every five of them joined at least one rebellion. Co-op-sponsored MPs were easily the most rebellious, and trade-union-sponsored Members were the least.

*Table 18: Labour Party Discipline and
Sponsorship 1955–59*

Rebellious % out of number of revolts (Total 9)	0%	1–33%	34% Plus	
Trade-union-sponsored MPs (102)	70%	28%	3%	(101%)[1]
Co-op MPs (21)	57%	19%	24%	(100%)
Non-sponsored MPs (167)	69%	23%	9%	(101%)

Labour MPs who entered parliament for the first time before 1945 were clearly the least rebellious Members of the PLP, and most trouble was caused by those who were newly elected in 1955.

*Table 19: Labour Party Discipline and
Date of Entry to the House 1955–59*[2]

Rebellious % out of number of revolts (Total 9)	0%	1–33%	34% Plus	
Pre-1945 MPs (35)	77%	17%	6%	(100%)
Post-1945 MPs (140)	71%	19%	10%	(100%)
Post-1955 MPs (13)	38%	39%	23%	(100%)

[1] Caused by rounding.
[2] Trade-union-sponsored Members have been eliminated.

As Table 20 indicates, Labour MPs educated at a university joined considerably fewer demonstrations against party politics than those Members who had not attended a similar institution.

*Table 20: Labour Party Discipline and
Formal Education 1955–59*[1]

Rebellious % out of number of revolts	0%	1–33%	34% Plus	
University-educated MPs (105)	74%	20%	7%	(101%)
Non-university-educated MPs (83)	59%	22%	18%	(99%)[2]

Although there were twenty-one public revolts in the Conservative party and nine in the Labour party, no MP was expelled or had the whip withdrawn during these four years. Nine Conservatives sat in the House as Independents, but they withdrew from the whip on their own accord.

[1] Trade-union-sponsored Members have been eliminated.
[2] Caused by rounding.

7 Rebellions and Party Discipline 1959-1964

It's terrible. I've been bitchier about other members of
my party [Conservative] than I ever thought I could be –
a most unpleasant atmosphere to work in.[1]

In 1959 the Conservative party won its third successive victory
with an impregnable majority of 100. Although the Suez crisis
had caused disruption in the party from 1956 to 1958, by
September 1959 most people thought the Conservative party
was more united than Labour.[2] However, in the ensuing
parliament there were twenty-one public beckbench revolts in
the Conservative party, whereas the PLP had only thirteen.
The timing of the Labour revolts is significant because they all
occurred in the first half of the parliament, so that by the time
parliament was dissolved the Labour party was thought to be
more united than the Conservatives, and subsequently they
received an absolute majority of four seats in the 1964 general
election.

The tendency of Conservative backbenchers to express dissatisfaction with government policies by voting against their
whips continued to increase, and in this parliament Conservatives rebelled in the division lobbies more frequently than
in any parliament since the war. The revolts were very
diversified; difficulties arose over domestic and foreign policy,

[1] A Conservative party official, quoted in D. E. Butler
and Anthony King, *The British General Election of 1964*,
p. 83.
[2] In September 1959 a Gallup poll found that 61% of the
people considered that the Conservatives were united,
but that only 31% thought the same about the Labour
party.

local and national issues, scandals and ministerial purges. The few Conservative revolts in foreign affairs were over basic policies toward Africa and the European Economic Community. Labour rebellions were nearly all concerned with foreign affairs. Only on four occasions did Labour Members cross-vote, but several times they tabled EDMs which raised serious objections about different aspects of Britain's defence policy. These revolts occurred at a time when official Labour policies in foreign affairs were fluctuating, and therefore it is necessary to examine the timing of these revolts in relation to official policy. For example, the most serious Labour revolt occurred when Hugh Gaitskell and the PLP refused to accept the 1960 conference decision on nuclear weapons. This dissension in the Labour mass party over unilateralism was paralleled to a lesser degree in the Conservative party when the Macmillan government decided to enter the Common Market.

Both parties had to obtain new leaders before parliament was dissolved. Harold Macmillan was attacked by some Members of the Conservative party after his ministerial purge of July 1962, and especially after the Profumo affair. In 1963 Macmillan retired, ostensibly because of illness.[1] Dissension persisted behind the scenes after the controversial selection of Sir Alec Douglas-Home as Leader of the Conservative party, and reached a climax when the Tory party split over Resale Price Maintenance, nearly causing a government defeat. This unparalleled display of disunity was probably a factor in the party's electoral defeat in 1964. Meanwhile, the untimely death of Hugh Gaitskell and the consequent leadership contest in the Labour party was not followed by a period of uneasiness as was expected; instead the reconciliation of George Brown with the new leader, Harold Wilson, led to two of the least rebellious years that the Labour party experienced between 1945 and 1964.

[1] See McKenzie, *British Political Parties*, pp. 594a–594h.

THE CONSERVATIVE PARTY

Table 21: Conservative Revolts 1959–64

	Number of Revolts	Main Issues
Domestic	15	Beeching Plan for Railways
		Corporal and Capital Punishment
		Cotton Policy
		Hereditary Peerages (A. N. W. Benn Case)
		National Health Service
		Offices Bill
		Profumo
		Retail Price Maintenance
		Sea Fish Industries
		Schedule A Taxes
		Welsh Leaseholds
Foreign Affairs and Defence	6	Colonial Development Corporation
		Congo
		E.E.C.
		Enahoro
		Rhodesia

The first sign of unrest in the Conservative parliamentary party appeared on 16 December 1959 when backbenchers placed a motion in the Order Paper demanding that the government institute a scheme whereby private patients would be able to obtain pills and medicines at the expense of the National Health Service. By 4 April the dissidents had collected 178 signatures on this EDM, but even this was not enough pressure to force the government to change its policy.[1] The mass party was also concerned with this issue, and in February 1960 it staged one of its rare public demonstrations against official

[1] *Notices of Motions,* 16 Dec 1959.

policy when the Central Council passed a resolution declaring that free drugs should be provided for private patients.[1] The Cabinet was shaken by this disturbance but took no action.

Neither of the first two revolts in the division lobbies concerned major issues. The first minor disturbance occurred early in the parliament when Richard Marsh, a Labour MP, introduced a bill to implement the standard set by the Gowers Committee for working conditions in offices. During the Second Reading on 11 December 1959, Dennis Vosper, Under-Secretary of State in the Home Office, strongly objected to the measure, but the bill passed when a large number of backbenchers were absent for the division and six Conservatives plus Sir David Robertson voted with Richard Marsh.[2] Since it was a Private Members' Bill there was no talk about party discipline. The second minor disagreement occurred on 7 July 1960, when four Conservatives abstained on a government amendment which restricted the Colonial Development Corporation from expanding its activities in ex-colonial territories.[3] Conservative leaders did not appear to take any notice of these abstentions.

The first very significant revolt over domestic affairs followed unrest which arose within the Conservative party over whether or not hereditary peers should be allowed to renounce their titles in order to stand for parliament. On three occasions concerned with A. N. Wedgwood Benn's right to disclaim the Stansgate peerage, Conservative MPs voted against the Tory government. In the first division 13 Conservative MPs combined with the Labour party in an attempt to allow Lord Stansgate to speak in the House.[4] When this failed, 14 Conservatives opposed the government by voting for a change in

[1] *The Times*, 18 Mar 1960.
[2] 615 *H.C. Deb.*, col. 1003–6. *The Times*, 12 Feb 1960.
[3] 626 *H.C. Deb.*, col. 829. *The Times*, 8 Jul 1960.
[4] 638 *H.C. Deb.*, col. 561. Also see Cornelius O'Leary, 'The Wedgwood Benn Case and the Doctrine of Wilful Perversity'.

M

the law regarding the renunciation of peerages.[1] Later, after Wedgwood Benn was successfully returned in a by-election in Bristol South-East, six Conservatives voted with Labour in proposing that he should be allowed to take his seat.[2] The rebels, half of whom had been elected in 1959, came from both wings of the Conservative party. Their only other distinguishing characteristic was that all but one of them joined other rebellions during this parliament. The Conservative Whips' Office had adjusted the whipping instructions to two lines, but after these divisions the Whips made it clear that they would return to three-line whips in the future.[3]

Meanwhile, revolts over capital and corporal punishment which had plagued them for years continued to embarrass Conservative leaders. On 12 April 1961, Burnaby Drayson and Peter Kirk disregarded their Whips on a Labour clause to amend the 1957 Homicide Act so that the minimum age for the death penalty would be raised from 18 to 21.[4] A much larger and more significant revolt over penal affairs occurred after the Berry Committee concluded that corporal punishment should not be restored.[5] This decision conflicted with the views of the Central Council of the National Union of Conservative and Unionist Associations and with the opinion of many Conservative Members.[6] The recalcitrant backbenchers met several times to plan their strategy, and at the Report stage Sir Thomas Moore moved a clause calling for the cane to be used on young offenders under the age of 17, and the birch for those between 17 and 21. The Speaker chose the clause for a general debate on corporal punishment, and Sir Reginald Manningham-Buller, the Attorney-General, said that since the government opposed the clause there would not be a free vote

[1] 638 *H.C. Deb.*, col. 635.   [2] 640 *H.C. Deb.*, col. 71.

[3] *The Times*, 27 May 1961.

[4] 638 *H.C. Deb.*, col. 266 and 350. *The Times*, 13 Apr 1961.

[5] This committee had been set up by R. A. Butler.

[6] See the resolution passed by the Central Council in March 1960. *The Times*, 19 Mar 1960.

on his side of the House.[1] When the clause was forced to a division 69 Conservatives, including five PPSs, voted against the government.[2] This aberration again raised the question of party discipline, but none of the dissident PPSs lost their positions even though the press reported that the Chief Whip, Martin Redmayne, had reproached them.[3]

On 20 June 1961, 13 Conservatives, including two PPSs, voted against the government on the committee stage of the Finance Bill because they objected to Schedule A Tax.[4] There was no attempt to discipline the Members, and the two rebel PPSs retained their positions. The next month two more Conservatives voted against their leaders after the Welsh leaseholds debate.[5] One represented a Welsh constituency and the other a London constituency. They had wanted the government to provide legislation to enable owner-occupiers to purchase the freeholds of their homes at 'fair and reasonable prices'. The next occasion was on 3 April 1962 when six Conservatives and Sir David Robertson voted against the government because it would not subsidize the shellfish industry.[6] The fourth of these revolts was also over constituency interests. It occurred on 28 June over the government's cotton policy. After mass demonstrations and lobbying in front of the Palace of Westminster, five Conservatives voted against the government and

[1] 638 *H.C. Deb.*, col. 125.

[2] 638 *H.C. Deb.*, col. 57 and 145. Sir Thomas Moore, interview.

[3] Unpublished letter, Robert Cooke to author, 4 Jun 1965; Unpublished letter, John Brewis to author, 5 Jun 1965. *Daily Telegraph*, 19 May 1961. The five PPSs were John Brewis (PPS to William Grant, Lord Advocate), Eric Bullus (PPS to Peter Thorneycroft, Minister of Aviation), Robert Cooke (PPS to Lord John Hope, Minister of Works), Sir Beresford Craddock (PPS to Harold Watkinson, Minister of Defence), and Leslie Thomas (PPS to Charles Hill, Chancellor of the Duchy of Lancaster).

[4] 642 *H.C. Deb.*, col. 1393.   [5] 644 *H.C. Deb.*, col. 467.

[6] 657 *H.C. Deb.*, col. 261.

two ostentatiously abstained on an opposition motion calling for greater protection of the Lancashire cotton industry.[1] The Whips were not unduly disturbed by any of these four rebellions, and none of the recalcitrants was punished.

There was sporadic criticism of Harold Macmillan within the Conservative party from the beginning of the parliament, but it did not reach serious proportions until about the summer of 1961. In December 1960 Viscount Lambton launched a personal attack on Macmillan, claiming that he was responsible for the undue American influence in British affairs. This criticism was so vehement that the chairman of Lambton's local party resigned in protest.[2] Sir Harry Legge-Bourke joined the attack against Macmillan in February 1962. He resigned his position as chairman of the Conservative Defence Committee, and advised Macmillan that, '. . . the time is coming for you now to hand over these responsibilities to men whose fortune is not to have had to bear for so many grievous years the burdens you have borne.'[3]

Within a month of Legge-Bourke's criticism the Liberals won the Orpington by-election, and a more widespread opposition to Macmillan's leadership began.[4] In July Macmillan dismissed the Chancellor of the Exchequer, the Lord Chancellor, and five other Cabinet ministers. After this purge Macmillan was constantly opposed by a number of ex-ministers, and backbench revolts became much more serious.

The Beeching plan for modernizing British Railways provoked criticism from several constituencies, particularly where stations were to be closed. When the issue was forced to a division on 30 April 1962 six Conservatives publicly abstained on a two-line whip.[5] One of the rebels, Mark Woodnutt,

[1] *H.C. Deb.*, col. 1485. *Daily Herald*, 29 Jun 1962, and *Daily Telegraph*, 29 Jun 1962.
[2] *Daily Express*, 9 Dec 1960.   [3] *The Times*, 3, 10 Feb 1962.
[4] For a study of the Liberal success in Orpington see chapter 6 of Butler and King, *British General Election 1964*.
[5] 676 *H.C. Deb.*, col. 1027. *The Times*, 1 May 1963.

declared that he would resign the Conservative whip if he could not save a local railway on the Isle of Wight.[1] He did not resign and the railway services were still in operation in August 1965.

The most important single rebellion during Macmillan's premiership took place because of the Profumo scandal. The relationship between John Profumo and Christine Keeler which resulted in Profumo admitting that he had lied to the House caused considerable trouble in the Conservative party. When Profumo resigned the government called for a vote of confidence.[2] In order to ensure a large majority a three-line whip was issued. This caused extensive but inconclusive discussions about party discipline. For example, on BBC's *Gallery*, Lord Hailsham defended the use of a three-line whip by stating that 'Whips only tell Members to come, not how to vote'.[3] During the debate in the House of Commons, Nigel Birch said that Macmillan should retire so that the Conservative party could witness a 'glad, confident morning', and ended his speech with the following declaration:

> Ahead of us we have a Division. We have the statement of my right hon. and noble Friend Lord Hailsham, in a personal assurance on television, that a Whip is not a summons to vote but a summons to attend. I call the Whips to witness that I at any rate have attended.[4]

The Labour party was in an uproar over the possibility of a large Conservative revolt, and George Wigg attacked Lord Hailsham's interpretation of a whip.

[1] Unpublished letter, Mark Woodnutt to author, 9 Jun 1965.
[2] For a more detailed account of this event see Lord Denning's *Report*; Wayland Young, *The Profumo Affair: Aspects of Conservatism*; Randolph S. Churchill, *The Fight for the Tory Leadership*; Clive Irving *et al.*, *Scandal '63*. A copy of this whip was published in the *Sunday Times*, 16 Jun 1963.
[3] Lord Hailsham on *Gallery*, B.B.C. T.V., 13 Jan 1963.
[4] 679 *H.C. Deb.*, col. 99.

There is not a right hon. or hon. Gentleman on either side of the House who accepts Lord Hailsham's interpretation of what a three-line Whip means. The three-line Whip is the final appeal to loyalty on party lines, and Lord Hailsham knows it.[1]

Wigg's interpretation of a three-line whip was more accurate than Hailsham's, but Sir Henry d'Avigdor-Goldsmid combined realism about the meaning of a three-line whip with enough idealism to show why some Members rebel regardless of the whipping instructions.

Surely there is no one so humble as to come to this House and not feel flushed with the success of the hustings that one day in his turn he may take his place at the Dispatch Box. I must confess to being disappointed in that. But if I have now taken an action which will certainly exclude me from any prospect of that, it is not out of spite or personal pique. It is because over the years I have learned what so many have recognised before me, that Parliament is bigger than any of its Members and that its honour as an institution far surpasses any consideration of party advantage. When the Division bell rings tonight it will toll for all of us.[2]

In the division that followed, 27 Conservatives abstained rather than follow Macmillan into the Aye lobby.[3] They were

---

[1] *Ibid.*, col. 100. Later Lord Hailsham said that the 27 Conservative abstentions proved that he was right, and maintained that, 'A direction how to vote would be, I conceive, a direct contempt of either House, and certainly the Party I belong to has always taken that view.' Lord Salisbury agreed with Hailsham, but Earl Alexander reminded the Lords that a breach of a three-line whip sometimes led to, 'strange circumstances and happenings.' 250 *H.L. Deb.*, col. 1371–3.

[2] 679 *H.C. Deb.*, col. 153–4.

[3] 679 *H.C. Deb.*, col. 169. They were Humphry Berkeley, Nigel Birch, McNeil Cooper-Key, Cmdr. Anthony Courtney, Sir Henry d'Avigdor-Goldsmid, Wingfield Digby, Anthony Fell, Victor Goodhew, Philip Hocking, Robert Jenkins, Dr. Donald Johnson, Aubrey Jones,

mainly persistent rebels, and over half of them had earlier opposed the government's Rhodesian policy. None of them lost the whip, but a few had some trouble with their local parties because of their aberration. Nigel Birch's constituency association wrote to Macmillan and expressed dissatisfaction with their Member's action, but Birch did not apologize and his local party made no further reference to the incident. However, Dr. Donald Johnson's trouble in Carlisle was substantially increased by his participation in this rebellion (see chapter 10).

Before any more backbench revolts took place in the House of Commons Sir Alec Douglas-Home succeeded Harold Macmillan as Prime Minister.[1] Although there followed an extraordinary controversy about the succession, only two former ministers, Iain Macleod and Enoch Powell, refused to serve in the new government, and Home's succession did not cause any actual rebellions in the House of Commons.[2]

Shortly before the 1964 general election the Conservative party was badly split over the Resale Price Maintenance Bill which provoked widespread controversy in the country, especially among small shopkeepers.[3] A Resale Price Maintenance Committee was set up to co-ordinate the criticism, and Conservative MPs reported having received scores of letters from angry constituents and Chambers of Trade. This pressure led to the largest revolt over domestic affairs which had been experienced by the Conservative party since 1945. On the Second Reading of the bill 21 Conservatives voted against the

Peter Kirk, Viscount Lambton, Sir Harry Legge-Bourke, Martin Lindsay, Captain John Litchfield, Gilbert Longden, Anthony Marlowe, Robert Mathew, William Morgan, Norman Pannell, Miss J. M. Quennell, John Talbot, Ken Thompson, Patrick Wolrige-Gordon, and William Yates.

[1] See the *Sunday Times*, 20 Oct 1963. R. Churchill, *Fight for the Tory Leadership*.
[2] McKenzie, *British Political Parties*, pp. 594a–594h.
[3] *The Times*, 10 Feb 1964.

government and 17 publicly abstained.[1] Nevertheless, the bill had an easy passage at this stage because the Labour party abstained.[2] Criticism did not subside after the Second Reading, and approximately 180 partisan amendments were tabled. Behind the scenes a negotiating committee, composed mainly of members from the Conservative backbench committee on Trade and Industry, was set up. Two PPSs, Anthony Kershaw and Peter Walker, were selected to report the results of these meetings to the government.[3] On 20 March some compromise amendments were tabled and the rebellion appeared to have ended.[4] However, when a clause to exempt drugs and medicine from the bill was forced to a division in the Committee stage, the government won by only one vote because 31 Conservatives voted against the bill and an extremely large number abstained.[5] The rebel group was much too large to punish, and in fact Resale Price Maintenance hardly figured in the 1964 general election.

No Conservative MPs had the whip withdrawn during these five years, but two resigned it on their own accord. Sir William Duthie resigned in October 1961 because of the government's action in preventing drift net fishing for salmon. Dr. Donald Johnson also resigned the Tory whip when his Carlisle local party announced they would not readopt him for the 1964 general election. (For details of these two cases see chapters 9 and 10.)

Foreign policy issues raised difficult problems for the Conservative leadership, especially over African affairs, but at

---

[1] 691 *H.C. Deb.*, col. 377–80. *The Times*, 11, 12 Mar 1964. *Sunday Times*, 15 Mar 1964.
[2] One Labour MP, Clifford Kenyon, voted against the bill.
[3] *Sunday Times*, 22 Mar 1964.   [4] *The Times*, 21 Mar 1960.
[5] Sir Charles Mott-Radclyffe, a vice-chairman of the 1922 Committee, was included in the group which opposed the government. *New Statesman*, 7 Feb and 13 Mar 1964. The names of the purposive abstainers were not published in any of the national newspapers.

no time in this parliament did they pose the same serious threat to party unity as did domestic questions.

An important rebellion over colonial affairs did take place in February 1961. After the Conservative Colonial Committee heard Iain Macleod defend the government's policy for Rhodesia, a number of recalcitrants expressed the view that he was forcing events too quickly in Africa.[1] They indicated their opposition by tabling an EDM which stated:

> That this House calls on Her Majesty's Government in considering the constitutional future of Northern Rhodesia to maintain the basis of non-racial representation, laid down by Her Majesty's Government in 1958, within the Federation of Rhodesia and Nyasaland.[2]

One hundred Conservative backbenchers signed this motion. Lord Salisbury dissociated himself from the government's policies in Rhodesia, and resigned as President of the Hertford Conservative Association in order to show his disapproval. Other local party officials also resigned from the mass party in support of Salisbury and his ideas.[3] This led to a bitter quarrel in the House of Lords, and after Salisbury severely attacked Macleod, some of the Conservative dissidents removed their names from the controversial EDM.[4]

Several months later, troubles in the Congo dominated the African scene. The crisis caused some unrest in the Conservative party, but although controversy and speculation about the Katanga Lobby abounded, only one division occurred in the

---

[1] *The Times*, 10 Feb 1964.
[2] *Notices of Motions*, 9 Feb 1961.
[3] *The Times*, 11, 20, 23 Mar 1961.
[4] *The Times*, 9 Mar 1961. In the House of Lords Lord Kilmuir and Lord Hailsham attacked Salisbury for saying that Macleod was 'too clever by half'. Two other EDMs about Rhodesia, which were placed in the Order Paper during the parliament, have not been considered here because they neither opposed party policy nor attacked the government.

House of Commons. In December 1961 nine Conservatives abstained ostentatiously on a Labour motion which criticized the government's Congo policy.[1] The rebels were all right-wingers who rebelled on other occasions during the 1959 parliament, but the Conservative Chief Whip did not punish any of them.

It was well over a year before the next rebellion concerning Africa took place. This time it occurred over the Nigerian Chief Enahoro, and Henry Brooke, the Home Secretary, received the brunt of the criticism because of the way he exercised his ministerial power. The Labour party put down a motion on 10 April 1963 condemning the Conservative government for refusing political asylum to the Nigerian chieftain. In the two divisions which followed, Lt. Col. J. K. Cordeaux and Dudley Smith both voted against the government and a number of Conservatives appear to have been absent without a reason.[2] The government decided to deport Enahoro to Nigeria so he could be tried for treason, and immediately the Labour party forced another division on which six Conservatives cross-voted and two publicly abstained.[3] After the government's decision was implemented a censure motion against Henry Brooke was proposed by the Labour party. Robert Jenkins voted in favour of this motion, while Lt. Col. Cordeaux and Sir Harry Legge-Bourke abstained.[4] All the rebels in these divisions were from the right-wing of the Tory party and nearly all of them were persistent rebels, but none were punished.

[1] 651 *H.C. Deb.*, col. 757. *The Times*, 15 Dec 1961. The number of rebellions does not include the trouble over unemployment in the North East on 17 Dec 1962 or the Commonwealth Immigrants Act on 16 Nov 1961 because there were no cross-votes, and the few abstentions were kept private. 669 *H.C. Deb.*, col. 1019, and 649 *H.C. Deb.*, col. 811.

[2] 675 *H.C. Deb.*, col. 1369 ff.

[3] 677 *H.C. Deb.*, col. 1451. *The Times*, 16 May 1963, and *Guardian*, 16 May 1963.

[4] 678 *H.C. Deb.*, col. 1051. *The Times*, 28 May 1963.

The government proposal that Britain should enter the Common Market caused the only other Conservative rebellions over foreign affairs. Although the leadership favoured Britain's application to enter the Common Market, a large number of Tory backbenchers and much of the mass party were violently opposed to this move. In May 1961 four right-wing MPs indicated their disagreement with the policy by publicly abstaining in a division on foreign affairs.[1] A few weeks later 49 Conservatives signed a motion which criticized the idea of surrendering sovereignty to the EEC.[2] Two ex-ministers, Sir Derek Walker-Smith and Robert Turton, led a country-wide campaign to prevent Britain from entering the Common Market, but the 1962 Conservative party conference readily accepted the government's policy. In the divisions on 8 November 1962 and 12 February 1963 over joining the Common Market there were neither cross-votes nor ostentatious abstentions.

LABOUR IN OPPOSITION

Table 22: Labour Revolts 1959–64

	Number of Revolts	Main Issues
Domestic	0	
Foreign Affairs and Defence	13	Air and Army Estimates
		German Troops in Wales
		NATO and Germany
		Nuclear Weapons Policy
		Polaris Submarines

[1] 640 *H.C. Deb.*, col. 1677. *Daily Telegraph*, 19 May 1961. They were John Biggs-Davison, John Eden, Viscount Hinchingbrooke, and Paul Williams.
[2] *Notices of Motions*, 26 Jul 1961.

A very short time after parliament reconvened R. H. S. Crossman and John Mendelson sponsored the tabling of an EDM which condemned '. . . the supply to Western Germany by the North Atlantic Treaty Organization, and with full consent of Her Majesty's Government of tactical atomic weapons and missiles of nuclear capabilities'.[1] The sponsors maintained that the motion simply interpreted party policy, but Labour officials feared that it might initiate another major dispute over German rearmament.[2] By February 1960, 116 Labour Members signed the motion, and Labour leaders reacted by putting their own compromise motion in the Order Paper stating that the arming of German forces with nuclear weapons before the summit talks would prejudice the discussions.[3]

The distrust with which many Labour backbenchers viewed Germany was expressed again in early March when Emrys Hughes and Frank Allaun tabled an EDM which proposed that British bases should not be used by the Luftwaffe and the German army. Only 13 Labour MPs signed this motion, but it embarrassed Labour leaders because of its implicit criticism of Germany's role in NATO.[4]

Some militant Labour backbenchers were still extremely concerned to change Britain's nuclear policy. On 16 February 1960 Stephen Swingler tabled an EDM signed by 48 MPs calling for the rejection of nuclear arms for Britain. The motion declared that Britain should renounce both the testing and production of nuclear weapons, and restrict the use of British territory for nuclear bases. This form of unilateralism was of course totally unacceptable to the Labour leadership

[1] *Notices of Motions*, 2 Dec 1959.
[2] *The Times*, 16 Dec 1959.
[3] For a discussion of these EDMs see *The Times*, 29 Jan and 25 Feb 1960. Two other EDMs have been omitted because of their timing and the small number of signatories. *Notices of Motions*, 30 Nov and 8 Dec 1960.
[4] *Notices of Motions*, 8 Mar 1960.

because it, like the motions on Germany, implied a rejection of Britain's role in NATO.

The controversy over whether or not Clause Four of the 1918 constitution should be amended began after Gaitskell hinted broadly that it was time for the Labour party to abandon the bulk of its nationalization proposals. This direct attack on a socialist fundamental evoked bitter comments about Gaitskell but it did not prove to be as intractable a problem as that of nuclear weapons. On 16 March the NEC was able to agree to a compromise which retained Clause Four and yet had only one opponent.[1] Much later at the 1960 labour party conference even the platform's proposal of a very mild addition to the words in Clause Four was defeated by a vote of 4,153,000 to 2,310,000.[2] The defeat ended this domestic controversy, but in the meantime weapons policy continued to cause dissension. Frank Cousins continually castigated Gaitskell for his nuclear weapons policy, and his action was reinforced by continual agitation from the Campaign for Nuclear Disarmament and Victory for Socialism.[3]

The strength and resolve of the dissident Labour MPs was shown on 1 March 1960 when 43 of them abstained on an official Labour defence motion.[4] These critics of Labour defence policy basically agreed with the position of R. H. S. Crossman and George Wigg, who had been trying to change Labour policy at least since the Sandys White Paper of 1957.[5] After the 1 March division a PLP meeting was called, and Hugh Gaitskell asked for a vote of confidence. According to *The Times*, only five Members admitted having voted against Gaitskell.[6]

---

[1] *The Times*, 16, 17 Mar 1960. R. T. McKenzie has provided an excellent description of the Clause Four controversy in his *British Political Parties*, pp. 607–12.
[2] *LPCR*, 1960, p. 221.
[3] See Driver, *The Disarmers*, pp. 93 ff.
[4] 618 *H.C. Deb.*, col. 1157. *Daily Telegraph*, 3 Mar 1960.
[5] Driver, *The Disarmers*, p. 25.
[6] They were Harold Davies, Emrys Hughes, Sydney Silverman, Stephen Swingler and Konni Zilliacus. *The*

The Whips also announced at the meeting that harsh measures would be used if any Members voted against the Service Estimates.[1]

Because of R. H. S. Crossman's part in the rebellion of 1 March and his criticism of official policy on nuclear weapons, Gaitskell told him that if he was to stay on the frontbenches he would have to accept the official policy on defence and 'for that matter, on any issue as decided by the party meeting'.[2] Crossman moved to the backbenches and asserted that '. . . the extension (with very minor concessions) of the doctrine of collective responsibility from the 12 members of the Shadow Cabinet to a numerous Shadow Administration means that no less than 59 members of the Parliamentary Labour Party are now only permitted to express in private any deep-felt criticism they may feel of the present party line'.[3] Crossman's local party gave him a vote of confidence, and expressed regret that he was no longer on the frontbenches.

Outside parliament the debate on nuclear policy became more bitter. *Tribune* attacks on official policy were censured by the NUGMW, and as would be expected the newspaper responded that it would print what it wanted.[4] Ian Mikardo told Gaitskell that he was out of touch with party opinion, and Woodrow Wyatt accused Frank Cousins of being the 'bully' of bloc votes.[5] VFS demanded that Gaitskell resign as leader of the party, but three prominent Members objected to this provocative request and resigned their membership in the group.[6]

Times, 4 Mar 1960. All five were members of VFS, and all but Hughes were on its executive. Two of them later lost the whip, and a third was suspended from the party.

[1] *Daily Telegraph*, 4 Mar 1960.
[2] *Daily Telegraph*, 15 Mar 1960, and *The Times*, 4 Mar 1960.
[3] *The Times*, 15 Mar 1960.
[4] *Tribune*, 17 Jun 1960, and *The Times*, 15 Jun 1960.
[5] *The Times*, 17 Jun 1960.
[6] They were Judith Hart, Walter Monslow, and Albert Oram. *The Times*, 20, 30 Jun 1960.

Criticism of Labour's defence policy multiplied after the government cancelled the Blue Streak missile. In response the NEC and TUC drafted a new defence policy which was still based on support for NATO. In September the TUC passed a resolution in favour of the NEC–TUC statement, but also accepted Frank Cousins' unilateralist proposal. Then at the 1960 Scarborough conference Gaitskell's defence policy was defeated when a unilateralist motion was narrowly accepted. A majority of constituency parties voted for Gaitskell's policy, but over 50 per cent of the unions' votes were cast in favour of unilateralism.[1] Hugh Gaitskell rejected this conference decision, and said that as long as the PLP accepted his policy it would remain in force. The Campaign for Democratic Socialism was then established to provide systematic support for Gaitskell and opposition to the unilateralists.

Two prominent Labour Members soon showed their disapproval of Gaitskell's decision. Anthony Greenwood resigned his position in the Shadow Cabinet, and in November 1960 Harold Wilson made an abortive attempt to replace Gaitskell as leader of the party.[2] Gaitskell considered his victory over Wilson a sign that the PLP wanted him to continue opposing unilateral disarmament. Nevertheless, 30 Labour MPs showed their dissatisfaction with Gaitskell's nuclear policy by signing an EDM which opposed the establishment of a United States' Polaris base in Scotland.[3] A much more important revolt occurred on 13 December when 72 Labour MPs disregarded a three-line whip and abstained on an official Labour defence motion.[4] Three days later the Labour party issued a three-

---

[1] Keith Hindell and Philip Williams, 'Scarborough and Blackpool'.

[2] *The Times*, 14 Oct and 4 Nov 1960.

[3] *Notices of Motions*, 1 Nov 1960.

[4] 632 *H.C. Deb.*, col. 351. *Daily Herald*, 15 Dec 1960, and *Daily Telegraph*, 15 Dec 1960. One of the rebels was Arthur Probert who had resigned his position as a party Whip only two days before the revolt. *Daily Telegraph*, 13 Dec 1960.

line whip calling for abstention on Harold Davies's motion which declared that there should not be submarine bases at Holy Loch, but 48 Labour MPs voted in favour of this motion.[1]

Before these last revolts took place Konni Zilliacus attacked Labour officials in a pamphlet entitled *The Anatomy of a Sacred Cow*.[2] George Brown requested that Zilliacus attend a meeting to discuss the pamphlet, but the dissident Member said that he would not go because the PLP had no authority over activities outside the House. Therefore at the next PLP meeting the leadership successfully instigated a resolution which condemned attacks on individuals in the party, and resolved that the whip could be withdrawn for such offences. It stated that:

> This meeting of the Parliamentary Labour Party accepts and endorses the statement made on behalf of the Parliamentary Committee, namely, that the parliamentary party maintains its right to deal with personal attacks; that it condemns such attacks; and reaffirms that part of the resolution agreed to by a party meeting on October 23, 1952, which called upon all members to refrain from making personal attacks on one another, either in the House, the press, or on the platform.[3]

Within a few weeks Zilliacus was called to a meeting with the NEC because of an article he published in the Communist international journal *Problems of Peace and Socialism*. The NEC was not satisfied with Zilliacus's defence and suspended him from the party on 22 March 1961.[4] The whip was automatically withdrawn from him, and his suspension was not rescinded at the 1961 annual conference.[5] (This important case is discussed more fully in chapter 9.)

In March 1961 the PLP decided to abstain in all divisions

---

[1] 632 *H.C. Deb.*, col. 839.
[2] Another critical pamphlet written by Zilliacus had been published in 1959 by VFS. The VFS executive at that time was composed of Sydney Silverman, Konni Zilliacus, and Ian Mikardo.
[3] *The Times*, 15 Dec 1960.   [4] *The Times*, 23 Mar 1961.
[5] *LPCR*, 1961, p. 247.

concerning the Service Estimates because it was thought that the public would interpret votes against the Estimates as meaning that the Labour party was against all defence proposals. Twenty-four Labour MPs would not accept this decision, and on 8 March 1961 they voted against the Air Estimates.[1] The Whips' Office issued warnings against dividing the House again, but William Baxter, S. O. Davies, Michael Foot, Emrys Hughes, and Sydney Silverman would not accept this ruling, and on 15 March 1961 they divided the House twice on the Army Estimates.[2] The fact that there were so few rebels meant that it was easy for the Labour leaders to punish them. The day after the division Herbert Bowden, Labour Chief Whip, asked that the whip be withdrawn from all five recalcitrants, and the PLP carried this proposal by a vote of 90 to 63.[3] The NEC merely noted that these Labour Independents had lost the whip and none of them had any difficulties being readopted for the next general election. The five whipless MPs continued to oppose the Estimates and voted against the government on a number of other occasions when the Labour party abstained.[4] (Chapter 9 discusses the cases of these five MPs in detail.)

The decision to withdraw the whip from the five Members did not stop rebel activity. On 19 July seven Labour MPs joined the five whipless Members in voting contrary to a PLP

[1] 636 *H.C. Deb.*, col. 639.

[2] S. O. Davies only supported the rebels on one of them. 636 *H.C. Deb.*, col. 1529, and col. 1533.

[3] *The Times*, 17 Mar 1961. The 1961 annual conference could not find any time to discuss the five MPs who had been deprived of the Labour whip.

[4] 637 *H.C. Deb.*, col. 159–69. On 24 May 1962, they forced a division in opposition to the method of handling debates on foreign affairs expenditures. 660 *H.C. Deb.*, col. 682–99; and on 7 Jun 1962 they forced a division on the EEC when the official Labour party abstained. 661 *H.C. Deb.*, col. 799. And lastly, they forced a division on the question of sending troops to Thailand on 24 May 1962. 660 *H.C. Deb.*, col. 697.

decision which supported the government's plan to allow German troops to train in Wales.[1] The seven Members were interviewed by the Chief Whip, deputy leader, and leader of the Labour party, and subsequently were censured by the PLP.[2] At the time there were no Standing Orders in the PLP because they had been replaced in 1959 by a Code of Conduct.[3] However, this series of rebellions caused a reconsideration of the 1959 Code, and on 13 December 1961 the PLP accepted a new set of Standing Orders which were more detailed and explicit than any of the former rules. Members were still allowed to abstain on matters of conscientious conviction, but were specifically instructed that this did not 'entitle Members to cast votes contrary to a decision of the Party Meeting', and Members were to delay motions, amendments, and prayers 'for one sitting day' if party officials so requested.[4]

In early 1961 the NEC, PLP, and the TUC held talks about nuclear weapons policy which resulted in a compromise agreement, but these discussions did not terminate the party conflict because no clear decision was made about NATO or about whether Allied bases should be allowed on British soil.[5] By autumn three large and several small unions had reversed their opinions on unilateralism.[6] At the 1961 annual conference they cast their votes in favour of Gaitskell's policy, thus defeat-

[1] 644 *H.C. Deb.*, col. 1405.

[2] *Daily Herald*, 28 Jul 1961. Victor Yates, interview.

[3] Discussed in chapter 2.

[4] *LPCR*, 1962, p. 85. Also see appendix III.

[5] *The Times*, 26 Jan, 20, 30 Feb 1961. Unilateralism was not the only cause of dissension in the Labour party at this time. In Sep 1961 Labour Members wrote to Kennedy and Khruschev advocating a radical disengagement policy for Central Europe. It suggested a recognition of both the Oder–Neisse line and East Germany, neither of which was in line with official Labour policy. *The Times*, 26 Sep 1961.

[6] Hindell and Williams, 'Scarborough and Blackpool', p. 311. More than half the constituency votes were still cast against a unilateralist policy.

ing Frank Cousins' unilateralist motion, and forcing an acceptance of the NEC's 'Policy for Peace'. However two minor motions critical of the leadership were carried: one of these objected to the stationing of German troops in Britain, and the other opposed having Polaris submarine bases in the country.[1] Gaitskell and the PLP would not accept either of these resolutions and did nothing to put them into effect.

After some hesitation Hugh Gaitskell opposed Britain's entry into the Common Market, and prevented the development of another major conflict in the Labour party. The newly established party calm was disturbed however by the death of Gaitskell on 18 January 1963. A leadership contest developed between Harold Wilson, George Brown and James Callaghan but contrary to all expectation the withdrawal of Callaghan and the final victory of Harold Wilson over George Brown ended all public revolts within the PLP until after the 1964 general election.[2]

After Wilson's election, the five Independent Labour Members were readmitted to the PLP. Only Alan Brown, who had resigned the Labour whip in March 1961 because he could not accept the 'new Labour defence policy', did not rejoin the Labour party. He accepted the Conservative whip,[3] and was defeated in his former constituency of Tottenham in the next election. (See chapter 9.)

The Conservative party had been in a state of uneasiness since the pay pause in the summer of 1961, but under the leadership of Harold Wilson the Labour party approached the general election more unified than at any time since 1945.

---

[1] *LPCR*, 1961, p. 194.
[2] After the first ballot James Callaghan withdrew from the leadership contest, and on the second ballot Wilson received 144 votes compared to 103 for George Brown.
[3] *The Times*, 23 Mar 1961, and *Daily Telegraph*, 5 May 1962.

In this period there were 396 Conservative MPs and each had an opportunity to join at least one revolt. No ministers engaged in any rebellions, but 14 Members joined one or more revolts in the parliament and then later became ministers, and one minister joined a rebellion after he had lost his office.[1] Three out of every four backbenchers were willing to make their critical views public by joining at least one of the revolts. The 39 Conservative PPSs were considerably more loyal than the average backbencher.

Table 23: Conservative Party Discipline and Parliamentary Private Secretaries 1959–64

Rebellious % out of number of revolts (Total 21)	0%	1–10%	11–24%	25% Plus	
PPSs (39)	23%	67%	7%	3%	(100%)
Backbenchers (291) (including PPSs)	25%	44%	25%	6%	(100%)

The year in which Tory Members were first elected to the House of Commons made little difference in the number of rebellions which they joined. On the other hand, Conservative MPs who had not attended a university were slightly more rebellious than those who had gone to such an institution; 8% of the non-university MPs joined at least five rebellions.

The two Conservatives who resigned the whip during these five years joined more rebellions than the average Conservative MP: Dr. Donald Johnson joined five of the revolts and Sir William Duthie was associated with those demonstrations concerning free drugs for private patients, the EEC, and Resale Price Maintenance.

[1] Kenneth Thompson rebelled in the division over John Profumo.

Table 24: Conservative Party Discipline and
Formal Education 1959–64

Rebellious % out of number of revolts (Total 21)	0%	1–10%	11–24%	25% Plus
Non-university-educated MPs (133)	18%	44%	30%	8% (100%)
University-educated MPs (158)	30%	44%	21%	6% (101%)[1]

Five Labour MPs had the whip withdrawn from them, and one Labour Member joined the Conservative party. The five independent Labour MPs joined many more revolts than the average Labour backbencher; William Baxter 80%, S. O. Davies 60%, Michael Foot 90%, Emrys Hughes 100%, Sydney Silverman 80%.

Table 25: Labour Party Discipline and
Sponsorship 1959–64

Rebellious % out of number of revolts (Total 13)	0%	1–20%	21–59%	60% Plus
Trade-union-sponsored MPs (99)	45%	35%	16%	5% (101%)
Non-sponsored MPs (146)	47%	19%	22%	12% (100%)
Co-op-sponsored MPs (18)	33%	11%	33%	22% (99%)[1]

[1] Caused by rounding.

Well over half of the Labour backbenchers joined at least one revolt.[1] As usual Co-op-sponsored Members were much more rebellious than other Labour MPs, and union-sponsored MPs were by far the least rebellious.[2]

Labour MPs educated at a university were no more rebellious than those who had not attended such an institution. The most rebellious Labour MPs were the newly elected members.

Table 26: Labour Party Discipline and Date of Entry to the House 1959–64[3]

Rebellious % out of number of revolts (Total 13)	0%	1–20%	21–59%	60% Plus
1945 and pre-1945 MPs (107)	47%	19%	23%	12% (101%)[4]
Post-1950 MPs (43)	51%	13%	22%	14% (100%)
Post-1959 MPs (14)	29%	36%	14%	21% (100%)

[1] During these years there were 284 Labour MPs, but only 263 of them were in the House when a rebellion occurred.
[2] It should be remembered that both the 1960 and 1961 Co-op conferences voted in favour of unilateral disarmament. *The Times*, 19 Apr 1960, and 1, 3 Apr 1963.
[3] Union-sponsored MPs have been eliminated.
[4] Caused by rounding.

8 Analysis of the Pattern of Revolts

Party discipline never prevented anyone from rebelling.[1]

The first seven chapters demonstrate that there were a significant number of revolts in parliament between 1945 and 1964. The fact that a number of rebellions took place made it possible to analyse statistically the revolts in each parliament to determine whether certain types of MPs were more rebellious than others. This chapter compares the statistics compiled for each parliament. It also studies some significant factors in party cohesion other than the rewards and punishments which will be discussed in Part III.

Party revolts are concerned with issues and policies and hence their occurrence is related to many complex factors. Moreover, the personalities of the Members and the ethos of the parties play major roles in determining the size and type of revolts. However, there is statistical evidence to suggest that two mechanical factors are also of some importance. They are (a) whether a party is in government or opposition, and (b) the size of the government's majority.

The first tentative conclusion to be drawn from the history of party revolts between 1945 and 1964 is that there were normally more rebellions in both parties when they were in office than when they formed the opposition. Governments are obliged to handle day to day administrative problems, and this function gives rise to factional demonstrations within the government party more readily than the activity of opposition results in backbench revolts in the opposition party. This con-

[1] Exclaimed by a Labour MP in an interview.

clusion agrees with Maurice Duverger's observation that
'. . . the exercise of power always creates divisions within the
party in office'.[1] Governments are confronted with concrete
situations and must make substantial decisions, not simply
present new declarations. This often induces government backbenchers to revolt when prescribed party policy cannot be put
into effect.

The occurrence of revolts in the Conservative party corres-
ponds completely with the generalization that there are more
revolts in the government party than in the opposition. It has
been shown that between 1945 and 1951 there were no significant Tory rebellions, but this number of revolts increased in
each succeeding parliament in which they formed the government. Moreover, the 1945 Labour government experienced a
large number of parliamentary rebellions, but very few
occurred while they were in opposition between 1955 and 1959,
and even fewer in the latter half of the 1959 parliament. This
suggests a major objection to this tentative conclusion. Opposition parties sometimes have to settle broad questions of policy
and these may lead to revolts in parliament. Between 1951
and 1955, and again between 1959 and 1961, the Labour party
was in opposition, and yet it was almost torn to shreds by inter-
necine strife and party dissension. Much of this turmoil occurred
outside parliament. Nevertheless, the issues of German rearmament and unilateralism were so important that they
caused a number of parliamentary revolts while Labour was
in opposition.[2]

The number and form of revolts in the government party
altered with the size of the majority. This phenomenon is well
known to politicians; Harold Wilson told Herbert Morrison

[1] Duverger, *Political Parties*, p. 404.
[2] The Conservative revolts at the end of 1965 over
Rhodesia may also suggest objections to the above conclusions, but the growing number of Labour rebellions
in early 1967 leads this author to conclude that the above
analysis is still essentially correct.

shortly before the 1964 general election that for this reason he hoped his majority would be small.[1] A survey of the attitudes of Whips on both sides of the House confirms that they all regard the size of the majority as being the most important single factor in determining the size and style of revolts. In the last twenty years whenever there was a small majority, rebels on the government side restricted their cross-voting and abstaining, and confined themselves to engaging in other rebellious activities. More specifically, the Labour government of 1950–51 encountered many of the same problems as the 1945 parliament, but it had far fewer revolts. This was largely because Labour rebels could not revolt in the division lobbies without causing a government defeat and a possible dissolution of parliament. As the Conservative party increased its majority in each election after 1951 its parliamentary revolts became more numerous. By the latter half of the 1959 parliament Conservative Whips were complaining that most of their difficulties were due to their large majority, and one of them declared that 'revolts are catching on because there are too many idle backbenchers'.

When the government party has a large majority neither cross-voting nor abstaining on a small scale can defeat the government, and dissidents can more freely show their dissatisfaction in the division lobbies. This factor was mentioned by all Tory Whips who were interviewed. An increase in the number of revolts in a government party with a large majority may also be due to the simple fact that there are more individuals to rebel. Prime Ministers have a limited number of offices to award to members of their party, and therefore more MPs have to be disappointed when there is a large majority. Furthermore, if one party forms the government for a number of years there will be several former ministers free to contribute to party dissension.

Another factor in the cohesion of the government party is

[1] Herbert Morrison, interview. It is doubtful that Wilson welcomed the extremely small majority which the Labour party received.

collective responsibility; following the normal constitutional practice in Britain not one minister joined a revolt throughout the years 1945 to 1964.[1] Shadow administrations have not accepted this doctrine to the same extent, and on a few occasions office-holders in the opposition have rebelled without resigning their positions.[2] Until the law was changed in 1965 only 70 MPs could be bound by the doctrine of collective responsibility because the Disqualification Act of 1957 limited the number of office-holders in the House of Commons.[3] However, Prime Ministers increased this number by appointing Assistant Whips and PPSs neither of whom came under the Disqualification Act because they were unpaid. Whips are now ministers and believe that it is incorrect to rebel, but they also think PPSs may do so on occasion. During the period covered by this book Whips almost never joined public backbench demonstrations against their party leadership, but the loyalty of PPSs was more flexible.

Whips do not expect complete loyalty from Parliamentary Private Secretaries, and do not regard them as 'unpaid ministers'. Although complete loyalty has never been realized, PPSs joined far fewer revolts than did ordinary backbenchers between 1945 and 1964. There are several reasons for this. Parties sometimes have special regulations which apply only to Parliamentary Private Secretaries. In 1965, for example, Labour PPSs were not permitted to sign EDMs without permission from the Chief Whip. More important is the fact that

[1] For a discussion of the concept of collective responsibility see Marshall and Moodie, *Problems of the Constitution.*
[2] A recent example of this occurred on 3 May 1965, when Sir Keith Joseph abstained on the Second Reading of the Race Relations Bill.
[3] This Act was simply the bringing together of various laws of the last two hundred years which had been enacted to prevent the House from being controlled by the Crown's patronage. *The Public General Acts, 1957,* pp. 81–115.

PPSs consider themselves to be part of the government and this increases their tendency to be loyal. Although not strictly applicable to them, the doctrine of collective responsibility also plays a role in preventing PPSs from joining public revolts. Five Labour PPSs were removed from their positions because they joined a rebellion, and PPSs from both parties resigned in order to join public revolts.[1] Moreover, some PPSs may hope that loyalty will be rewarded. Approximately one out of every three junior ministers in both parties between 1918 and 1963 spent some time as a PPS.[2]

Nevertheless, PPSs have always been prepared to rebel when their loyalty was strained too much and a number have done so since 1945 without losing their positions.[3] Prime Ministers are wary of causing bad publicity for their party by dismissing PPSs who rebel only on a few occasions, and ministers can often protect their PPSs. There is also evidence that some ministers actually favoured the revolts joined by their PPSs, but could not participate themselves because of the doctrine of collective responsibility.

Sponsorship was the most important and consistent factor in Labour party cohesion. Sponsorship refers to an individual's appointment to a union's panel of candidates. The aspirant

[1] In 1945 James Callaghan resigned as a PPS because he wanted to oppose the Labour government's policy over the United States loan. Two years later he was appointed Parliamentary Secretary in the Ministry of Transport. In 1957 a Conservative, John Rodgers, resigned as PPS to Sir David Eccles. The next year he was made Parliamentary Secretary at the Board of Trade. Early in the 1964 parliament Edmund Dell resigned as a PPS and in 1966 he was made a Joint Parliamentary Secretary for the Ministry of Technology.

[2] Philip W. Buck calculated that 39·3% of Conservative junior ministers and 31·5% of Labour junior ministers first served as PPSs. *Amateurs and Professionals in British Politics 1918–59*, p. 115.

[3] An interesting recollection of the role of PPSs is presented by Sir Richard Denman in his *Political Sketches*, p. 64.

still requires adoption by a constituency party before he becomes an official candidate, but once this occurs the union pays for much of his election expenses and often gives him a small salary in addition. What degree of loyalty can be expected from these sponsored candidates when they are elected? As Table 27 shows, the average union-sponsored MP has joined by far the least number of party rebellions in every parliament since 1945, and Co-op-sponsored Members have joined the most. This average percentage may not be too meaningful because it prevents analysis of those members who joined no revolts and does not allow for tests of statistical significance. Table 28 shows the total number of revolts joined by Labour Members between 1945 and 1964. A *chi*-square test for statistical significance provides a result of 25·309 which indicates a very high significance indeed.[1] There can be little doubt that sponsorship is related very closely to cohesion or the lack of rebellions in the Labour party.

Labour Members reported that nearly everyone with experience in the trade-union movement believes in loyalty and discipline. One former sponsored MP even maintained that

Table 27: Labour Party Discipline and Sponsorship A

| | Average % of Rebellions Joined by MPs who were | | | |
	Union-sponsored MPs	Co-op-sponsored MPs	Non-sponsored MPs	All MPs
1945–50	6	13	10	10
1951–55	11	23	19	18
1955–59	7	17	9	11
1959–64	12	29	18	20

[1] This chi-square value is high even at the ·001 level. For an introductory essay on these tests see chapter 15 of Hubert M. Blalock, *Social Statistics* (N.Y., 1960).

Table 28: Labour Party Discipline and Sponsorship B

	The Number of Members who Joined the Following Percentage of all Revolts for all Parliaments		
	0–20%	21% Plus	Total
Union-sponsored MPs	347	58	405
Co-op-sponsored MPs	52	29	720
Non-sponsored MPs	545	175	81
	944	262	1206
		$\chi^2 = 25 \cdot 309$	

discipline and loyalty are more important than any policy.[1] Union-sponsored MPs have also tended to be older than the average Labour MP, and this may have been a factor in their lack of vigorous opposition to party leaders.[2] Moreover, Members have sometimes been kept quiet by their own unions. Roy Mason wrote that '. . . on occasions trade union MPs are actually gagged. When a deputation from a trade union is in negotiation with a Government Department, all too often a hint is passed to the union's MP – "No questions in the House on this issue, please. They might be embarrassing" '.[3] There seems to be considerable truth in I. R. Thomas's assertion that 'During the past ten years, when the wranglers were wrangling and the unity of the parliamentary party was threatened, it was the "solid, loyal and dull" phalanx of TU members that brought its weight and influence to bear on difficult situations'.[4]

[1] Percy Collick, interview.
[2] Robert E. Dowse, 'The Parliamentary Labour Party in Opposition'.
[3] Quoted in Mackintosh, *The British Cabinet*, p. 470. Characteristically, Mason's comment was attacked by the trade union group of MPs. *The Times*, 29 Nov 1959.
[4] I. R. Thomas, letter to the editor, *New Statesman*, vol. 65 (5 Apr 1963), p. 489.

Although there is no factor such as sponsorship in the Conservative party, there was a tendency for the formal education of Members in that party to be related to the number of rebellions which they joined. Members who had attended a university usually joined fewer overt rebellions than those who had not attended such an institution. This result was somewhat caused by the fact that many non-university-educated MPs favoured corporal and capital punishment which were persistent issues throughout these nineteen years.

*Table 29: Conservative Party Discipline and
Formal Education A*

| | Average % of Rebellions by MPs who were | |
	University-educated	Non-University-educated
1951–55	13	17
1955–59	5	5
1959–64	9	11

This relationship was not arrived at by a chance happening. The association between formal education and rebelliousness in the Conservative party proved to have a *chi*-square value of 5·363.[1] In the Labour party no statistical significance could be found to indicate a similar type of relationship.

Whether an MP has been newly elected or is an experienced parliamentarian has often been thought to influence his rebelliousness. This has not been the case to any significant degree in either the Conservative or Labour parties. It is true that in certain parliaments newly elected MPs in one or the other party were the most rebellious, but the overall significance of this is statistically negligible. A statistical significance test showed little association between the two phenomena. Nevertheless, it

[1] Significant at the ·05 level.

Table 30: Conservative Party Discipline and
Formal Education B

	Number of Members who joined the Following Percentage of Revolts for all Parliaments		
	0–10%	11% Plus	Total
University-educated MPs	334	130	464
Non-University-educated MPs	226	125	351
	560	255	815
		$\chi^2 = 5 \cdot 363$	

is possible that the fact that newly elected MPs hold fewer offices than more experienced MPs is a significant personal factor at the individual level which does not show up in general statistics. One former Chief Whip commented that new MPs rebel because they 'don't know how much influence they can have behind the scenes'.

The type of constituency and the size of a Member's electoral majority have often been considered to be factors of great importance in his rebelliousness and in party discipline generally. Interestingly, neither of these factors appears to have affected the Conservative party between 1945 and 1964 except for a very slight tendency for Members with electoral majorities of less than 5% to be somewhat more rebellious than Members from safer constituencies. In the Labour party, on the other hand, both factors proved to have statistically significant relationships. Non-trade-union Members with majorities of 17% or greater joined considerably fewer revolts than those with smaller majorities. The *chi*-square value of 4·214 on Table 31 is significant.[1]

[1] Significant at the ·05 level. Trade-union-sponsored Members, unopposed Members and Members from multiple-member constituencies have been eliminated.

Table 31: Labour Party Discipline
and Size of Majority

| MPs with Size of Majority | Number of Members who Joined the Following Percentages of Revolts for all Parliaments[1] | | Total |
	0–20%	21% Plus	
0–16%	286	122	408
17% Plus	291	89	380
	577	211	788
		$\chi^2 = 4 \cdot 214$	

It is normally thought that Labour is an urban-oriented party and that the Conservatives are more rural-oriented. It was postulated, therefore, that there should be more urban rebels in the Conservative party and more rural rebels in the

Table 32: Labour Party Discipline and
Rural/Urban Members

| | Number of Members who Joined the Following Percentage of Revolts from 1951–64 | | Total |
	0–20%	21% Plus	
Rural MPs	376	144	520
Urban MPs	17	20	37
	393	164	557
		$\chi^2 = 45 \cdot 867$	

[1] Since sponsorship has been shown to be a factor in Table 27, trade-union-sponsored Members have been eliminated from Tables 31 and 32.

Labour party. This proved incorrect for the Tories, but was statistically significant in the Labour party. Rural Labour Members joined by far the most revolts against established party policy during the years 1951 to 1964.[1]

[1] Table 32 had a *chi*-square value of 45·867 which is more than significant at the ·001 level, but the reader should notice the unequal marginals which seriously decreases the conclusiveness of this statistic. Trade-union-sponsored Members have been eliminated.

o

Part III

Virtually every MP in recent years has been a Member of a political party, and in practice this has meant that parties have controlled not only the business of the House, but also the career of every parliamentarian. This party dominance has sometimes led to the notion that Members rarely revolt against established party policy, and that when they do rebel they are punished by their leaders. Moreover, it has often been thought that Members are rewarded if they refrain from participating in revolts.

Although Part II has demonstrated that there were a significant number of rebellions between 1945 and 1964, disciplinary measures were employed on only the rarest occasions. It remains to be determined how effective the various sanctions employed by Whips and local parties were in penalizing dissident MPs, and to assess whether or not rewards were important in maintaining parliamentary cohesion. The first half of chapter 9 examines each case of expulsion, withdrawal of the party whip, and loss of office. The second half discusses the rewards that party leaders have given to loyal party Members. Chapter 10 examines the history of MPs who experienced trouble with their constituency organizations, and discusses certain factors in local party control. Chapters 9 and 10 show that sanctions and local party pressures have been used very sparingly against rebellious MPs, but that they still played some part in maintaining party cohesion. These chapters suggest that when parties became extremely cohesive in the twentieth century, discipline was rarely concerned with destroying MPs' careers, but that it was still significant in the dialogue between leaders and backbenchers.

Chapter 11 examines the strategy and attitudes of rebels and Whips toward party discipline. It is found that they expect backbenchers to be able to influence party policy even though a high degree of solidarity is also required, and they agree that there are very few devices for punishing dissidents which can be effective in practice. Rebels and Whips both think that a private and subtle process of accommodation takes place in the Labour and Conservative parties and that rebellion and discipline are only public symptoms that this process has failed to operate. The final chapter posits a somewhat speculative conclusion about stability and change in parties in which revolt and discipline have a part to play.

9 Parliament and Party Discipline

There is more nonsense spoken and written about the
iniquities of the British party system and in particular
of the part played by those gentlemen, known as Whips,
. . . than almost any other part of our legislative and
governmental tradition.[1]

Much of the academic discourse about party discipline has
been about rewards and punishments. The three penalties controlled by party leaders and Whips are often thought to include
expulsion, loss of office, and withdrawal of the party whip. The
rewards are usually considered to include promotion, minor
awards such as trips abroad, and patronage in the form of
honours and non-ministerial positions.

Penalties and rewards are often less obvious than these categories would indicate. Members who express strong views
against their parties sometimes take positive actions to set themselves apart from their parties, thus actually penalizing themselves because they prefer to select their own fate rather than
accept the punishments which they anticipate from their parties,
or they act basically to assert their extreme disagreement with
party policy. The main avenues open to MPs in such events
are – resignation of the whip, crossing the floor, or simply
becoming Independents. On the other hand, Members may
receive rewards which are much less tangible than those mentioned above. Although this chapter is primarily concerned
with mechanical rewards and punishments, the psychological
fulfilment of joining in collective action may indeed be as
significant as a cause of behaviour.

The first part of this chapter attempts to determine how effective the use of sanctions was in penalizing dissident MPs in the

[1] Baker, *My Testament*, p. 252.

short run, and to assess whether or not the penalties did permanent harm to their future careers. In order to determine if a Member's persistence in joining revolts had any effect on whether or not he was punished, each dissident Member's past political career was studied. It was also important to know if the Members who were disciplined experienced any informal pressures and whether or not they were concerned that something worse might happen to them. Members who were punished were interviewed about their reactions to party discipline, and this obviously meant that more details were available about some forms of party discipline than others. For example, a number of MPs have lost the whip but very few have been expelled.

The second section of the chapter examines the rewards which were given to party Members. The number and significance of the revolts joined by recipients is analysed, and this makes it possible to posit some conclusions about how significant party loyalty was to leaders in selecting these MPs.

EXPULSION

Expulsion is the strongest disciplinary action that can be taken against a Member, and as such it has rarely been used. In the last twenty years no Conservative MPs and only five Labour Members have been disciplined this harshly. Of these expelled Labour Members, four were thought to be fellow-travellers,[1] and the fifth was on the right-wing of the party.

[1] It is debatable whether the four expelled MPs were card-carrying members of the Communist party. According to Douglas Hyde, *I Believed*, there were at least eight or nine 'cryptos' in the House of Commons in addition to the two publicly-acknowledged Communist MPs. This is certainly not enough proof to accuse any particular Labour MP of being a Communist. Further enlightenment was given in 1950 by Harry

The four Members who were expelled during the 1945 parliament were John Platts-Mills, Leslie Solley, Konni Zilliacus, and Lester Hutchinson. Another well-known Labour MP, D. N. Pritt, had been expelled a few years earlier in 1940, and before discussing the above four incidents it is worthwhile to look briefly at his case because he became leader of the crypto-communists in the House during the 1945 parliament. Pritt had represented Hammersmith North from 1935 to 1940 as a Labour MP, and had been a member of the National Executive. In 1940 he was expelled for opposing the official Labour policy towards Russia and Finland, and consequently in the 1945 election he stood as an Independent Labour candidate in his former constituency. He won 64% of the votes cast while the official Labour candidate lost his deposit. However, his success was short-lived, and in 1950 he was defeated along with the other Independent Labour candidates.

John Platts-Mills (Finsbury) was suspected of being too much in sympathy with Communist policies even before the Nenni telegram because it had been customary for him to take an extreme left-wing approach on most issues. He was associated with many demonstrations about Eastern Europe and was a leading member of the British-Soviet Friendship Society. The attention of the NEC focused sharply on Platts-Mills after he declared that the *coup d'état* in Czechoslovakia was 'a great victory for the workers'.[1] On 13 April 1948, the NEC Sub-

Pollitt, General Secretary of the British Communist party. He advised Communists: 'We hate the Tories, and we despise those who suck up to them. We shall urge you to vote Communist where a Communist candidate is standing, and we shall also urge you to vote for such splendid independent Labour representatives as D. N. Pritt, Leslie Solley, Lester Hutchinson, and John Platts-Mills.' *Communist Policy Special*, Jan 1950. John Platts-Mills and D. N. Pritt have also been publicly accused of being leading members of Communist front organizations. See Neil Wood, *Communism and British Intellectuals*.
[1] Burns, 'The Parliamentary Labor Party in Great Britain', p. 868.

Committee of Officers and Chairmen met and decided to ask him to make a statement about his rebel activity. The invitation, which was marked 'personal and urgent', asked him to attend a committee meeting to assist in the investigation of a series of statements he had made which appeared to be 'subversive of party policy'.[1] On 21 April Morgan Phillips sent Platts-Mills a charge sheet which listed his rebellious actions, but did not mention his voting record in the House of Commons. The charges included extracts from Platts-Mills' articles, statements, and speeches made between 1946 and 1948. They were presented to him again at the sub-committee meeting, and Herbert Morrison asked him if there were any issues on which he disagreed with the Communist party. According to Morrison, Platts-Mills could not provide a satisfactory answer to this question, and the sub-committee consequently decided that he would have to furnish assurances about his future loyalty if he was to remain a member of the party.[2] Platts-Mills wrote to the NEC on 24 April, but his letter did not satisfy Labour officials possibly because of its reference to his 'solemn undertaking to exercise the rights of criticism accorded to minorities in the party. . . .'[3] Within a week the NEC decided that in view of his 'general conduct', and not just because of his activity concerning the Nenni telegram, he was expelled from membership in the Labour party.[4] Two days later Platts-Mills received a letter from Carol Johnson, secretary of the PLP, which said that since he had been expelled the whip was withdrawn from him.[5]

Soon after his expulsion Platts-Mills claimed that the Labour

[1] Unpublished letter, Morgan Phillips to John Platts-Mills, 28 Apr 1948.
[2] Morrison, interview.
[3] Unpublished letter, John Platts-Mills to Morgan Phillips, 24 Apr 1948.
[4] Unpublished letter, Morgan Phillips to John Platts-Mills, 28 Apr 1948.
[5] Unpublished letter, Carol Johnson to John Platts-Mills, 30 Apr 1948.

government had betrayed their electoral promises while he had tried to live up to his election pledge 'to fight for a free, happy, prosperous, and independent Socialist Britain'.[1] He declared that the NEC had neither given him any prior warning about bad behaviour, nor produced any evidence that they had formally withdrawn recognition from the Nenni Socialists.[2]

The NEC reported the expulsion of Platts-Mills to the 1948 annual conference. According to party regulations an expelled member cannot speak at a conference unless the Orders are waived. Therefore Edgar Duchin of the Haldane Society asked that the Orders be suspended in order to allow Platts-Mills to speak to the delegates. He argued that 'no warning had been given at any time that his [Platts-Mills] conduct might be subject to the drastic penalty imposed on him'.[3] He also reminded the audience that there was a precedent for allowing an expelled Member to speak. Stafford Cripps had done so after he had been expelled, and he had later risen to high office.[4] After Duchin's motion was seconded, Morgan Phillips spoke for the NEC. He first made the constitutional point that the conference was not responsible for party discipline but that 'The National Executive is responsible for all matters of discipline of organizations and individuals'.[5] He rejected the proposal to suspend the Orders because he said it would be a precedent for allowing people expelled by local parties to come before the conference. Critics of Phillips' point might argue that a difference should be drawn between MPs who had been expelled and ordinary members of the party, but the conference

[1] *Daily Herald*, 29 Apr 1948.
[2] *Manchester Guardian*, 29 Apr 1948.
[3] *LPCR*, 1948, p. 120.
[4] Martin Harrison's statement in *Trade Unions and the Labour Party Since 1945*, p. 218, that 'the Conference has never accepted a motion to suspend Standing Orders to hear an expelled member' is false if it refers to pre-1945 history but it is true for post-1945. For example, see chapter 9 of Eric Estorick, *Stafford Cripps*.
[5] *LPCR*, 1948, pp. 120–1.

agreed with Phillips and turned down the motion by a vote of 2,563,000 to 1,403,000.[1]

The GMC of the Finsbury Labour party accepted the expulsion, but suggested that Platts-Mills should be given a chance to reinstate himself. There was also considerable pressure from constituents and from the *Islington Gazette* for Platts-Mills to be retained as the Labour candidate. Scores of letters were published in the local paper demanding his readoption, and M. Cliffe, chairman of the Finsbury Labour party, resigned temporarily because of the NEC's action.[2] The local party was badly divided. The Management Committee told 27 members of the borough council who had sent a letter of support to Platts-Mills that they would be forced out of the party if they did not recant. Nine of them would not retract their support and were expelled.[3]

Platts-Mills stood as an Independent in the revised constituency of Shoreditch and Finsbury in 1950. He obtained only 18% of the vote, and was defeated by the official Labour candidate who received 53%.[4] Despite Platts-Mills' repeated

---

[1] *Ibid.*

[2] In 1949 Platts-Mills received enough local support to be elected to the Finsbury borough council. *Islington Gazette*, 30 Apr and 11 May 1948; 5 May 1949. In 1958 Cliffe was elected as the official Labour candidate for Shoreditch and Finsbury.

[3] J. M. Burns' figures of 24 signatories and 8 expulsions are not completely accurate because three members signed the letter later, and a Mrs. D. Schild was not expelled at the same time as the eight. *Islington Gazette*, 11 May 1948 and 8 Oct 1948; and *Daily Telegraph*, 5 May 1948. Compare to Burns' article, 'The Parliamentary Labor Party'.

[4] To show that an expelled MP still has the rights of any MP in parliament and to illustrate Platts-Mills' character, it is significant to note that a study by D. N. Chester and Nona Bowring showed that Platts-Mills asked more starred questions than any Labour MP between Oct and Dec 1948. *Questions in Parliament*, p. 194.

attempts to rejoin the party, the NEC has always rejected his applications.[1]

The next MP to be expelled was Konni Zilliacus who represented Gateshead East. His case is somewhat different from the other three left-wing rebels because he was pro-Tito, refused to sign a left-wing pamphlet, and as we have seen earlier he was not praised by Harry Pollitt, the General Secretary of the Communist party as the other three were. In December 1948 the Gateshead East CLP asked the NEC Elections Sub-Committee to endorse their sitting Member as an official Labour candidate. Two months later, on 23 February, the NEC subcommittee announced their refusal to endorse Zilliacus because of his opposition to official policy.[2]

Before Zilliacus's first meeting with the NEC to discuss his left-wing activity he was provided with a 'charge sheet' which listed the complaints against him. Most of the charges connected him with the Communist party, and were documented with speeches he had made in the House and articles he had written in the *Labour Monthly* and *Daily Worker*.[3] In the meantime Zilliacus attended the World Peace Congress where he attacked the Atlantic Pact even though he knew this action would be embarrassing for the Labour government. At his meetings with the NEC he was accused of advocating his own policy, of taking 'a prominent part in the deliberations of the Communist inspired World Peace Congress', and of being a member of its permanent committee.[4]

According to Zilliacus the sub-committee decided by a vote of 9 to 0 to endorse him, but Attlee was against the endorsement and the NEC accepted his opinion.[5] The Gateshead East

---

[1] Arthur Skeffington, interview.　　[2] *LPCR*, 1949, p. 18.
[3] It is also true that in October 1947 Zilliacus endorsed the new Cominform declaration, and that in a speech in Prague he criticized Labour party policy.
[4] K. Zilliacus, *Why I Was Expelled*.
[5] *Ibid.*, p. 40. Harold Laski later suggested that the expulsion of Pritt and Zilliacus was carried out with 'an

Labour party voted 42 to 4 to retain Zilliacus as their candidate, but their protests to the NEC did nothing to change the final decision.

Zilliacus accused the NEC of interfering with his aid to world peace, and advocated a backbench revolt against the Labour government's foreign policy. He said that if peace was important it was necessary for Labour MPs to kick up more rows, be less loyal to leaders, and more loyal to principles.[1] He expanded this argument in *Why I was Expelled*, a pamphlet which he wrote to justify his stand on foreign affairs and which he intended to be an election manifesto. In fact, inserted within the pamphlet was a circular appealing for funds for his election campaign. The pamphlet also included some statements that indicate why Zilliacus had caused difficulties for the Labour party. For example, he wrote:

> And yet Mr. Attlee is an exceptionally honest and upright man – as honourable and scrupulous as Sir Edward Grey, the British Liberal Foreign Secretary, who similarly misled the country and the House, including his own back benchers, when they asked him questions about the British foreign policy that ended in the first world war.[2]

According to Zilliacus his expulsion was simply the conclusion of a long series of attempts by the NEC to get rid of him. As he described it the NEC had earlier attempted to dissuade the local party from readopting him.

> They hoped to do so by stirring up the Catholics against me and as far back as February successively approached two Catholic M.P.'s who had lost their seats in the re-shuffle. But they refused to stand against a colleague and objected to

unjustifiable and disproportionate harshness'. *Reflections on the Constitution*, p. 89.
[1] *The Times*, 19 May 1949.
[2] Zilliacus, *Why I Was Expelled*, p. 17.

having their religion exploited for a political intrigue. So did a third 'displaced' M.P. who was approached.[1]

The Gateshead East CLP adopted A. S. Moody as their candidate for the 1950 general election, and Zilliacus was forced to stand as an Independent.[2] Moody was elected with 45% of the vote while Zilliacus polled 15%.

A third Labour Member, Leslie Solley (Thurrock), was expelled on 18 May 1949 along with Zilliacus. By that time Solley had already been called before a sub-committee of the NEC, and presented with evidence about his alleged misconduct. The evidence included extracts from four of his speeches in the House, two newspaper articles, and the Nenni telegram was also mentioned.[3] The NEC declared that Solley was expelled for his activities and attitudes between 1945 and 1948.[4] At first the Thurrock Labour party voted by an 80% majority to retain him, but finally it selected another candidate.[5] Solley stood as an Independent in the next election and received 10% of the vote while 53% was cast for the official Labour candidate.

At the 1949 annual conference J. R. Sandys (USDAW) put forward a motion that Zilliacus and Solley be allowed to speak, but this was defeated by a vote of 3,032,000 to 1,993,000.[6] A delegate from Gateshead East, G. C. Esther, said that the report

---

[1] *Ibid.*, p. 21. The only name obtained was Hugh Delargy, who did stand as the official candidate against Leslie Solley in Thurrock. Interview.

[2] *The Times*, 2 May 1955.

[3] *Essex and Thurrock Gazette*, 28 May 1949.

[4] *LPCR*, 1949, p. 18.

[5] *Manchester Guardian*, 1 Jun 1949, and *Daily Telegraph*, 22 Jun 1949.

[6] It has often been suggested that if the unions had not been allowed to vote Zilliacus and Solley would have been permitted to speak to the meeting. But, Martin Harrison has calculated that '. . . the constituencies split evenly, or slightly in favour of the NEC'. *Trade Unions and the Labour Party since 1945*, p. 220.

about Zilliacus was false because the NEC had not officially approached the local party about Zilliacus' conduct. According to him, their Member's action had caused neither a drop in finances nor in membership, and yet the CLP had '. . . suffered nothing else but threats and intimidation from the Press spokesmen of Transport House and of the Regional Council: "either you drop Zilliacus, or else!" '[1] When the conference would not accept Esther's views he resigned from the party, and his later attempts to rejoin were vetoed.[2] Support for Solley was not as vigorous as it was for Zilliacus, but E. T. Wootton reported that the Thurrock CLP was not given any notice that there was a possibility of action against Solley, and that his CLP had voted 55 to 17 against the expulsion.[3]

Several other members of the Labour party complained about such harsh disciplinary action against MPs. Geoffrey Bing said that '. . . what we cannot afford to be is a Party of rubber stamps'. T. G. Healey declared that the Labour party should not 'remove people and defeat their ideas by bureaucratic expulsion'.[4] N. Whine argued that other MPs had attended the Peace Congress and had not been expelled, and concluded that there was an 'intolerance . . . creeping over the Movement'.[5] Harold Davies underlined this warning by declaring that a fear of criticism was creeping into the party.[6]

Only two speakers, Arthur Deakin and Sam Watson, defended the action of the NEC. Watson said that Solley and Zilliacus had '. . . consistently opposed the policy of the Party in relation to foreign affairs as decided by Annual Conference'.[7] It would have been difficult to prove that these two Members had flouted conference decisions, but they were certainly out of step with the foreign policy of the PLP and especially that of Ernest Bevin. The proposal to refer the NEC Report back

---

[1] *LPCR*, 1949, pp. 120–1.
[2] *Manchester Guardian*, 24 Jan 1952.
[3] *LPCR*, 1949, p. 122.   [4] *Ibid.*, p. 121.
[5] *Ibid.*, p. 122.   [6] *Ibid.*, p. 123.   [7] *Ibid.*, p. 126.

to committee was overwhelmingly defeated by 4,721,000 votes to 714,000.[1]

After their respective defeats in the 1950 general election, Solley and Zilliacus continued to seek readmission to the party. Solley was not accepted as a party member until 1958, and his subsequent attempts to be nominated as an official party candidate have failed.[2] Zilliacus was readmitted to the party in 1952 despite the opposition of Herbert Morrison, and he returned to parliament in 1955 when he was elected as the Member for Gorton.[3] His experience as an Independent did not lessen his individualism, and he continued to participate in most left-wing revolts. In 1961 Zilliacus was suspended from the Labour party for publishing articles in the Soviet and East European press, and especially for an article in the Communist journal *Problems of Peace and Socialism*. At the 1961 annual conference R. Spurway challenged this suspension, and Ray Gunter, chairman of the Organization Sub-Committee of the NEC, replied that Zilliacus had 'used language of the gutter' towards civil servants of the party.[4] The conference voted down Spurway's resolution, but in 1962 the suspension was lifted and Zilliacus again became a full member of the PLP.

Lester Hutchinson (Rusholme) was the fourth MP to be expelled from the Labour party.[5] He would probably have been expelled at the same time as Solley and Zilliacus but he was not in the country at that time. In 1949 Hutchinson sought nomination from the Ardwick Labour party because his constituency had disappeared in the redistribution. Ardwick

---

[1] *Ibid.*, p. 127.   [2] Interview.

[3] Morrison, interview. Transport House tried to get Gorton to adopt Sir Frank Soskice as their candidate instead of Zilliacus, but the selection committee selected Zilliacus by a vote of 39 to 36. *The Times*, 26 Apr and 2 May 1955.

[4] *LPCR*, 1961, p. 247. In 1959 Zilliacus received 38 votes when he stood for membership in the PLP committee.

[5] *Daily Herald*, 3 Feb 1949.

would not accept him, possibly because the NEC had announced that although he was a MP he still required NEC endorsement. Although all Labour MPs require endorsement it was unique for the NEC to announce this about a particular MP. Finally the Middleton and Prestwich local party adopted Hutchinson as their candidate, but when they asked the NEC for his endorsement he was expelled from the party. The NEC said that Hutchinson would not accept the policies of the party, and had publicly declared his independence on foreign policy questions.

In June 1949 the five Independent Labour MPs (not to be confused with the ILP) formed their own parliamentary group, and before the 1950 general election all of them except Zilliacus signed a manifesto entitled *Crisis and Cure*. Hutchinson accepted the request of a rebel group in Walthamstow to stand against Prime Minister Attlee. Although Hutchinson had changed constituencies and there had been some redistribution in Wal-

Table 33: Labour Rebel Elections – 1950[1]

Candidates	Rebel Vote %	Official Labour Vote %
H. L. Hutchinson (Walthamstow W.)	2	60
J. Platts-Mills (Shoreditch and Finsbury)	18	53
D. N. Pritt (N. Hammersmith)	25	40
L. J. Solley (Thurrock)	10	53
K. Zilliacus (Gateshead E.)	15	45

[1] Adapted from a table by Butler, *Electoral System in Britain Since 1918*, p. 165.

thamstow, the above table clearly illustrates the fate of the expelled Labour MPs.

The fifth Member to be expelled was Alfred Edwards. Edwards was elected as the Labour Member for Middlesbrough East in 1935 and 1945, but in 1948 he opposed the Labour government's decision to nationalize road haulage and electricity, and declared that the Iron and Steel Act was 'sheer madness'.[1] Edwards, who was a company director in the iron industry,[2] argued that civil servants could not be trusted to run large corporations, and finally he offended trade-unionists by attacking the principle of strike action.[3] As early as April 1946 party officials had reprimanded him for being absent on a number of three-line whips.[4] The next year the Northern group of Labour MPs complained about his speeches on party policy, and in March 1947 he was criticized at one of their meetings.[5] On 21 May 1947 the Northern group decided to take action into their own hands by recommending that the whip should be withdrawn from him. By the end of 1947 Edwards had alienated a great number of Labour MPs; as he later recalled 'Some leaders of the Party have not spoken to me for a year'.[6]

Shortly after Edwards voted against the Iron and Steel Act the Middlesbrough local party passed a resolution which declared that they had 'lost all confidence' in him.[7] The NEC investigated Edwards' activities, and on 12 May 1948 he attended a sub-committee meeting at which he was confronted with a dossier of quotations from his articles, interviews and

[1] *The Times*, 13 May 1948.
[2] Allen Potter, *Organized Groups in British National Politics*, p. 292.
[3] *The Scotsman*, 21 Apr 1947.
[4] Unpublished letter, William Whiteley to Alfred Edwards, 3 Apr 1946.
[5] Unpublished letter, Alfred Edwards to E. Popplewell, 11 Mar 1947.
[6] *Daily Mirror*, 11 May 1948, and *Daily Graphic*, 8 May 1948.
[7] *Evening Gazette* (Middlesbrough), 17 Apr 1948.

P

speeches.[1] He was asked to prepare a statement regarding his future conduct, but he replied that he could not make any promises. Consequently, the NEC expelled him because of his 'general political conduct'.[2] Edwards had rebelled in the House on only three occasions, but each time he had opposed clearly established principles of the Labour party.[3]

Edwards accepted the NEC decision, joined the Conservative party, and accepted their whip. In 1950 he stood as a Conservative in his former constituency of Middlesbrough East where there was a boundary change and Liberal intervention. The new official Labour candidate, Hilary Marquand, held the seat with a vote of 62·2% while Edwards received 26·7%. In 1951 Edwards was defeated as the official Conservative candidate in Newcastle upon Tyne East.

The history of the five expelled Labour Members illustrates several factors about the disciplinary structure of the Labour party. Although the five Members vigorously opposed certain aspects of party policy, none of them was expelled solely because of his voting record in the House; a significant number of other Labour MPs had been just as rebellious as these five Members in that respect. The main evidence produced against the expelled MPs came from their speeches and articles. There is no doubt that the Labour leaders believed that the four left-wingers were associated with the communists and that Edwards was aiding the Conservatives. Therefore, the NEC was chiefly concerned with preventing the recalcitrants from damaging the party's reputation in the country.[4] The large Labour majority meant that they could not be defeated in the House, but that they could be in a general election.

Another most interesting fact about the expelled MPs is that

[1] *LPCR*, 1948, p. 17.   [2] *Ibid.*
[3] He voted against the government on the Direction of Labour Bill, the Civil Aviation amendment, and the Iron and Steel Act.
[4] Morrison, interview.

four of them stood for safe seats and the NEC knew that the fifth seat would disappear because of redistribution. Platts-Mills, Solley, and Zilliacus had impregnable majorities, and Edwards' seat was very comfortable.[1] The NEC had little fear that the rebels would split the vote sufficiently to allow the Tories to gain these constituencies. Only Hutchinson's constituency of Rusholme was marginal (he had captured it by only 10 votes in 1945) but it was destined to disappear, and hence party officials had absolutely no fear of losing this seat.

The expelled MPs were all deprived of party membership during a period when the Standing Orders were suspended, and in every case they were given an opportunity to explain their rebellious actions either to the Organization Sub-Committee or a special sub-committee. Very little detail was made public about these committees even when they reported to the annual conference. In each case the committee interviewed the MP, and made its own decision before reporting to the NEC. The NEC then made the final decision and submitted its conclusions to the annual conference. Very little information was released at the conference because the NEC argued that party discipline was their prerogative.

In four of the above cases expulsion completely ended the Members' political careers, and in at least one of them it damaged the MP's career outside parliament. In the latter case the Member had a profitable private career while he was a member of the PLP, and his success increased as he became more rebellious, but after the expulsion his business declined for two years and he was forced to rely on another means of gaining a livelihood.[2] However, expulsion has not always ended

---

[1] This statement employs the scale used in Finer *et al.*, *Backbench Opinion in the House of Commons, 1955–1959*: marginal 5% or less; semi-marginal 6–11%; comfortable 11–16%; safe 17–31%; impregnable over 31%. For the Labour rebels the 1955 and 1964 election figures have been used.

[2] Interviews.

a Member's political career. Zilliacus was readmitted to the party in 1952 and has been re-elected to the House of Commons in each general election since then. Earlier in 1939 Stafford Cripps (Bristol East), Aneurin Bevan (Ebbw Vale), and George Strauss (North Lambeth) were expelled for advocating a 'Popular Front' with the Communists.[1] Bevan and Strauss were readmitted to the party between 1939 and 1940 after they pledged not to campaign against official party policy, and Cripps returned to the party after 1945. All three later rose to high office in Labour governments.

There is implicit in this whole discussion the question of whether or not the external organization of the Labour party has controlled the actions of MPs. In 1945 it was shown that the NEC chairman, Harold Laski, could not control Clement Attlee, and this was confirmed by Hugh Gaitskell's action after the 1960 annual conference.[2] However, the NEC has expelled a few Members from the party, and terminated their political careers. Len Williams, Secretary of the Labour party, declared in 1955 that:

> The belief that a person can hold any opinion he likes and yet be a member of the Labour party is incredibly naive. An organisation is formed to fulfil certain purposes: anybody who joins with a view to winning the organisation for other purposes is always in danger of expulsion.[3]

Nevertheless, this power has not been used to punish MPs for disobeying the party whip in the division lobbies, and this casts some doubt on the idea that it will be used for this purpose in the future. Furthermore, the power to expel a MP from the Labour party has been used very rarely indeed, and may even have atrophied as a weapon since it has not been employed for almost twenty years. There are several reasons why expulsion of MPs may not be used again. Because of the lack of adequate party organization in 1945 many Labour candidates were not

[1] See *Labour Party, Notes for Speakers,* 10 Feb 1939.
[2] See chapter 7.
[3] A. L. Williams. 'Expelled for Opinions?'.

given the kind of screening that is now possible, and the vast Labour majority may, therefore, have swept many Members into office that party officials might not have accepted as candidates in more settled times. Even more important, the increased fear of fellow-travellers during the hysteria over Communism in Europe in the late 1940s added motivation for expelling the four extreme left-wingers which is unlikely to occur in the same form or intensity again. The expulsion of a MP from a political party provides very bad publicity, and this fact has been increasingly realized by Labour leaders.

LOSS OF OFFICE

It is well known that Members who hold official positions in the government are bound by the doctrine of collective responsibility.[1] The enforcement of this principle reinforces the natural inclination of Members holding official positions to resign before cross-voting, abstaining or joining any public demonstrations against party policy. Between 1945 and 1964 only nine ministers are known to have resigned because they openly opposed party policy.[2] They were Stanley Evans (Agricultural Subsidies) on 16 April 1950; Aneurin Bevan, Harold Wilson, and John Freeman (Budget proposals) on 23–24 April 1951; Anthony Nutting (Suez) on 31 October 1956; Sir Edward Boyle (Suez) on 5 November 1956; Enoch Powell, Peter Thorneycroft, and Nigel Birch (Economic Policy) on 6 January 1958.[3]

[1] The application of this principle to the opposition party was discussed in chapter 8.

[2] See S. E. Finer, 'The Individual Responsibility of Ministers'.

[3] Since 1964 Christopher Mayhew, Minister of Defence for the Royal Navy, and Frank Cousins, Minister of Technology, have resigned because they opposed government policy but as yet it is too early to analyze how this will affect their future careers.

Of these nine only Anthony Nutting had serious trouble with his local association because of his action. The other eight were all returned to parliament in the election following their resignations. Stanley Evans was later denied readoption because of his revolt over Suez, and John Freeman retired in a few years. Nigel Birch remained on the backbenches of the Tory party, but the remaining five MPs all received promotions within a few years. Aneurin Bevan was later elected deputy leader of the Labour party, and Harold Wilson held many positions before finally becoming Prime Minister. Sir Edward Boyle, Enoch Powell, and Peter Thorneycroft were subsequently made ministers of Education, Health, and Defence respectively.

No Conservative MPs are known to have lost minor government positions because they rebelled between 1945 and 1964, but five Labour PPSs were replaced for voting against the Ireland Bill in 1949, and three Labour Whips were removed in 1954 for supporting an amendment to the Atomic Energy Bill.[1] What happened to these MPs?

Three of the five PPSs were union-sponsored, one was unsponsored, and one was sponsored by the Co-op. None of them were very rebellious in the parliament in which they lost their positions; only J. P. W. Mallalieu demonstrated his left-wing

---

[1] For more details about the revolts see chapters 3 and 5. The PPSs were Frank Beswick, William Blyton, J. P. W. Mallalieu, Robert Mellish, and George Rogers. The Whips were Kenneth Robinson, Charles Royle, and John Taylor. On 11 May 1967 seven Labour PPSs were dismissed because they abstained during a division on the government's decision to apply for membership in the Common Market. It is too early to analyse how this action will affect the careers of the following rebel PPSs – A. Eadie, PPS to the Minister of Social Security, M. English, PPS to the President of the Board of Trade, R. Fletcher, PPS to the Minister of Defence (Equipment), D. Kerr, PPS to Mrs. Hart at the Commonwealth Office, A. Morris, PPS to the Minister of Agriculture, L. Pavitt, PPS to the First Secretary, and T. Watkins, PPS to the Secretary for Wales.

views by signing the Keep Left manifesto. None of the former PPSs had trouble with their local parties, and all of them were readopted and elected in the 1950 general election.

The subsequent careers of these five PPSs indicate that they were not prevented from being awarded other official positions. A year after he was removed from office, Frank Beswick was promoted to the position of Parliamentary Secretary in the Ministry of Civil Aviation, the same ministry to which he had been attached in 1949. George Rogers and Robert Mellish were reinstated as PPSs in 1950, and in 1954 Rogers became a Labour party Whip. When the Labour party was elected to office in 1964 three of these former PPSs, J. P. W. Mallalieu, Robert Mellish and George Rogers, became junior ministers; two others, Frank Beswick and William Blyton, were made Life Peers.

Only one of the three Whips who were asked to resign in 1954 had a marginal seat, and none of them were sponsored candidates. Two of them joined very few revolts before they lost their positions, and John Taylor joined only the revolt for which he lost his office.

All three former Whips were readopted and elected in 1955. Two of them did not go back to the Whips' Office, but John Taylor returned after only a few days. Royle was made a Life Peer in August 1964 and Kenneth Robinson became Minister of Health when Labour formed its 1964 government. Whips are not allowed to become publicly involved in party controversies, and very rarely participate in debates in the House of Commons. It was quite reasonable for the Whips to lose their positions for rebelling because when Whips want to join a revolt they are expected to resign their positions, as, for example, John Dugdale did before he joined the Bevanite cabal.

In very few cases when ministers resigned because they disagreed with government policy, or when PPSs or Whips were removed for joining revolts, were their future careers damaged. The study of PPSs and their rebelliousness in chapter 8 showed that they did join revolts on occasion, and it has now been established that even on the very few occasions when they were punished their futures were not impaired. Whips, on the other hand, have become ministers through the Ministerial Salaries Act of 1965 and can no longer rebel without resigning their positions.

LOSS OF PARTY WHIP

One of the most frequently discussed disciplinary weapons is loss of the party whip.[1] Ten Labour Members have had the whip withdrawn since 1945, but this measure has not been used in the Conservative party since May 1942.[2] On the latter occasion an outspoken Conservative, A. S. Cunningham-Reid, had the whip withdrawn because he promoted a 'People's Movement' for attaining total efficiency in the war, and because part of his local association disliked some of his political opinions and objected to his personal affairs.[3]

[1] An interesting letter concerning the withdrawal of the whip was written by Sir Robert Peel to a dissident MP in 1844. 'My reason for not sending you the usual circular was an honest doubt whether I was entitled to send it – whether towards the close of the last Session of Parliament you had not expressed opinions as to the conduct of the Government in respect to more than one important branch of public policy, foreign and domestic, which precluded me, in justice both to you and to myself, from preferring personally an earnest request for your attendance.' Quoted in C. S. Parker, *Sir Robert Peel*, p. 146.

[2] The only other Conservative to have the whip withdrawn in the twentieth century was Sir B. Peto, Barnstaple, who lost it in July 1928.

[3] According to *The Times*, 15 May 1942, the whip was withdrawn from Cunningham-Reid because he had associated himself 'with Mr. W. J. Brown, Independent member for Rugby, Mr. Edgar Granville, M.P., who recently resigned from the Liberal National Parliamentary Party, and some private citizens in the formation of a "People's Movement", which is to have constituency committees and whose object is "to attain total efficiency in this total war".' Cunningham-Reid received a vote of

Between 1945 and 1964 no Labour Members resigned the whip and later rejoined their party, but a number of Conservatives did so.[1] Patrick Buchan-Hepburn, Conservative Chief Whip 1948–55, suggested to some Members that they should resign from the whip, and often maintained that 'withdrawing from the whip was only grander than having it taken away'.[2] This opinion was supported by Sir John Mellor, who said that Conservative Whips preferred Members to resign the whip.[3] However, it is known that Martin Redmayne maintains that he had never encouraged a Member to take such action because it would leave the Chief Whip 'in a weak position'.[4] The next section examines the history of the Labour Members who had the whip withdrawn and compares them to the 16 Conservative Members who chose their own fate by withdrawing from the whip.

LABOUR PARTY – WITHDRAWAL OF THE WHIP

Ten Labour MPs have had the whip withdrawn on a permanent basis since the Second World War and 24 have been given a one month suspension. The first instance was in December 1954 when the whip was withdrawn from seven Labour MPs who had rebelled over German rearmament. They were George Craddock, S. O. Davies, Ernest Fernyhough, John McGovern,

confidence from the Marylebone Conservative association, but a group broke away and formed another local party which was finally accepted by the Conservative Central Office as the official association. In 1945 he stood as an Independent in Marylebone, but was defeated by the official Conservative candidate.

[1] Reginald Paget, Northampton, resigned the Labour Whip on 8 December 1966 because he opposed the government's decision to invite the United Nations to impose selective sanctions on Rhodesia. On 6 June 1967, he asked to receive the Whip again, and shortly thereafter he became the first Labour Member since 1945 to receive the Whip after a resignation.

[2] Interview.　　[3] Sir John Mellor, interview.　　[4] Interview.

Emrys Hughes, Sydney Silverman, and Victor Yates. Three months later Aneurin Bevan was also denied the party whip ostensibly because he had embarrassed Attlee in the House. In 1961 five Labour MPs, three of whom had earlier lost the whip, were deprived of membership in the PLP because they revolted over the Service Estimates. They were William Baxter, S. O. Davies, Michael Foot, Emrys Hughes, and Sydney Silverman.[1]

None of the Labour Members who had the whip withdrawn were suspended or expelled by the NEC. All of them had the whip returned, were readopted, and elected in the general election following their punishment. These facts severely diminish the importance of the assessments of Samuel Beer and Peter Richards that withdrawal of the whip means a Member will 'almost certainly' or 'normally' be deprived of his seat in the next election.[2] Their evaluations would be correct if the whip were not returned to a Member, but this has not happened for at least the last 20 years.

Three questions will now be considered. First, what events took place before these Labour MPs lost the whip? Second, what happened to the Members when they were without the whip? And lastly, how did they regain membership in the PLP?

Similar events preceded the disciplinary actions of 1954 and 1961. The recalcitrant MPs all joined over half the revolts that took place in the parliament in which they lost the whip.[3] Moreover, on each occasion the annual party conference had only narrowly accepted the policy of the party leader.[4] In view of the controversy over party policy, the PLP decided to avoid a party split by calling for abstention in the House, and on both occasions MPs who voted against the Conservatives were

[1] See chapters 5 and 7.
[2] Samuel Beer, 'The Conservative Party of Great Britain', p. 67, and Peter Richards, *Honourable Members*, p. 150.
[3] Only John McGovern had not joined half of the rebellions.
[4] The issues involved were discussed in chapters 5 and 7.

deprived of the whip. In both incidents a three-line whip was issued, and special appeals were made to Members. In 1954 the whip was accompanied by a letter from Attlee requesting Members to abstain. In 1961 Labour leaders were quite angry with MPs for rebelling in an earlier division and announced that no revolts would be tolerated on the defence estimates.

All ten rebels made their dissatisfaction with party policy known to their local constituency organizations long before the issue came before the House, but none of them consulted the officers of their local parties immediately before they rebelled. Some of the rebels sought advice from close friends and relatives. Victor Yates, who later described his revolt over German rearmament as his 'finest hour', apparently gave considerable thought to what the consequences of rebellion would be.[1] Approximately one hour before the division he was summoned to Herbert Morrison's office for a discussion about how he would vote in the division lobbies. Afterwards Yates consulted some relatives, and decided to rebel even though he knew that he might have to return to his former career as a clerk. Ernest Fernyhough made the same decision, and to avoid a confrontation with the Whips he stayed away from the House until it was time for the division.[2] In 1961 the rebels did not decide to vote against the defence estimates until a few hours before the division. Thus, even if they had wanted to inform their local parties, they could not have done so.[3] Moreover, they maintained that the vote involved conscientious scruples and thought that therefore it was not an issue to be decided by their local parties. William Baxter thought that he had 'covered all cases' by telling his selection committee in 1959 that whenever a matter of conscience was involved he would vote according to his own principles.[4]

None of the rebels were threatened by party officials, but most of them were approached by their area Whips and told that 'it would be best not to rebel'. Victor Yates maintained

[1] Victor Yates, interview. [2] Ernest Fernyhough, interview.
[3] Michael Foot, interview. [4] William Baxter, interview.

that the Whips tried to convince him to speak against the proposal in the House, but then to follow the whipping instructions and abstain. According to Emrys Hughes the Whips did not even try to change his opinion.

In every case the PLP withdrew the whip on the recommendation of the party leaders. This was disadvantageous to the rebels because the leaders' authority became involved in the decision. In 1961 the rebels complained that the decision to withdraw the whip was taken at a special PLP meeting. The Members were notified about the meeting only one day before it took place, and therefore a number of them did not know that there would be a vote on the rebels.[1] In both cases the dissident Members were allowed to defend themselves at a PLP meeting, but their speeches won few votes and sometimes lost them.[2] After the vote the names of the whipless MPs were reported to the NEC, and only in the case of Aneurin Bevan was a sub-committee set up to make a further investigation. The NEC merely 'noted' that the whip had been withdrawn from the other MPs, and this inaction allowed the whipless Members to tell their local organizations that the party was not ostracizing them.

While the Labour MPs were without the whip they did not receive the weekly whipping instructions, and they could not attend meetings of the PLP or the specialist backbench committees. They no longer received guidance about the relative importance of bills, but the significance of this should not be

[1] This provoked some controversy in the PLP meeting, and Joyce Butler resolved that three days notice should be given before a meeting was called about withdrawing the whip, and that a two-thirds majority should be required to make the decision. According to *The Times*, this proposal received only 11 votes. 17 May 1961.

[2] One member recalled that in 1954 S. O. Davies challenged the PLP meeting by declaring – who will defeat me in Merthyr Tydfil? This apparently angered many Members, and damaged the rebels' chances of defeating the resolution.

exaggerated. Many of the Labour Independents borrowed whips from their friends. They also received help from party officials who could not be sure how soon it would be before the rebels would be readmitted to the party. For example, whipless Members were sometimes helped to prepare their speeches by the Research Department of the Labour party.[1]

Another penalty was imposed on some of the MPs who lost the whip. Membership on Select Committees is determined through the 'regular channels', and the Whips' proposals are always accepted.[2] Since Victor Yates was not a member of the PLP, the Labour Whips did not nominate him to the Estimates Committee. Yates had been a member of this committee for seven years and had held official positions on it. A number of MPs were angry that Yates was not made a member, and they forced a debate and division on the membership of the Select Committee. The debate was conducted in a rather lighthearted fashion, but the whips were applied by both parties. Yates' nomination was defeated in the division by a vote of 152 to 33; the government and opposition frontbenches agreed that all committee nominations should be made through the Whips' Offices.[3] In a parallel case Sydney Silverman was not nominated to the Select Committee on Private Bill Procedure.

Whips and other party officials generally paid little attention to the whipless Members. In 1961, for example, the whipless MPs were not told to apply for accommodation in the proposed new office building, and only found out about it from friends

---

[1] Geoffrey Gibson, interview. Even professionally Independent MPs received help from the Whips, consulting them and voting according to their desires. This was because these MPs needed help to organize their attendance and activity at the House, and as A. P. Herbert pointed out, to get support on Private Members' Bills. For a discussion about the activity of one Independent MP see A. P. Herbert, *Independent Member*.

[2] K. C. Wheare, *Government by Committee*, p. 209.

[3] 536 *H.C. Deb.*, col. 804 ff. *Manchester Guardian*, 2 Feb 1955.

in the PLP.[1] None of the Labour Independents thought that Members changed their attitudes towards them after they lost the whip. Yates remarked that there was a 'strange' feeling towards him, but the other rebels maintained that their friends or 'in group' remained loyal, and that they experienced no unpleasant social pressures. Personality was very important in this regard. Konni Zilliacus declared that it did not matter what other MPs thought about him: 'I spend my time in the library!'[2] Socially-minded Members might be more concerned about the reactions of other MPs.

The local parties of the whipless Labour MPs did not cause any serious difficulties for their Members. The Ladywood GMC feared that the NEC might retaliate against them, and passed a compromise resolution which asked Victor Yates to regain the whip, but which also gave him a unanimous vote of confidence.[3] While Ernest Fernyhough was without the whip, Aneurin Bevan went to his colleague's constituency and spoke on his behalf. The Jarrow GMC nearly all supported Fernyhough, and wrote to the NEC asking why he had lost the whip.[4] The executive of the Ayrshire South Labour party divided over what action to take when Emrys Hughes lost the whip. Although some members of the executive feared an early election and some councillors were worried that they might lose their positions, a small majority gave Hughes a vote of confidence.[5] Harold Wilson went to Scotland and spoke for William Baxter. The West Stirlingshire executive wrote to the NEC and asked what action they should take towards Baxter, but since the executive took no action the NEC must either have urged them to do nothing or their advice was disregarded. When Michael Foot lost the whip the Ebbw Vale GMC announced that their Member's action was '. . . in full accord with his election pledges and the policy of this divisional Labour party'.[6] But in private the GMC was pleased that the NEC had taken no action

[1] Michael Foot, interview.   [2] Konni Zilliacus, interview.
[3] Victor Yates, interview.   [4] Ernest Fernyhough, interview.
[5] Emrys Hughes, interview.   [6] *The Times*, 21 Mar 1961.

against Foot, and asked him when he would receive the whip again, and what would happen if a general election was announced. All the Labour Independents maintained that they received more letters from constituents supporting their action than complaining about it.

There were several other reasons why the whipless MPs did not have difficulties with their local parties. They all had left-wing GMCs and considerable support in their constituencies. All the Labour MPs interviewed said that they were on good terms with their executives and were particularly friendly with their chairmen and secretaries. Each thought that he had enough support to remove his local party chairman if it was necessary, and all said that their agents were not very important in their constituency organizations.

Some unions were concerned about Members who lost the party whip. Craddock and Fernyhough each collected £200 yearly from the USDAW, and Aneurin Bevan received a retainer of £150 from the NUM. The USDAW was in a dilemma. The TUC had voted against German rearmament, and its decisions were binding on USDAW members, but at the same time all sponsored candidates had to have the Labour whip, and the whip had been taken away from Craddock and Fernyhough because they had voted in accord with the TUC decision. Only the USDAW annual conference could remove a Member from the sponsored panel of MPs, and since the whip was returned to both Fernyhough and Craddock within a very short time, the conference was never given an opportunity to decide on this disciplinary action. Although there was considerable controversy about whether or not Aneurin Bevan would lose his retainer from the NUM, nothing came of it.[1] The belief that rebels cannot be sponsored by a union is still prevalent among Labour MPs, and Victor Yates maintained that this was the reason he did not become a sponsored candidate until before the 1964 general election.[2]

[1] See chapter 5.
[2] Victor Yates, interview. Union-sponsored MPs have

It has sometimes been suggested that there is a relationship between the size of a Member's majority and whether or not he can be disciplined.[1] The theory is that a local party can more easily get rid of a rebellious Member if the seat involved is safe, but that if the seat is marginal, the local party must be more wary about what action it takes. None of the ten Labour rebels stood for marginal seats; only two of the seats were even semi-marginal, one was comfortable, three were safe, and four were clearly impregnable. Thus, since none of the whipless Members had any serious difficulties with their local parties, there is some evidence in favour of the theory. However this evidence is far from conclusive because the local Labour parties involved in these cases approved of their Members' action, and the question of whether or not they should discipline their Members did not arise to any great extent.

In 1954 all of the rebels, except John McGovern, who asked individually, applied simultaneously to receive the whip, and their request was granted. In 1961 the rebels waited until Harold Wilson became leader of the party before they applied for readmission.[2] They were then told to apply individually, and to indicate their willingness to accept the decisions of the PLP. After private consultations between some of the rebels and party leaders the whipless Members each sent a letter to the PLP requesting the whip, and this was granted on the recommendation of the Parliamentary Committee. Thus, all Labour Members who had the whip withdrawn after 1945 had it returned before a general election was called.

been less rebellious than other MPs. See the summary to chapters 3, 5, 6, 7, and especially the conclusions in chapter 8.

[1] See the tentative conclusions in Epstein, 'British M.P.s and their Local Parties: The Suez Cases'.

[2] The whipless MPs were assisted by VFS in their request to rejoin the party, and also by 78 Labour MPs who signed a letter supporting their application. *Daily Mail*, 21 Mar 1961, and *The Times*, 21 and 22 Mar 1961.

In January 1968 a novel and extraordinary punishment was employed by the Labour party. The government, encountering severe financial difficulties, decided to limit expenditures. While the left wing of the party was pleased with the new policy for the Far East, it objected to the government's decision to reintroduce charges on prescriptions, make cuts in public sector housing, and to postpone the raising of the school-leaving age. These members, joined by a few loyalists who opposed the lack of discipline in the party, abstained in the division on 18 January 1968 concerned with the reduction in public spending.

John Silken, Chief Whip, acted immediately by telling the rebels that they no longer would be admitted to meetings of the Parliamentary Labour party. After charges that Silkin had exceeded his powers, the dissidents were allowed to attend a PLP meeting to decide their fate. On 31 January the PLP withdrew the whip from 24 Labour members for a period of one month.[1] This suspension was an extremely mild measure, and while it indicates a new form of discipline, it does not mean that the careers of these rebels will actually be damaged in the long run. The press will probably devote as much attention to this extremely mild discipline as to other much more severe measures, and it remains to be seen whether it will continue to be used with any regularity.

CONSERVATIVE PARTY – RESIGNATION OF THE WHIP

Sixteen MPs withdrew from the Conservative whip between 1945 and 1964, but none of them crossed the floor to join another party.[2] They withdrew either because they disagreed with party

---

[1] *The Times*, 1 Feb 1968
[2] They were Colonel Cyril Banks, John Biggs-Davison, E. L. Gandar Dower, Sir William Duthie, Anthony Fell, Viscount Hinchingbrooke, Dr. Donald Johnson, Sir Harry Legge-Bourke, Patrick Maitland, Angus Maude, Sir Frank Medlicott, Sir John Mellor, Sir Victor Raikes, Sir David Robertson, Lawrence Turner, and Paul

policy or because they had serious trouble with their local associations. Eleven Conservative Members resigned over Suez and five on other issues. Of the eleven who resigned over Suez, nine did so simply as a protest against party policy, and two, Col. Cyril Banks and Sir Frank Medlicott, resigned because their local associations indicated that they would not be readopted. Of the five who resigned on other issues, three simply opposed party policy and the other two, Dr. Donald Johnson and E. L. Gandar Dower, resigned because they were in difficulties with their local parties. (Their readoption problems are discussed in chapter 10.) The background of Members who resigned the whip over the Suez issue was examined in chapters 5 and 6, but the history of the three MPs who resigned the whip on other issues, Sir John Mellor, Sir David Robertson, and Sir William Duthie, must be outlined here.

Sir John Mellor resigned the Conservative whip in June 1954 because he objected to a proposed increase in Members' salaries, and in particular to Churchill's handling of the situation.[1] Although his friends thought it was hopeless to oppose Churchill, Mellor believed that it was necessary for someone to make a public demonstration against the party leader.[2] Another Conservative MP, Sir David Robertson, resigned the Conservative whip in January 1959 after his Private Members' Bill for improving Scottish economic problems was 'talked out'.[3] He said that the Conservative government was not doing enough for Scotland, and claimed that the high unemployment rate in Caithness and Sutherland justified his action.

Williams. In July 1966 Geoffrey Hirst, Conservative MP for Shipley, resigned the whip because he thought the Conservative party should make 'a more decisive and clear-cut expression' of its intentions, especially on the Prices and Incomes Bill. The executive council of the Shipley Conservative Association passed a motion of unanimous support for Hirst, but at the time of writing this situation was not resolved.

[1] *The Times*, 3 Jun 1954.   [2] Sir John Mellor, interview.
[3] Sir David Robertson, interview. *The Times*, 31 Jan 1959.

Sir William Duthie resigned the Conservative whip in October 1961 because he was dissatisfied with the government's decision to stop drift net fishing for salmon off the Scottish estuaries. This case is a good example of Conservative back-bench behaviour. In March 1961 newspaper agitation began against drift net fishing for salmon. Many people, and especially landed proprietors, opposed fishing in the 'salmon highways' because they thought it would destroy all salmon fishing.[1] Behind the scenes a sub-committee of the Scottish Unionist Members Committee was appointed to study the problem.[2] The sub-committee, of which Duthie was a member, met on 29 June and 13 July. Duthie was not able to attend the second meeting, which co-opted two proprietors of fishing rights in Scotland, John Morrison and Marcus Kimball. At this vital second meeting the committee decided to oppose drift net fishing for salmon, and informed John Maclay, Secretary of State for Scotland, of this decision on 18 July.[3] No minutes of the meeting of 13 July were sent to Duthie, and it was rather surprising that the Fisheries Committee, of which Duthie was chairman, was not even consulted about the decision.[4] This breakdown of communications angered Duthie almost as much as the decision to stop the salmon fishing,[5] and on 16 October he informed Maclay that he was resigning the Conservative whip. A few days later Duthie discussed the matter with the Prime Minister, and later told him that he would support all other

[1] It was first discussed in the House of Lords, see 232 *H.L. Deb.*, col. 766–805.
[2] It consisted of Sir Colin Thornton-Kemsley, Forbes Hendry, Patrick Wolrige-Gordon, and Sir William Duthie.
[3] Unpublished letter, Sir William Duthie to Hon. J. S. Maclay (Sec. of State for Scotland), 4 Aug 1961.
[4] The responsibility for the breakdown of communications is a matter of dispute, and the unpublished letters of Maclay to Duthie, 14 Sep 1961 and Duthie to Maclay, 20 Sep 1961 do not resolve the problem.
[5] 649 *H.C. Deb.*, col. 202–320.

Conservative policies, but that he had to resign the whip because of the 'fishery folk'.[1]

Of the sixteen Conservative Members who resigned the whip only five did not have it returned. Angus Maude and Sir Victor Raikes retired from politics while they were without the whip. Raikes did not enter politics again, but Maude was welcomed back after three years in Australia, and automatically received the Conservative whip when he was re-elected in 1963. E. L. Gandar Dower did not take back the Conservative whip after 1948, and retired from politics within two years. Sir David Robertson and Dr. Donald Johnson both became Independents, and did not attempt to regain the whip. If the latter two MPs had wanted the whip returned they would have had to assure the Whips' Office that they would not oppose the Tory candidates who had been selected to take their places. According to Martin Redmayne this would have been required of any Tory MP who had been refused readoption by his local party.[2]

Six of the seats held by Members who resigned the whip were marginal, one was semi-marginal, five were comfortable, four were safe, and only one was impregnable. These cases provide no evidence for the theory that local associations can most easily discipline Members with large majorities because two of the Members who had readoption problems held marginal seats and the other two stood for comfortable seats.

The most persistent rebel of the sixteen MPs was Dr. Donald Johnson. He joined rebellions in the 1959 parliament over issues as diverse as RPM, Profumo, Rhodesia and corporal punishment. On the other extreme were Gandar Dower and Sir David Robertson, who joined almost no rebellions in their years in the House of Commons. Nine of the sixteen MPs rebelled at least once in favour of corporal punishment. Two of the Members, Banks and Medlicott, opposed the attack on Egypt, but

[1] Unpublished letter, Sir William Duthie to the Prime Minister, 19 Oct 1961.
[2] Martin Redmayne, interview.

thirteen of those who resigned the whip were diehards on the Suez question at one time or another. Of the four MPs who had readoption problems, only Medlicott was not readopted solely because of his rebellion in the House.[1]

Resignations from the whip are usually tendered in a very polite manner. Sir Harry Legge-Bourke sent his resignation to the Chief Whip, Patrick Buchan-Hepburn, with a warm account of his affection for the Whips' Office, and received an equally polite letter which said that the Whips regretted his decision and thanked him for the compliment.[2] The next week Legge-Bourke received a letter from the Whips' Office marked 'For Information', which was the usual whip without the underscoring.[3] The more usual response of the Whips' Office is illustrated by Edward Heath's letter to Lawrence Turner:

> The Prime Minister has already seen your letter of the 13th May ... and he has asked me to express to you his regret that you no longer wish to receive the whip. I should let you know that it is customary for the Governments' Whips' Office to send to Independent Members a copy of the Business Statement and of the All-Party notices for their information.[4]

Sir William Duthie only opposed the government on one issue, and therefore Martin Redmayne, in a 'Private and Confidential' letter, told Duthie that the Whips' Office would send him the business statement and list of divisions, and that in this special situation they would also indicate which divisions were important. Duthie wrote to Redmayne that he did not wish

[1] See chapter 10.
[2] Unpublished letter, Sir Harry Legge-Bourke to Patrick Buchan-Hepburn, 14 Jul 1954, and unpublished letter, Patrick Buchan-Hepburn to Sir Harry Legge-Bourke, 16 Jul 1954.
[3] Conservative whip, 19 Jul 1954.
[4] Unpublished letter, Edward Heath to Lawrence Turner, 14 May 1957.

this privilege, and wanted to withdraw completely from the Conservative whip.

Lack of the party whip is little more than a formality because all Members have friends who will give them the information they require, and even without the whip some MPs can find out from the Whips' Office the number of lines that have been issued for specific divisions.[1] A more serious consequence of the resignation of the party whip is loss of party privileges. Whipless MPs cannot attend the meetings of the 1922 Committee or go to the annual conference as MPs. This practice has been rigorously upheld, and it has definitely diminished the influence of the MPs concerned. But the whipless MPs still found out from friends what happened at the various meetings, and they attended the annual conferences as either journalists or delegates from their local parties.

Conservative MPs who have resigned the whip cannot hold official party positions. Sir Harry Legge-Bourke, Viscount Hinchingbrooke, and Angus Maude had to yield their positions on the executive of the 1922 Committee when they resigned. Sir Victor Raikes lost the chairmanship of the Fuel and Power Committee, Sir William Duthie resigned his positions on the Fisheries Committee and the Unionist Committee, and Viscount Hinchingbrooke was deprived of the chairmanship of the Foreign Affairs Committee. However, resigning the whip may or may not cause a Member permanent harm when he tries to regain an official party position. Legge-Bourke was immediately re-elected to the executive of the 1922 Committee when he rejoined the party whereas Viscount Hinchingbrooke found it impossible to be selected to a party position.

Conservative MPs who were deprived of the party whip also found it impossible to be selected for House of Commons Standing Committees. Sir William Duthie and Sir David

---

[1] Anthony Fell, interview. Another former Conservative MP also suggested that when a MP is without the whip for a length of time other Members become very cautious about what they tell him. Interview.

Robertson wanted to be members of a Fisheries Committee, and there is no doubt that they both had the proper qualifications for nomination. But neither of them was accepted. Sir David complained to the House of Commons, and the chairman of the Selection Committee wrote a letter to Robertson saying that the reason he and Duthie were not eligible for the committee was 'not because I have been thwarted by the Whips' but 'because you are unfortunately no longer Members of the Conservative party'.[1] In fact, the Whips had not recommended them for committee positions so they had not received any.

How were the Independent Conservatives treated by other Members of the House of Commons? Most Independents thought that party officials had an 'air of hostile neutrality' towards them, but some of them met their former area Whips to discuss party policy and the possibility of returning to the party.[2] Sir David Robertson thought that the Whips controlled speeches in the House and that they had prevented him from being called to speak in an agriculture debate.[3] He also maintained that on one occasion the Prime Minister avoided his question, which was third on the list, by transferring it to the Secretary of State for Scotland where it was so far down the list that it was never answered.[4]

Many of the whipless Members found that they were treated politely by other MPs, and that there was little social pressure. For example, Sir Victor Raikes, who lost his position as chairman of the Conservative Fuel and Power Committee, remained chairman of the Commonwealth and Empire Industries Committee while he was without the whip. (This was an all-party House of Commons committee which was largely dominated by Conservatives.) Lawrence Turner found that ministers treated him no differently when he was without the Conservative whip. He asserted that when he and a constituent approached the

---

[1] 655 *H.C. Deb.*, col. 201–5. Also see the above discussion about Sydney Silverman and Victor Yates.

[2] Patrick Maitland, interview.

[3] Sir David Robertson, interview. [4] *Ibid.*

Minister of Colonial Affairs, Alan Lennox-Boyd, about the Mau Mau, they were 'treated very cordially'. On the other hand, a few Members felt that it had been an 'unpleasant period'. One MP suggested that there had been 'systematic whispering campaigns' about him, a second MP discovered that some friendships seemed to 'cool', and another MP thought that some of the 'lick-spittles' did not want to be seen with him. Some of the whipless Members said that they were no longer invited to social parties, one was asked to leave a private dining club, and another maintained that his wife 'lost many of her bridge friends'.

Some of the whipless MPs thought they had been denied company directorships because of their rebelliousness. One declared that 'hints were dropped' to the 'business fraternity' that certain rebel MPs were not suitable for directorships. A second MP stated that he was deprived of a position with a company when he was without the whip. And a third Member described a parallel and serious instance. When he resigned the Conservative whip he was a director of a company which had an important member of the Conservative leadership on its main board. Apparently while he was without the whip he did not receive his customary salary rise, but when he rejoined the party the rise was given to him.

Most of the MPs who were without the Conservative whip had cordial relations with Central Office. Sir Harry Legge-Bourke received the following message from Lord Woolton:

> Of course I am sorry about the step that you have taken, but no one will doubt for a moment that your action was a matter of conscience – and that is an issue that one must follow.[1]

When the eight Conservatives resigned the whip over Suez, however, Oliver Poole told a reporter that the rebels would receive neither help nor support from Central Office, and that a Member's readoption was '. . . a matter for each association,

[1] Unpublished letter, Lord Woolton to Sir Harry Legge-Bourke, 22 Jul 1954.

which is entirely autonomous, to deal with, and for each of these particular Members to decide whether to remain outside the party or rejoin'.[1] Some minor and petty irritations also occurred. The whipless MPs were no longer invited to speak at local party meetings, and in at least one case Central Office discontinued the Member's weekly supply of party literature and propaganda.

Conservative MPs who resigned the whip because they were not readopted by their local parties are discussed in chapter 10 but the relationship between the other whipless Members and their local associations is considered here.

The Isle of Ely Conservative Association called a meeting to discuss Sir Harry Legge-Bourke's resignation. According to Sir Harry, the Eastern Area Office applied pressure to his local association, but it had no effect because the executive was only concerned with local affairs. The executive passed a resolution drafted by Legge-Bourke which gave him a vote of confidence but suggested that he should regain the whip.[2] The agent then told a reporter that the resolution was 'perfectly satisfactory' to Central Office.[3] Legge-Bourke received fewer critical letters from his constituents when he resigned the whip than later when he attacked Harold Macmillan. He was selected in 1955, 1959, and 1964 and re-elected in each contest.

Neither Sir John Mellor nor Sir William Duthie received much criticism from their local constituents when they resigned the whip. They both retired before the next election, but not because their local parties were disturbed at their action in parliament. Duthie thought he was too old to stay in parliament, and Mellor had tired of politics and was dissatisfied with the redistribution of his seat.

All right-wing Members who resigned the whip because of the government's decision to leave the Suez canal zone were readopted by their local parties. Anthony Fell, Angus Maude,

---

[1] *The Times*, 20 May 1957.
[2] Sir Harry Legge-Bourke, interview.
[3] *Cambridgeshire Times*, 6 Aug 1954.

Sir Victor Raikes, and Viscount Hinchingbrooke received votes of confidence after they resigned the whip. Fell and Hinchingbrooke were readopted, but Maude and Raikes retired before the 1959 general election. John Biggs-Davison did not receive a formal vote of confidence from the Chigwell party because no executive meeting was even called: the officers simply expressed faith in him.[1] He was selected as a candidate again in both 1959 and 1964. Patrick Maitland received a vote of confidence from his local association, but not until after his chairman was approached by the Chief Whip and another Whip telephoned his agent.[2] This pressure from the Whips' Office was later raised in the House as a possible breach of privilege.[3]

When Lawrence Turner rebelled over Suez the Oxford Association passed the following resolution:

> This Executive Council thanks Mr. Lawrence Turner for having requested and addressed this meeting, and places on record its appreciation of his services to the constituency and his unwavering support of British and Commonwealth interests, and is fully aware of his support and work for the Conservative party. The Council gives Mr. Turner its full support. . . .[4]

Nevertheless, he had considerable trouble with some officers of the Oxford Association, and decided not to stand for re-election in 1959. Turner's decision was influenced by his controversy with the local party, but just as important was the fact that his company went bankrupt, and at the same time he was divorced.[5] The Area Agent attended all of Turner's meetings with the Oxford executive, and Lord Poole attempted to have a private talk with the local chairman, but was told that Turner had to be present.

Paul Williams (Sunderland South) had no serious readoption problems, but he experienced some rather petty irritations

---

[1] *The Times*, 1 May 1957.   [2] Patrick Maitland, interview.
[3] Discussed in chapter 6.   [4] *Oxford Mail*, 12 Jun 1957.
[5] Lawrence Turner, interview. The proceedings of the divorce and bankruptcy have been made public.

while he was without the whip. He was not allowed to use party offices, or the Tory van with its loudspeakers, and he was informed by his local chairman that it would be inappropriate for him to sit on the platform when the Prime Minister visited the constituency.[1] Some local party officers apparently warned Williams that he might not be readopted, but it is thought that Williams replied that he would stand as an Independent, split the vote and let Labour win the seat. Central Office took no official stand, but apparently Lord Poole contacted some of the local party officials and the Area Office 'made things difficult' for the Member. After Williams regained the whip his relations with the Sunderland South party returned to normal. He was readopted and held the seat in 1959, but was defeated there in 1964.

The Conservatives who resigned the whip were unanimous in their belief that they would be readmitted to the party, and this presumption was correct for all of those who applied. In each case the whipless Members had an excuse for asking for readmission to the party, and the leader made the final decision allowing them to regain the whip.

Sir Harry Legge-Bourke did not ask to rejoin the Conservative party until after the failure of the European Defence Community. The Chief Whip referred the matter to Churchill, who agreed that Legge-Bourke should be readmitted.[2] When Sir John Mellor resigned the whip, the Sutton Coldfield Association heard him 'in camera'. The association wanted him to regain the whip immediately, but he would not take it back until Winston Churchill retired.[3] When Eden replaced Churchill as Prime Minister in April 1955 Mellor asked to rejoin the party, telling his area Whip that if he was not reinstated soon he would go on a holiday. Within a fortnight he received the Tory whip.

[1] Interviews.
[2] Sir Harry Legge-Bourke, interview. *Cambridge Independent News*, 22 Oct 1954.
[3] Sir John Mellor, interview.

Sir William Duthie (Banff) did not attempt to regain the whip until Harold Macmillan was replaced by Sir Alec Douglas-Home. He had a private conversation with the Scottish area Whip, and then saw Martin Redmayne, the Conservative Chief Whip. Since Duthie had earlier indicated his inclination to retire, the Banff Conservative Association had chosen a new candidate. Redmayne asked Duthie if he would support this choice. Duthie replied that he would not publicly oppose the new candidate, but neither would he support him. Duthie then wrote directly to the Prime Minister, and shortly afterwards received the whip.[1]

Sir David Robertson was also told that he would not receive the whip unless he supported the new Conservative candidate for his constituency. Robertson did not really want the whip returned, and said that he would not support Patrick Maitland as Conservative candidate for Caithness and Sutherland under any circumstances. He then sponsored an Independent Conservative, J. M. Young, in the 1964 general election. A Liberal won the seat, but although Robertson's opposition to Maitland caused considerable controversy in the constituency, Young did not poll enough votes to have caused the Liberal victory. (Lib. 36·1%, Lab. 30·3%, Cons. 20·8%, and Ind. 12·8%.)

Six of the eight MPs who resigned the whip over Suez asked for it to be returned. Behind the scenes the chairman of the Scottish Unionist party spoke to party leaders on behalf of Patrick Maitland, and the Chief Whip called Maitland to a private meeting to discuss the application. At Christmas, when it was thought there would be less publicity, Maitland became the first Suez rebel to regain the whip.[2] After that Maitland asserted that he would never resign the whip again because 'one is more influential within a party even if its policy is wrong.[3]

After Maitland was readmitted to the party, three of the whipless MPs, John Biggs-Davison, Anthony Fell, and Paul

[1] Duthie did not openly oppose the Banff candidate in the 1964 general election.
[2] *The Times*, 24 Dec 1957.   [3] Patrick Maitland, interview.

Williams, became worried about their constituency associations and informed the other Independents that they desired to rejoin the party. Lawrence Turner was indifferent to the proposal because he was about to retire, and Viscount Hinchingbrooke knew he would eventually go to the Lords. All five MPs waited until the White Paper on Cyprus was published, and then asked for the whip to be returned. The Chief Whip readmitted them to the party and Edward Heath's letter to Turner was typical of the correspondence which took place:

> I have informed the Prime Minister of our recent talk following your letter to me of the 25th June; he is glad to hear of your request and agrees that you should receive the party whip again.[1]

Two MPs, Colonel Cyril Banks and Sir Frank Medlicott, were not readopted by their local associations but both of them were readmitted to the Conservative parliamentary party before the next election. Neither MP was asked to support his local party's new candidate, and neither stood as an Independent in 1959. Both cases are discussed more fully in the next chapter, but it is important to note here that Banks did not attend any party functions after the whip was returned because he thought he was unpopular.[2]

REBELS WHO CROSSED THE FLOOR

A number of MPs ended their parliamentary careers by resigning from their party. These included Members who crossed the floor to join another party and others who became Independents. In many of these cases the Members merely resigned before their leaders could punish them for being rebellious.

[1] Unpublished letter, Edward Heath to Lawrence Turner, 11 Jul 1958.
[2] Interview.

Between 1945 and 1964 two Labour MPs chose to cross the floor and join the Conservative party. They were Ivor Bulmer-Thomas and Alan Brown. In this period no Conservatives did the same in order to join the Labour party.[1]

Ivor Bulmer-Thomas was first elected for Keighley in 1942, and in the 1945 parliament he held the positions of Parliamentary Secretary in the Ministry of Civil Aviation and Under-Secretary of State for Colonies. In 1948 it became public that he opposed the nationalization of steel, and wanted to retain the delaying power of the House of Lords.[2] On 15 October, in a letter to *The Times*, Bulmer-Thomas suggested that the government should renounce all contentious legislation, and referred explicitly to the Iron and Steel Act and the Parliament Bill.[3] In the debate on the Address he went so far as to declare that the country was drifting towards an omnipotent and totalitarian state.[4] This speech was especially disliked because in 1946 Bulmer-Thomas had announced that iron and steel had to be nationalized because they were the '. . . real centre of Tory privilege and power'.[5]

Bulmer-Thomas often abstained from voting in divisions when he disagreed with government policy, and William Whiteley, Labour Chief Whip, had condemned his actions. Undoubtedly Bulmer-Thomas must have disliked this personal criticism, and it would be uncommon for a Member not to harbour some ill feelings after being removed twice from

[1] This does not include two Labour MPs (Evelyn King and Aidan Crawley) who were defeated and later stood as Conservatives, or two Liberals (Lady Megan Lloyd George and Edgar Granville) who were defeated as Liberals and later stood as Labour candidates.
[2] Another Labour MP, Walter Scott-Elliott, said that he agreed with Bulmer-Thomas' opposition to steel nationalization, but that he would not resign from parliament. He did not contest a seat in the 1950 general election.
[3] The Keighley Labour party repudiated this statement. *Keighley News*, 23 Oct 1948. *The Times*, 15 Oct 1948.
[4] 457 *H.C. Deb.*, col. 108–19.   [5] *The Times*, 5 Aug 1946.

government office. Moreover, the fact that he was financially independent probably helped Bulmer-Thomas to decide to leave the Labour party.

Bulmer-Thomas's relationship with his local party was also far from satisfactory. He declared that the Keighley party had fallen into the hands of extremists and Communists, but many of his constituents thought that he was not interested in their views.[1] At the same time as Bulmer-Thomas tendered his resignation, the local party declared that he was not a suitable candidate for the next election.[2] Obviously private negotiations had been taking place for some time because on the day that Bulmer-Thomas crossed the floor to join the Conservatives, he was adopted as a prospective candidate by the Newport Conservative Association. The Keighley Labour party demanded that Bulmer-Thomas resign from parliament, but he refused.

Alan Brown resigned from the Labour party on 23 March 1961 because he was not prepared to accept the new official Labour defence policy. The Tottenham Labour party demanded that Brown resign from parliament, but he refused, and on 4 May 1962 he accepted the Conservative whip. At the 1964 general election he contested his former constituency for the Conservatives and lost.

The three former Labour MPs, Bulmer-Thomas, Brown, and the expelled Member Edwards, contested at least one election as Conservatives. They were all defeated, and the fact that they had been Labour Members does not appear to have had a significant effect on the elections in their constituencies. Ivor Bulmer-Thomas changed constituencies and was defeated in Newport in 1950 (Lab. 51%, Cons. 35%, Lib. 14%). Alfred Edwards stood in his former constituency of Middlesbrough East in 1950, and was defeated (Lab. 63%, Cons. 27%, Lib. 10%, Comm. 1%). And in 1964 Alan Brown was defeated in Tottenham (Lab. 55%, Cons. 33%, Lib. 11%).

[1] Ivor Bulmer-Thomas, interview. *Keighley News*, 10, 17 Mar 1945, and 23 Oct 1948.
[2] *Keighley News*, 30 Oct 1948. *The Times*, 29 Oct 1948.

Rebels Who Became Independents

Since 1945 only one Labour and two Conservative Members have resigned the party whip and contested the next election as Independents.[1] They were Sir Richard Acland (who opposed Labour policy on nuclear weapons), Dr. Donald Johnson (who had constituency difficulties), and Sir David Robertson (who opposed Conservative policy for the Scottish Highlands). In 1955 Sir Richard Acland split the vote in Gravesend such that the official Labour candidate was defeated and a Conservative won the seat. (Cons. 46·2%, Lab. 40·1%, and Ind. 13·7%).[2] In 1964 Dr. Donald Johnson did so badly that the percentage of votes cast for him did not significantly affect the results. However, Labour won Carlisle from the Conservatives. (Lab. 45·6%, Cons. 40·5%, Lib. 11·0%, and Ind. 2·9%). Sir David Robertson held Caithness and Sutherland as an Independent in the 1959 general election, but the Unionist association did not adopt a candidate to oppose him and actually provided

[1] Two other Labour MPs resigned their party whip but neither of them stood for public office again. E. Walkden resigned after the Garry Allighan case in November 1947 and Raymond Blackburn resigned in August 1950. Blackburn was in difficulty in the constituency of King's Norton because of his personal affairs, and knew that he might not be readopted. Neither of these two former Labour MPs took the Conservative whip. On 18 January 1968, Desmond Donnelly, Pembroke, resigned the Labour whip because he opposed the government's *East of Suez* policy. At the time of writing this situation was unresolved.

[2] Sir Richard Acland, a former Liberal M.P., founded the Commonwealth party in the 1940s and was elected as a Commonwealth Member in 1945. Soon afterwards he joined the Labour party, and the Commonwealth party did not sponsor any more candidates.

him with *de facto* support. (Ind. 65·4%, Lab. 34·6%).[1] The only other Independent candidate elected to the House between the 1949 Representation of the People Act and 1964 was George Forrest in Mid-Ulster. Two Members were disqualified from representing Mid-Ulster between 1955 and 1956, and this complicated the 1956 by-election. Forrest was elected as an Independent, but the Ulster Unionists did not adopt a candidate and gave Forrest informal support. In 1959 Forrest was elected as an official Ulster Unionist.[2]

REWARDS

Although only a very few Members have been punished for rebelling, there is considerable evidence to suggest that a large number of MPs have received various rewards for loyalty. Of course, psychic satisfaction in seeing your party successful, in witnessing the implemention of your party programme, and even in loyalty itself may possibly be as important as tangible rewards in maintaining cohesion, but here we shall only deal with rewards such as promotion, patronage, and trips abroad.

Naturally, the most significant reward is to be appointed a government minister, and the longer a party is in office the more of these rewards it will be able to offer. Prime Ministers have well over a hundred such positions to fill and there is little doubt that a Member's former loyalty to his party and especi-

---

[1] Sir David's activities in the 1964 election are discussed above in this chapter.

[2] *The Times House of Commons 1959*, and *Vacher's Guide for 1959* report that Forrest was an Independent candidate in 1959, but this was a mistake. Unpublished letter, John Maginnis to author, 2 Jun 1965. See Butler, *Electoral System in Britain Since 1918*, and Commander Stephen King-Hall, 'The Independent in Politics'.

R

ally to the person who is Prime Minister are important factors in the selection. Several Chief Whips have reported in interviews that they were consulted about all appointments of junior ministers and that the main question they were asked was whether or not the MPs had been loyal party supporters. Although the appointment to ministerial office is the most important reward that can be used to reward loyalty, it is analytically impossible to use statistical methods to relate loyalty to such appointments in this study because the time period is too short. Moreover, this would require studying the rebelliousness of Members while their party was in opposition and before they achieved a position in the government, and although the Conservatives technically could have been analysed, they had no serious revolts while they were in opposition. Regardless of this problem it should be borne in mind that ministerial appointments are the most important rewards for loyalty, and that a former minister has a much greater chance than a backbencher has to be given other patronage in the form of honours or appointments to boards, commissions, and corporations.

Several MPs receive ministerial positions, but most backbenchers can only hope to receive lesser benefits. A Chief Whip commented that he could sometimes help financially embarrassed MPs to 'find the right friends' and another reported that the Whips' Office 'made an almost daily selection of MPs' names' for some minor awards or enticements. For example, the government Chief Whips, on their own initiative, have been able to place individuals on such things as hospital boards and to send them to Foreign Office dinners. There was general agreement between Whips and rebels that honours and trips abroad were the most important minor rewards, but some MPs believed that the minor enticements included invitations to embassies, to the Queen's garden parties, and to the Prime Minister's table for dinner. One Conservative MP even thought that London hostesses asked the Whips' Office to supply lists of names for dinner parties.

DELEGATIONS ABROAD

Almost every MP interviewed said that free trips abroad were awarded for loyal party service, and maintained that rebel MPs were deprived of these trips to foreign countries. In interviews, former Chief Whips confirmed that the Whips' Office knew which MPs wanted these trips, and that they used them to reward loyalty.

There are three kinds of delegations, only two of which are controlled by the Whips' Office.[1] The Inter-Parliamentary Union and the Commonwealth Parliamentary Association both send MPs on delegations but not as official representatives of the House of Commons. The sub-committees of their executives select the delegates, and the Chief Whip is not allowed to scrutinize the list. The Speaker of the House holds an important position on both of these committees because he is Joint President of the IPU, and Honorary President of the CPA.

The second type of delegation officially represents the House of Commons. These delegations are sent to countries for such events as independence ceremonies for former colonies. Technically, the Members are selected by the House, but the actual process is as follows. The Speaker of the House of Commons instructs his secretary to write to the Chief Whips and ask them to send lists. The Whips canvass their party to see who would like to go, and then the Chief Whip chooses the delegates from his party. The Speaker automatically accepts this list, and a formal resolution in the House confirms it.

The third form of delegation is not confirmed by the House. The Western European Union, the NATO Parliamentary Conference, and the Council of Europe ask the Speaker to send British delegations to their meetings. The Speaker's secretary asks the Chief Whips for a list of MPs to be sent on the delegations, and these are automatically accepted by the Speaker.

[1] Interviews.

The individual ministries also send groups of MPs to see new government projects. These come under the control of the appropriate minister, but the Whips' Office is often consulted. One exception to this general rule occurred in the 1959–64 parliament, when the selection of members to go on Air Ministry visits was made by officials of the Air Sub-Committee of the Conservative party.

It is impossible to obtain complete lists of the Members who have gone on these various trips, but one very high official has remarked that 'it is surprising how often the same individuals continue to be put on these lists'. Loyalty in itself may not assure a backbencher of several trips abroad, but constant rebellion will almost certainly lessen his chances of being selected.

PATRONAGE

It is impossible to disentangle the complex factors that the Prime Minister and his Patronage Secretary consider when they select backbenchers for rewards. They are, of course, distributed mainly on a party basis, but very little information is made public about how the choices are determined. One Chief Whip admitted that the rewards went to MPs whom he regarded 'most highly', and that loyalty was 'important' in the selection. In order to establish how important party loyalty was in the distribution of honours, a study has been made of every Member elected after 1945 who received either an honour or a non-ministerial post by December 1964. All Members who held government positions have been eliminated from this analysis because their loyalty was affected by the doctrine of collective responsibility.

Nine backbench Labour MPs were given hereditary Peerages after 1945, and 13 were awarded Life Peerages after the 1958 Life Peerages Act and before December 1964. Neither of the Labour governments awarded Baronetcies or Knighthoods to Labour MPs (except the Law Lords), but four Labour Members received Knighthoods from Conservative governments. On the other hand, the Conservatives awarded 15 Baronetcies, 63 Knighthoods, 7 hereditary and 2 Life Peerages to backbenchers who had never been ministers at any time in their career.

Most Members who received Peerages had been consistently loyal to their parties. Only two Conservative backbenchers who became Peers had joined any party rebellions after 1945; one of them had revolted over corporal punishment and the other over Suez. Five of the nine Labour Members who were awarded hereditary Peerages had not joined any rebellions, and the remainder had joined only minor revolts on conscription and civil aviation. However, one Labour Peer had signed the controversial Berlin telegram.

The two Conservative MPs who were made Life Peers had joined no serious revolts, nor had five of the Labour Life Peers. Three Labour Peers had joined some serious rebellions in the 1945 parliament, but this was almost ten years before they received their awards. In December 1964 Harold Wilson broke the tradition of awarding Life Peerages to MPs who had been loyal to the party. All five Life Peers appointed by him had been associated with a number of revolts in the 1945 parliament; three of them had joined most of the Bevanite revolts, and two, Frank Bowles and Fenner Brockway, continued to revolt until 1964. In this case long service and possibly loyalty to Harold Wilson were more important than rebellion against Attlee and Gaitskell.

Five of the Conservative MPs who were made Baronets never joined a revolt, and four joined none during the parliament in which they received their awards. The fact that Members accepted Baronetcies did not stop them from rebelling at a later date; in fact most of them revolted more frequently. For example, Sir Thomas Moore advocated corporal and capital punishment before he was made a Baronet, and afterwards he continued to oppose official Conservative policy on both of these issues.[1]

[1] Sir Harry Legge-Bourke is another prime example of

The four Labour backbenchers who were given Knighthoods during these years officially received them from the Queen on the recommendation of the Conservative Prime Minister, but in fact they were the result of consultations between party leaders. Two of the Labour backbenchers had joined no rebellions before they were knighted, and Barnett Janner, a leading member of the Zionist Federation, had only opposed Labour policy over Palestine. The fourth Labour MP, Barnett Stross, joined a very large number of Bevanite rebellions, but he did not receive his Knighthood until Harold Wilson became leader of the Labour party.

In the Conservative party there is no doubt that Knighthoods are awarded for loyalty and long party service. In February 1963 the following telling exchange took place in the House of Commons:

> EMANUEL SHINWELL: When does the right hon. Gentleman propose to conduct another review? When he does, will he take into consideration the fact that there are many of his hon. friends who have not yet been awarded an honour?
>
> HAROLD MACMILLAN: After the next twelve years of our being in office that will no doubt be remedied.[1]

Between 1945 and 1964 Conservative leaders awarded 63 Knighthoods to their backbenchers. The average recipient spent 12 to 15 years in the House, but long service was not the only prerequisite because a number of backbenchers served far more than 15 years without receiving an honour. Although most of the Tory MPs who were given Knighthoods had been loyal to their party, a few, such as Beverley Baxter, Gerald Nabarro, and William Teeling, had been persistent rebels. Another significant factor was that two out of every three backbenchers who received Knighthoods were right-wing on such issues as the National Health Service and corporal and capital punishment.

a MP whose rebelliousness did not terminate when he was knighted.

[1] 672 *H.C. Deb.*, col. 232.

Backbench MPs were rarely appointed to non-ministerial positions such as High Commissioners and Judges of the Court of Session, but those few who were appointed had been extremely loyal party members.[1]

MPs often desire honours for the officers of their local parties, and extensive use is made of this patronage. Conceivably the Patronage Secretary would be more likely to award an honour to someone suggested by a loyal party Member than by a rebel, but this is very complex and would involve many questions besides the loyalty of the Member such as the personality of the candidate, his work for the party, and the number and quality of other candidates for the honours. Nevertheless, Chief Whips realize that Members are concerned with obtaining honours for some of their constituents, and this desire provides the Whips with one more minor reward. Some MPs have also promised honours to local party officials in order to offset criticism of their own parliamentary behaviour.

According to Labour MPs patronage is more important to Conservative Members than to them. This is reasonable given the party's ideology and, moreover, the chances of political rewards are much greater for Conservative MPs. Most Conservative MPs who were interviewed agreed with this evaluation, and thought that patronage helped to keep the Conservative party united. However, a number of Conservatives said that patronage was more important for the wives of politicians and for local party officials than for MPs. Patronage may not be the 'secret' of discipline in the Conservative party,[2] but it is certainly a significant factor in the relationship between Tory leaders and backbenchers.

[1] A list of all Members who received non-ministerial posts was compiled by Peter G. Richards in *Patronage in British Government*, pp. 77 ff.
[2] Suggested by A. N. Wedgwood Benn in 582 *H.C. Deb.*, col. 494.

This chapter has discussed the various penalties and rewards which the Whips and party leaders have employed for maintaining party cohesion. The sanctions included expulsion, loss of government office and withdrawal of the whip. Whereas the Labour party used all three methods, the Conservatives employed none of them. Withdrawal of the whip and loss of office have been temporarily harmful to recalcitrant MPs, but in the long run have not damaged their careers. Probably the most lasting effect of these punishments was their reinforcement of attitudes about the omnipotence of parties in Britain. The most extreme disciplinary device was expulsion because it ended the careers of five Members of the Labour party, but this weapon has not been used for almost twenty years and, as was shown above, is unlikely to be employed again.

Conservative leaders have chosen more subtle methods of handling their backbench Members than have Labour leaders. No Conservatives lost minor positions for rebelling, and Tory backbenchers resigned the whip but did not have it withdrawn. While both parties stressed loyalty as a factor in the selection of ministers and junior ministers, Conservative leaders gave a greater number of enticements such as honours to their Members.

The amount of party discipline employed by the Whips was extremely small in relation to the significant number of public rebellions against party policy between 1945 and 1964. Since few harsh measures were used by Whips in parliament, possibly greater pressures were exerted by local parties on their representatives. The following chapter examines that aspect of party discipline.

10 Constituency Parties and Party Discipline

Only a poor MP can't control his local party.[1]

Virtually every Member of parliament elected since 1945 was selected by a local constituency organization of one of the three political parties. This selection process was vitally important because, among other things, once a candidate was elected his readoption was rarely challenged. However, a few Members were refused readoption because they rebelled over Suez, and this gave rise to many arguments about the proper relationship between a Member and his local party, and to coherent theories about party discipline being caused because of constituency pressures.

The opponents of local party control were inspired by Edmund Burke's theory about the ideal relationship between a Member and his local party, and like M. Ostrogorski they were worried that the development of mass parties meant that Members would become servants of their party organization.[2] Their arguments were based on the premise that MPs would not rebel in parliament if they feared their readoption might be challenged, and they therefore implied that local parties should have little control over their representatives. On the other hand, two former Prime Ministers declared that Members had

---

[1] Interview.
[2] For a discussion about whether or not Burke's ideas were relevant to his own age see Ernest Barker, *Essays on Government*, ch. 6. Ostrogorski's greatest fears never materialized. See McKenzie, *British Political Parties*, pp. 9–10 *et passim*.

to be willing to accept the dictates of their local parties.[1] These arguments were often devoid of evidence about the actual relationship between Members and their local parties, and this chapter attempts to remedy this situation by studying the history of Members who had their readoption challenged between 1945 and 1964.

CENTRAL PARTY CONTROL

The Conservative and Labour local parties are linked vertically to Central Office and the NEC respectively, and Members have connections with both their local parties and party headquarters. Therefore, the relationship between Members and the party organization is essentially triangular. The structure of the central organization of both parties has been described in detail by R. T. McKenzie and Austin Ranney,[2] but one small point must be added because it is referred to later in the chapter. Prior to 1959 matters affecting the choice of Labour party candidates were handled either by a special Elections Sub-Committee or by the Chairmen's Committee (composed of the chairmen of all the NEC sub-committees). After 1959 the Organization Sub-Committee officially dealt with all matters concerning candidates. But, in fact, the Organization

---

[1] Earl Attlee wrote 'When a Member finds that he is in disagreement with his party on a major issue, his right course is to put the matter to his local association. If they wish him to continue to represent them, well and good; but if not he should resign'. 'Party Discipline is Paramount', pp. 15–16. On 23 Nov 1958, Harold Macmillan said on T.V. that it did not matter if a Member fell out with his party, but he must keep his local association with him.

[2] McKenzie, *British Political Parties*, and Austin Ranney, *Pathways to Parliament*.

Sub-Committee set up a secret three man committee, known as the Enquiry Committee,[1] to deal with these matters.

In general, central control of Members is based officially on the authority of the National Executive Committee and the Standing Advisory Committee on Candidates to veto any candidates selected by constituency organizations, and central control over local parties is based on their power to disaffiliate constituency organizations from the national parties. Moreover, as the following cases illustrate, in both parties much depends on informal linkage, and articulation does not depend solely on formal structure.

Each party has a list of approved would-be candidates, and official party candidates must have their names on this list.[2] Theoretically the central organization can prevent a name from being placed on the list, but this has been done very rarely. The NEC has interfered in the selection of candidates on at least ten occasions since 1945, but the SACC has interfered only once.[3] In 1950 the Chorley Conservative Association selected A. Fountaine as their candidate, but the SACC would not accept him because of his avowed anti-Semitic views. He

[1] Some Members of the NEC wanted it to be called the Disciplinary Committee, but this suggestion was defeated. In 1964 its members were Ray Gunter, A. V. Hilton, and Arthur Skeffington.

[2] A detailed study of candidate selection has been made by Ranney, in his *Pathways to Parliament*. Also valuable are McKenzie, *British Political Parties*; R. L. Leonard, *Guide to the General Election*, ch. 7; William Rees-Mogg, T. E. M. McKitterick, Philip Skelsey, 'Selection of Candidates'; Allen M. Potter, 'The English Conservative Constituency Association'.

[3] Ranney, *Pathways to Parliament*, p. 164. One Labour candidate, Harold Lawrence, received NEC sponsorship, but Attlee would not give him a letter of support because Lawrence would not support the official Labour defence policy. *The Times*, 10 Feb 1951. In Mar 1957, Lawrence contested the Bristol West by-election as an official Labour candidate and lost.

became the only locally adopted candidate that the SACC vetoed between 1945 and 1964.[1] Nevertheless, the Chorley party showed their independence by supporting him and he almost won the seat. (Lab. 47·6%, Ind. Cons. 46·9%, and Lib. 5·5%.) This was a close enough result to tempt the Chorley Association to keep Fountaine as their candidate for the next election. However, the SACC not only reaffirmed that they would not approve Fountaine, but they added a new threat; if the Chorley Association insisted on readopting this candidate, the association would lose its membership in the National Union. This combined pressure was great enough in the end to force the association to drop Fountaine and choose a new candidate. Thus, when it came to a showdown over a candidate the constituency association had to back down for fear of being disaffiliated from the National Union.

Neither Conservative nor Labour sitting MPs are known to have been refused endorsement, and only one former MP has had his endorsement rejected since 1945.[2] Tom Braddock was elected for Mitcham in 1945, and was defeated as their official Labour candidate in 1950. Braddock had always been a left-winger in the Labour movement, and during the 1945 parliament he was one of the most rebellious Labour MPs.[3] After his defeat in 1950 he sought re-endorsement as the Labour candidate for Mitcham, but the NEC had taken his name off the B list. In October 1950 Braddock was summoned to a meeting with Morgan Phillips, R. T. Windle, and D. Dixon (chairman of Mitcham CLP) to discuss why he had not received endorsement. At the meeting Morgan Phillips criticized Braddock for having said that he would vote against his party if he thought it was necessary in the interests of the workers. He went on to declare that the party could not tolerate rebels in the 1951 parliament because there was a good chance that the general

[1] *The Times*, 5, 19 Mar 1949.
[2] The five expelled MPs were discussed in chapter 9.
[3] He maintained he has never been a member of the Communist party. Tom Braddock, interview.

election would only produce a small Labour majority. Consequently, Braddock promised not to vote against the party whip, or abstain from voting if there was risk of a Labour defeat, and said that he would not speak for, or be a member of, a proscribed organization.[1] However Braddock was not endorsed and the NEC would give no reasons. Later complaints by Braddock were simply 'noted' by the NEC.[2]

In 1953 Braddock's name was suggested for adoption by the Kingston-upon-Thames Labour party. The National Agent wrote to the association and told them that:

> I would, however, draw your attention to the nomination of Mr. T. Braddock. On several occasions the N.E.C. has refused to endorse the nomination of Mr. Braddock and I am quite sure that were he selected by your Constituency Labour Party their attitude on this matter would be the same. I therefore recommend that Mr. Braddock's name be deleted from the list of nominations to be submitted to your selection conference.[3]

The GMC put forward Braddock's name but he was not chosen. In early 1954 he was selected by his own CLP for the safe Conservative seat of Wimbledon. Subsequently the chairman of the NEC called Braddock to a private meeting, after which Len Williams informed the Wimbledon chairman that Braddock would not be endorsed as an official Labour candidate. Williams would not say why this decision had been made, only that clause 9 of the constitution gave the NEC the right to refuse endorsement.[4] When the Secretary of the Surrey

[1] R. T. Windle asked Braddock in a letter of 27 Oct 1950, to give this assurance because Braddock had been an editor of *Socialist Outlook*, and an outspoken member of the proscribed Socialist Fellowship.

[2] Unpublished letter, A. L. Williams to Tom Braddock, 30 May 1952.

[3] Unpublished letter, Secretary-Agent to Tom Braddock, 25 Jun 1953.

[4] Unpublished letter, A. L. Williams, to H. Shindler, 1 Jun 1954.

Federation of Labour parties contested the fact that no reasons were given, Len Williams informed him that the NEC had acted on 'legal advice'.[1]

The Wimbledon GMC voted 32 to 3 for Braddock to be endorsed and this was approved unanimously by the local Trades Council, but it was to no avail. Braddock attended another meeting of the Organization Sub-Committee in March 1955. This time the committee was composed of Attlee, Gaitskell, Edith Summerskill, the Wimbledon chairman, and, significantly, the Chief Whip. Braddock was questioned about his votes and attitudes in the 1945 parliament, and about the correspondence between the chairman of the Mitcham GMC and Morgan Phillips.[2] The NEC still would not endorse Braddock, and in May it threatened the Wimbledon party with disaffiliation and finally forced the selection of another candidate.[3]

Braddock continued to try to get on the B list. In 1957 a Wimbledon CLP committee studied all the documents, and decided in his favour.[4] The NEC still refused to endorse him, now complaining that he was too old.[5] Braddock replied that this personal slight adversely affected his practice as an architect.

In 1958 Braddock was selected for Kingston-upon-Thames, but the NEC objected to the fact that there was only one name on the short list. Two names were added, but Braddock was still selected. He was then called before the Elections Sub-Committee again, and asked if he would support the party manifesto. He answered in the affirmative, and was finally

---

[1] Unpublished letter, A. L. Williams to N. L. Bryon, 19 Aug 1954.
[2] *Wimbledon Boro' News*, 22 Apr and 6 May 1955.
[3] *Wimbledon Boro' News*, 6, 13 May 1955. The Wimbledon GMC had been visited by Frank Shephard, the Southern Regional Organizer.
[4] Unpublished letter, F. J. Parker (Hon. Sec.) to Tom Braddock, 1 Mar 1957.
[5] Braddock was then 70 years old.

placed on the B list.[1] Kingston-upon-Thames was a safe Conservative seat, and Braddock was defeated there as the official Labour candidate in 1959 and 1964. Apparently the NEC had decided that Braddock was the only serious candidate for this seat, and that his candidature would not harm the party.[2]

No Conservative MPs have been refused endorsement since 1945, but the SACC intervened in a dispute in Newcastle upon Tyne North, and subsequently favoured the non-readoption of a Member. In 1940 Sir Cuthbert Headlam stood as an Independent and defeated the official Conservative candidate, Howard Grattan-Doyle, son of a former MP. When Sir Cuthbert was elected to parliament he immediately accepted the Conservative whip, but discontent continued behind the scenes and in 1949 Headlam was readopted by the Conservative association by a vote of 481–301, despite the opposition of the Executive Council. The officers of the association, therefore, grew even more vehement in their attempts to have Headlam removed. Shortly after he was re-elected in 1950, his supporters formed a new Conservative association which the Executive Committee of the National Union investigated and officially recognized.[3] Later, Sir Cuthbert announced his retirement, and said that the new association represented Conservative opinion in the constituency.[4] The new association adopted a former Liberal MP, Major Gwilym Lloyd George, who stood in 1951 as a Liberal and Conservative candidate. The old association also sponsored a candidate and he actually saved his deposit, but Lloyd George was elected and became Minister of Food in the new government. (Cons. 51·1%, Lab. 36·3%, and Ind. 12·6%.)

The central organization of the Conservative party states

[1] Tom Braddock, interview.
[2] Interview. In 1966 Braddock was the official Labour candidate in the safe Conservative seat of Wimbledon.
[3] *The Newcastle Journal and North Mail*, 13 Aug 1951. *The Times*, 21 Nov 1949, 22 May 1951 and 19 Jun 1951.
[4] *The Times*, 19 Jun 1951.

its neutrality more clearly than the NEC does, but both try to influence local parties behind the scenes. Labour Regional Organizers and Conservative Area Agents are appointed by, and are responsible to, the Conservative party chairman or the Organization Sub-Committee of the NEC, but they work closely with the constituency agents and hence link party headquarters to the local organizations. They attempt to appear neutral in local disputes, but their role is very important because they act as channels for information between the local parties and their headquarters.

There is no formal link between the Whips' Offices and the local parties, but linkage is provided through other parts of the party organization. The Conservative Chief Whip is always in close contact with the party chairman, and therefore information flows via the party chairman to and from the local associations. The Labour Chief Whip keeps in contact with the local parties through his membership on the Organization Sub-Committee of the NEC. In both parties this linkage is informal and its strength depends on personal relationships. A former Chief Whip described it this way: 'I say to the party chairman – if the local chairman is a good chap why don't you phone him and suggest . . .'[1]

LOCAL PARTY CONTROL

Constituency control over MPs varies from semi-official hints by local party officers to formal decisions by the organizations not to readopt their Members as candidates. This control differs from party to party, constituency to constituency, and from one Member to the next. The relationship between a Member and his local party usually involves only a small group of party officers. In the Labour party disagreements are usually handled

[1] Interview.

by the General Management Committee or its Executive Committee. In the Conservative party these affairs are usually dealt with by the Executive Council or the smaller Finance and General Purposes Committee which is composed of the officers of the association.

The dialogue between Members and the officers of their local parties is continuous and complex, and on occasion Members are privately criticized for their actions. These disagreements sometimes become public, but local parties have only occasionally passed votes of no confidence in their Members and even more rarely have MPs been asked to resign. In only a very few of these rare cases has the constituency party action had anything to do with a Member rebelling in the House.

In both parties MPs must be readopted before every election, but this is almost always a formality. In the Conservative party there is a presumption that sitting Members ought to be readopted, and in the Labour party the Model Rules specify that before a GMC can get rid of an MP it must get a majority of its ward committees and affiliated organizations to pass a resolution asking the MP to retire.[1]

LABOUR READOPTION CONFLICTS

Since 1945 fewer Labour MPs than Conservatives have had their readoption challenged, and the NEC has been more prominent in defending its MPs than has Central Office. The motives for challenging the adoption of Labour Members were usually mixed, but the predominant reasons were: (*a*) for personal failings or inadequate local services (*b*) for supporting official Labour policy, and (*c*) for opposing official Labour policy.

[1] *Model Rules*, Set A, clause XII, section (7).

S

For Personal Failings or Inadequate Local Services

A number of Labour MPs have retired from parliament after disputes with their local parties. The following four were criticized either because of their personal affairs or because of inadequate service to their constituencies: J. D. Mack (Newcastle-under-Lyme), James Glanville (Consett), John Baird (Wolverhampton), and Neil Maclean (Glasgow, Govan).[1] The first two Members withdrew without much of a struggle, and the latter two had to be forced out.

Neil Maclean was first elected for Govan as an Independent Labour candidate in 1918. He then became an official Labour candidate until he was not endorsed for the 1929 general election.[2] He was elected as an Independent in 1929, and continued to hold the seat in 1945 as an official Labour candidate. In 1949 there were complaints that at 75 he was too old to be a MP, and consequently he was put on a short list, and defeated. After several delays and much quarrelling Jack Davis was selected as the official Labour candidate.[3] Maclean's age was the dominant factor in the dispute, but some newspapers also recorded the party chairman as saying that Maclean did not mix well, and that he had not 'kept in touch'.[4] Maclean had not been a rebel in the 1945 parliament, and had twice been a Labour Whip. He saw Morgan Phillips about the dispute, but the NEC would not intervene[5] so Maclean accepted the new candidate. The Govan constituency was won by the Conservatives in 1950, but there had been important boundary revisions.

[1] At least two other Labour MPs have been forced to retire since 1945 because they were known as habitual drinkers.
[2] *Telegraph*, 22 Mar 1927. *The Times House of Commons Guide 1929.*
[3] *Daily Herald*, 16 Jan 1950.
[4] *Daily Graphic*, 16 Jan 1950.
[5] *Glasgow Evening Citizen*, 18 Jan 1950. *Govan Press*, 14 Oct 1949, and 17 Feb 1950.

J. D. Mack was elected as an official Labour candidate for Newcastle-under-Lyme in 1942 and 1945. Mack was a well-known left-wing MP who had signed the Nenni telegram and joined other revolts against party policy, but he was not in any difficulty with the Whips or his left-wing GMC. Before the 1950 general election the managing director of Rist's Wire and Cables claimed publicly that Mack had promised that in return for a position with the business he would 'work things' in parliament for the firm. This allegation was denied, and Mack was re-elected in 1950.[1] Shortly after the election Mack declared that he would not stand again because of bad health. However, the Labour 'insiders' interviewed by Austin Ranney '. . . were sure that the Newcastle executive had forced Mack to resign because they believed there was substance in Rist's charges, and Mack had not fought back because he did not want any public controversy'.[2]

The constituency difficulties of James Glanville were both serious and amusing. Glanville was a former miner, who represented the miners' seat of Consett. He was a very loyal member of the PLP, but was known as a habitual drinker and had offended the teetotalling section of his constituents. In May 1953 he advocated in jest that free beer should be provided at all coronation ceremonies, and had to apologize for this statement because the Consett Labour party dissociated itself from his remark. A few months later he announced that he would not stand again because he was too old at 62.[3]

In early 1963 John Baird was advised by the Wolverhampton GMC that he should retire at the end of the parliament. A resolution was passed to this effect, and the GMC asked the NEC to allow them to select a new prospective candidate.[4] Baird declared that this attack was due to his vehement opposi-

---

[1] *Newcastle Times*, 24 Feb 1950.
[2] Ranney, *Pathways to Parliament*, p. 187.
[3] *Consett Chronicle*, 21 May and 15 Oct 1953; *Consett Guardian*, 11 Jun 1953.
[4] *The Times*, 7 Feb 1963, and *Guardian*, 8 Feb 1963.

tion to the Commonwealth Immigration Bill, but the GMC complained about personal failings and his long period of illness which had caused him to be absent from the House.[1] Baird had often been convicted for speeding, had sponsored the Direct Action Committee against Nuclear Warfare, and had publicly declared that George Brown should resign as deputy leader of the party.[2] Besides all this, Baird was known as an extremely rebellious left-wing Labour MP, but this could not have had a very great effect since there has always been a left-wing constituency party in Wolverhampton and in 1964 the party selected Renée Short as the official candidate.

Behind the scenes the NEC, PLP Committee, and the Chief Whip had consultations about the Wolverhampton party's desire to adopt a new candidate, and they agreed that it would be best for Baird to retire.[3] The NEC then announced that the Wolverhampton party had acted properly,[4] and that Baird would not be readopted.

None of these four MPs had readoption problems because they opposed official party policy, and only in Baird's case were any political reasons even suggested. The NEC did not defend any of them, and in at least Baird's case favoured the action of the local party.

For Supporting Official Party Policy

Before the 1955 general election the Labour party was badly divided over the Bevanite controversy. A number of local parties favoured Bevan's policies and caused trouble for Members who accepted official party policy. This type of readoption conflict severely limits the importance of statements about how local

---

[1] He was also absent from local party meetings. *Birmingham Mail*, 16 Feb 1963.
[2] *Birmingham Mail*, 21 Jul 1958. *County Advertiser*, 2 Feb 1961, and *Daily Telegraph*, 4 Jan 1961.
[3] Arthur Skeffington, interview.
[4] *The Times*, 8, 28 Feb 1963.

parties act to help keep the party united in the House of Commons. In these cases the local parties were trying to divide the party.

Elaine Burton was first elected for Coventry South in 1950, and during nine years in the House of Commons she never joined a revolt against party policy. In 1955 the GMC of the Coventry Labour party asked its three MPs to vote against taking the whip away from Bevan. Later, in a PLP meeting Miss Burton asked Attlee if he would consider it a vote of no confidence if she voted for Bevan. Attlee replied in the affirmative, and Miss Burton cast her vote against Bevan. The Coventry South divisional party took no action against her, but the GMC of the composite Coventry party passed a vote of no confidence in her (52–19). After a meeting with Sara Barker (Assistant National Agent), Reg Underhill (West Midlands Regional Organizer), and the GMC of Coventry South, the GMC announced that they regretted her action but that no further steps would be taken. In 1955 she was readopted and re-elected.

Several other Labour MPs had disputes with Bevanite factions in their local parties. Some Members, such as Denis Healey, were able to keep the criticism relatively private, but a few constituency parties informed the NEC that they supported Bevan.[1] Some local parties were split on what action to take in the Bevanite controversy. Percy Collick strongly opposed Bevan and indicated this by being absent from a meeting when Bevan came to his Birkenhead West constituency.[2] Collick's executive was somewhat split over his readoption in 1955, but vigorous support from the local Trades Council prevented any public criticism.

The Hayes and Harlington Labour party severely criticized Arthur Skeffington because of his approval of German rearmament and his opposition to Bevan. Contrary to some

---

[1] Denis Healey, interview. Also see the difficulties of Jack Jones in Rotherham. *Daily Telegraph*, 27 Mar 1952.
[2] Percy Collick, interview.

reports, the NEC did not intervene in the dispute because Skeffington kept the confidence of a majority of the GMC. However, according to Labour officials, if he had not been re-adopted the NEC would have intervened as they did in the cases of Herbert Butler and Bessie Braddock.[1]

Herbert Butler was first elected for Hackney in 1945. The Hackney local Labour executive was very pro-Bevan, and privately threatened not to readopt Butler in 1955 if he continued to uphold official party policy. The NEC opposed this threat, and sent a Regional Organizer to intervene in the dispute.[2] Butler was readopted without any further difficulties, and was elected in 1955.

Bessie Braddock was first elected for the Exchange division of Liverpool in 1945. In her first parliament she joined a large number of left-wing revolts, but from 1950 to 1964 she was not associated with any rebellions. In 1951 Kenneth Counsell, the Exchange agent, had 'considerable success' in influencing the local Labour party executive to accept the policies of Aneurin Bevan.[3] In view of this the GMC demanded that Bessie Braddock support Bevan. She refused, voted for German rearmament, and periodically attacked the Bevanites.[4] Consequently the local party stopped supporting her, and even denied her the use of their committee rooms for interviewing constituents.

In June 1954 the GMC asked the Exchange wards to decide whether or not another candidate should be selected. Two wards voted in favour of Bessie Braddock's retirement but the St. James ward asked the NEC to intervene. St. James declared that the GMC should have given reasons for not readopting Bessie Braddock, and that the GMC was supposed to wait until much closer to a general election before selecting a prospective candidate. Reg Wallis, the North-West Regional Organizer,

---

[1] Interview.　　　　　　　　[2] *Ibid.*
[3] Jack and Bessie Braddock, *The Braddocks*, p. 90.
[4] Millie Toole, *Mrs. Bessie Braddock, M.P.*, p. 180.
Also see *Daily Telegraph*, 29 Apr 1955; *The Times*, 29 Apr 1955.

concluded that the procedure used by the GMC was unconstitutional, and asked the NEC to investigate the situation. The NEC sent a committee, composed of Wilfred Burke (chairman of the Labour party), James Haworth (President of Transport Salaried Staffs Association), and Len Williams, to study the Exchange difficulties. On 27 October 1954 the committee reported that Bessie Braddock was to remain the candidate, and that the Exchange party had to be reorganized.

The GMC would not accept the decision of the NEC committee, and failed to pass a vote of confidence in their Member by 40 votes to 39. As it happened, seven members of the GMC lived outside the district, and their votes were invalid. Therefore, the NEC declared that Bessie Braddock was to remain Exchange's candidate until another investigation could be launched. After the second inquiry the NEC asserted that there were no other candidates available, and threatened to disaffiliate the Exchange party if Bessie Braddock was not readopted. As a result of this threat the GMC voted to retain her as their candidate by a vote of 31 to 7 (with 26 abstentions).

Later the Exchange GMC was disbanded, financial irregularities were found in the accounts, and the local agent absconded to Canada.[1] The chairman and secretary of the Exchange Labour party resigned, and Councillor Lawrence Murphy stood as an Independent in the 1955 general election. Despite this dissension Bessie Braddock easily held Exchange in 1955. (Lab. 56·1%, Cons, 35·4%, Ind. 8·5%.) Councillor Murphy was then expelled from the party for standing as a candidate in the election.[2]

For Opposing Official Party Policy

Only once since 1945 has a Labour Member had readoption problems because he opposed official party policy, and even

[1] J. and B. Braddock, *The Braddocks*, p. 91.
[2] *The Times*, 28 Jul 1956.

that occasion was substantially caused by personal factors.[1] Stanley Evans joined merely three revolts during his career as MP for Wednesbury from 1945 to 1956. In March 1950 he was made Parliamentary Secretary in the Ministry of Food, and within a short time he complained that the government's agricultural policy was 'feather-bedding' the farmers. Although there were virtually no farmers in Wednesbury, the National Union of Farmers condemned Evans' outburst and he was forced to resign from the government. Later, he helped to organize a right-wing revolt against the Labour party's official policy for the Central African Federation.[2]

In 1955 Evans had some difficulty being selected because one Wednesbury ward and the local branch of the AEU opposed his candidature. Wednesbury had been a trade-union seat, and Evans' successful business background did not appeal to many members of his local party. Moreover, Evans declared that he would not contribute to local charities and this outraged some Labour supporters.[3] In 1956 Evans began to advocate vigorous action over Suez, and in September of that year the Wednesbury GMC told him they opposed a British attack on Egypt. Within the next two months Evans abstained twice on Labour censure motions against the Conservative government's action in the Middle East. He claimed, correctly, that the Standing Orders of the Labour party allowed him to abstain, but this did not influence his local party. On 17 November the Wednesbury GMC voted unanimously that Evans should resign. Evans assented to this request, saying that '. . . a general without an army, and what is more living on borrowed time, seldom wields

---

[1] In 1966 Desmond Donnelly, Pembroke, Reginald Paget, Northampton, and Woodrow Wyatt, Bosworth, controlled constituency grievances over their criticism of government policy. William Warby's constant attack on party leaders caused serious constituency criticisms of his behaviour, but he retired without seeking the nomination again for Ashfield.

[2] See chapter 5.   [3] Interview.

much influence and lacks all dignity'.[1] Although Evans was not in any trouble with the Whips, he never returned to the House, and simply asked to be appointed to the Manor of Northstead.[2]

CONSERVATIVE READOPTION CONFLICTS

Conservative readoption conflicts can be examined under the following headings: (*a*) for personal failings or inadequate local services, (*b*) conflict over specific issues combined with criticism of a Member's activities, (*c*) for opposing official party policy.

For Personal Failings or Inadequate Local Services

A number of Conservative Members are known to have been refused readoption because they had personal failings or were thought to be ineffective as MPs. These included Nigel Fisher (Hitchin), E. L. Gandar Dower (Caithness and Sutherland), Captain Arthur Marsden (Chertsey), E. E. Gates (Middleton and Prestwich), Sir Gifford Fox (Henley), and Charles Challen (Hampstead). None of these six MPs was a party rebel, and Central Office made no attempt to intervene when their local associations caused difficulties for them.[3]

[1] *Daily Telegraph*, 21 Nov 1956.
[2] Interview. *Manchester Guardian*, 21 Nov 1956.
[3] In early 1966 Commander Anthony Courtney, Harrow East, successfully defeated an attempt to prevent him from being the official Conservative candidate for the general election. Courtney had been involved with a woman in Russia in 1961, and in the light of this knowledge his executive committee decided to look for other candidates. Arguing that Soviet authorities were trying to remove him from power he forced a meeting of the Harrow East Conservative Association which deplored the action of the executive committee by a

Nigel Fisher was elected for Hitchin in 1950 and 1951. In January 1952 he was divorced and his local chairman, backed by the Hitchin Conservative Association, publicly repudiated him.[1] Therefore, Fisher decided not to stand for Hitchin in 1955, and the executive selected a new candidate.[2] Fisher's political career was not permanently damaged because in 1955 he was elected as the official Conservative candidate for Surbiton and later became a junior minister.

Sir Gifford Fox and E. E. Gates were both accused by their local associations of being inadequate constituency representatives. E. E. Gates, Conservative Member for Middleton and Prestwich from 1940 to 1950, was faced with this accusation in 1951 by the Finance and General Purposes Committee of his local association. The committee asked Gates for his resignation, and although he vowed he would improve, he stood down before the 1951 general election.[3] The Henley association first complained about Sir Gifford Fox in 1945, saying that he was not adequately representing them, and that he was not making enough personal appearances in the constituency. Although Sir Gifford had represented them since 1932, they appointed a new selection committee, and he was defeated.[4]

There was little difference in the readoption difficulties of Captain Arthur Marsden, Charles Challen, and E. L. Gandar Dower. Marsden was elected for Chertsey in 1937, and it was not until 1949 that he had readoption problems. Allegedly Marsden had made large contributions to association funds,

vote of 454 to 277. Courtney remained the official candidate for Harrow East, and although he lost the election, the defeat was probably not caused by this constituency row.

[1] Nigel Fisher, interview.

[2] *Hertfordshire and Bedfordshire Express*, 5 Apr 1952.

[3] *Prestwich and Whitefield Guide*, 20 Jul 1951; *Middleton Guardian*, 28 Jul 1951, 22 Sep 1951. An earlier identical case concerned J. N. McKie (Galloway), but it was prior to 1945; see *The Scotsman*, 4 Jun 1945.

[4] *South Oxfordshire Standard*, 15 Apr 1949.

and there is some possibility that his popularity decreased after the adoption of the Maxwell Fyfe reforms which prevented Conservative candidates from making large donations to their local parties. However, the 1949 redistribution of seats was even more significant. When his constituency was divided, Marsden refused to stand for the new seat of Esher, and was not selected for Chertsey.[1] Both of these constituencies were won by the Conservatives in 1950.

Charles Challen was elected for Hampstead in 1941. In 1947 he was told that his readoption would not be automatic because he had not become a national figure. Although Challen's supporters contested the action, a short list was prepared which included the names of Challen, Henry Brooke, and two other candidates. Brooke was chosen by a vote of 46–21.[2] This decision was challenged, and on 15 August the whole association was given a chance to decide who would be the Conservative candidate for Hampstead.[3] Only 1,163 of the 7,500 eligible members cast their ballots, and Brooke received almost twice as many votes as Challen.[4] Brooke was elected in 1950, and met Hampstead's desire for a national figure by becoming a member of the government within four years, and Home Secretary in 1962.

E. L. Gandar Dower was elected for Caithness and Sutherland in 1945 by only six votes. During the election campaign he promised to resign and fight a by-election after Japan was defeated. When Japan surrendered, Gandar Dower asked his local party several times to let him apply for the Chiltern Hundreds, but the local executive refused, and would not even allow the association to vote on whether or not their Member should stand down. Finally, he made their refusal public.[5]

[1] *Surrey Herald*, 7, 21 Jan 1949.
[2] *Hampstead News*, 8 Dec 1949.
[3] It was not necessary for local party members to be present at the meeting in order to vote.
[4] *Daily Express*, 19 Aug 1949. In February 1950 Challen informed Lord Woolton that he would not stand. *The Times*, 10 Feb 1950.
[5] *The Times*, 16 Sep 1948.

There had been adverse criticism of Dower's service to the constituency, and the executive proceeded to select Sir David Robertson as their prospective candidate. Gandar Dower resigned the Tory whip, and retired from politics in 1950.

Conflict Over Specific Issues Combined with Criticism of Members' Activities

A few Conservative MPs had their readoption challenged because their local parties opposed their opinions on specific issues and also disliked some of their personal habits. They included Colin Turner (West Woolwich), Patrick Wolrige-Gordon (Aberdeenshire East), Dr. Donald Johnson (Carlisle), H. Montgomery Hyde (Belfast North), and two other Ulster Unionists.

The West Woolwich Conservative Association began to criticize Colin Turner in 1962 after he had been their MP for only three years. The local officers, and especially the chairman, said that Turner was interfering too much in local government, and was an inadequate representative for the constituency. According to Turner, there were also complaints about his opposition to the Wolfenden proposals.[1] In 1962 the Executive Committee attempted to replace Turner with Sir William Steward, his predecessor as MP and then president of the West Woolwich Conservative Association.

A selection committee placed Turner, Steward and two others on a short list, and Sir William was selected by 52 votes to 31.[2] This decision was reversed at two meetings of the local association, and Turner was readopted by a vote of 274–184.[3] In view of this decision, Steward (president of the association), Robert

[1] Colin Turner, interview.
[2] *The Times*, 13 Jan 1964. See also *Daily Mail*, 18 Oct 1962.
[3] Turner had been very much aided by the local Young Conservatives.

Fyson (chairman) and Eric Goodman (treasurer) resigned their positions. Turner was not able to replace these three with his supporters, and Leslie Smith, who also had opposed Turner, was elected chairman.

Turner was defeated in the 1964 general election, but he insisted that he should not have to contest his selection again. However, the agent asked him to submit his name along with the other candidates. Turner regarded this as an insult, resigned, and went into the market for another seat. Turner was neither helped nor hindered by any formal action from Central Office. He received some informal aid from Iain Macleod (chairman of the party), who presented a favourable report to the officers of the association.

Dr. Donald Johnson was first elected for Carlisle in 1955. His personality came to be disliked both in Carlisle and in Central Office, and this feeling intensified in 1963 when he criticized Macmillan's leadership. During the crucial division over Profumo he allowed the *Daily Express* to photograph him playing golf.

Johnson was dissatisfied with being a backbencher, and continually informed his local executive that if he was not given a government position he might not stand again.[1] These threats and Johnson's parliamentary revolts caused a large majority of the Carlisle executive to vote against his readoption.[2] The chairman told the press that it was up to the local association to decide when a Member's outspokenness was unreasonable.[3] At first Johnson said that he would resign, but later he decided to oppose the decision of the Executive Council. Some local newspapers supported Johnson, and he easily received the fifty signatures necessary to force a meeting of the whole association.[4] However, Johnson had little support in the party, and the

---

[1] Unpublished letter, Dr. Donald Johnson to R. D. Harrison, 14 Oct 1963. *Cumberland Evening News*, 3 Jul 1963.
[2] The meeting took place on 14 Oct 1963.
[3] *Cumberland Evening News*, 16 Oct 1963.
[4] See, for example, *Cumberland Evening News*, 15 Oct, 29, 30 Nov 1963.

meeting upheld the decision of the executive by a vote of 138 to 31.[1] Central Office made no attempt to intervene in this case because, as Johnson said, 'they thought I was a nuisance'.[2]

John Lett, a friend of Johnson, appealed to Central Office to allow a postal ballot as had been employed in the Nigel Nicolson case. Rule 19 of the Carlisle Association stated that all local disputes would be solved by Central Office. However, in 1951 the rules for the whole party had been changed so that disagreements were settled by the Executive Committee of the National Union of Conservative Associations. Therefore, Lord Blakenham, chairman of the party, refused the appeal because the Carlisle rules were out of date.[3] In parliament Johnson resigned the Conservative whip and sat as an Independent.[4] He announced to the press that: 'The Conservative Party is clearly undergoing a great sickness. . . . On all sides during the last four months I have encountered nobody but Rip Van Winkles still living in the days of Harold Macmillan. . . .'[5]

In June 1964 Johnson proposed a single transferable vote system for Britain, but this Private Members' Bill was not allowed to be introduced.[6] Nevertheless, Johnson announced that he intended to stand as an Independent in the 1964 general election. Labour won the seat, but Johnson's candidature was not a significant factor in the result. (Lab. 45·6%, Cons. 40·5%, Lib. 11·0%, and Ind. 2·9%.)

Patrick Wolrige-Gordon was first elected for East Aberdeenshire in a 1958 by-election. He was a vigorous campaigner for

[1] *The Times*, 31 Dec 1963.
[2] Dr. Donald Johnson, interview.
[3] Unpublished letter, Lord Chelmer to John Lett, 22 May 1964. *Carlisle Journal*, 5 Jun 1964.
[4] *Daily Telegraph*, 24 Jan 1964.
[5] *The Times*, 23 Jan 1964. For Johnson's attitude to the leadership of the Conservative party see his pamphlet, *On Being an Independent M.P.* For further enlightenment on this case, see also Johnson's autobiography, *A Doctor in Parliament*.
[6] The vote was 137 to 20. 696 *H.C. Deb.*, col. 251.

Moral Re-Armament, and in October 1961 his local executive asked him to refrain from making speeches for MRA. When he became engaged to Peter Howard's daughter the executive (especially the chairman and agent) was even more vocal in its complaints and declared that his MRA activities were taking time which should be devoted to political duties.[1] Wolrige-Gordon refused to announce that he would not stand again, and in April 1962 the executive passed a vote of no confidence in him.[2] He and his supporters collected enough signatures from constituents to force a meeting of the whole association on 25 April. The adversaries presented their cases, and the audience voted 463 to 185 to retain Wolrige-Gordon as their candidate.[3] The members of the executive who opposed their Member were then forced to resign.[4] In 1964 Wolrige-Gordon was readopted and elected for East Aberdeenshire.

Belfast North first elected H. Montgomery Hyde in 1950. Hyde lost much of his control over the executive in 1958 when a new Imperial constituency association for North Belfast was established to link the old divisions. In 1959 many complaints were made about Hyde's support for the Wolfenden proposals and the abolition of capital punishment.[5] It was said that he did not spend enough time in the constituency, and that he travelled abroad too frequently. He was also criticized for campaigning for the return of the Lane Collection from the Tate Gallery to Dublin,[6] and for publishing the Casement diaries and a list of the Kings of England who had homosexual tendencies.

Hyde went to Belfast North and solicited support shortly before the selection committee met to adopt their prospective candidate for the 1959 general election. He mustered enough

[1] P. W. Wolrige-Gordon, interview.
[2] *The Times*, 14 Apr 1963.   [3] *Ibid.*, 9 Apr 1962.
[4] *Ibid.*, 26 Apr 1962, and 29 Jun 1962.
[5] Although Hyde was not in trouble with the Conservative Whips, he was actually the most rebellious Tory in the 1955 parliament. See chapter 6.
[6] According to some North Belfast constituents this was his greatest mistake. *Irish Times*, 6 Jan 1959.

support to win the nomination by the narrow vote of 77–72.[1]
After this decision Hyde was so confident of his readoption
that he ignored a special invitation to attend a meeting to
ratify his nomination, and instead he went on a parliamentary
delegation to the West Indies.[2] The selection committee
presented Hyde's name to the whole association, but it was
rejected by 171 votes to 152.[3]

Acting on the advice of Nigel Nicolson, Hyde applied for a
postal ballot to be taken.[4] He declared that the meeting which
rejected his readoption had been irregular, and made an
attempt behind the scenes to convince the Secretary of the
Ulster Unionist Council to intervene. Both of these attempts
ended in failure when the GMC voted three to one against a
postal ballot.[5] Hyde was told to accept the fact that he was no
longer a candidate for the Ulster Unionist party, and was
reminded that he had made the usual pledge to abide by the
decisions of the association and had undertaken 'to support
whole-heartedly such person as may be selected by the Association as a candidate'.[6] Hyde did not contest the 1959 general
election, and retired from politics.

Conservative Members from England and Scotland can
normally expect to be automatically readopted, but in Northern
Ireland this is not the case.[7] This is illustrated by the 1963

---

[1] *The Times*, 13 Jan 1959.
[2] H. Montgomery Hyde, interview. Unpublished letter,
Elizabeth Noble to H. Montgomery Hyde, 10 Mar 1959.
[3] *Belfast Telegraph*, 9, 13 Jan 1959. *The Times*, 14 Feb
1959. Theoretically, over 2,000 members could have
voted at the meeting.
[4] Unpublished letter, Nigel Nicolson to H. Montgomery
Hyde, 1 Jan 1959.
[5] Unpublished letter, Elizabeth Noble to H. Montgomery
Hyde, 10 Mar 1959. *The Times*, 10, 19 Mar 1959, 4 Apr
1959.
[6] Unpublished letter, Elizabeth Noble to H. Montgomery
Hyde, 2 Apr 1959.
[7] See *The Times*, 27 May 1963, and *New Statesman*, 7 Jun
1963.

readoption difficulties of Captain Lawrence Orr (South Down), George Currie (North Down), and Knox Cunningham (South Antrim).[1]

Knox Cunningham was elected by a majority of 50,041 in the 1959 general election. In the spring of 1963 some local party members complained that Cunningham did not spend enough time working for the constituency because he was PPS to the Prime Minister, and others thought that he was too right-wing. According to Cunningham, his chairman, vice-chairman, and treasurer joined in a secret effort to get another candidate.[2]

In South Antrim it is not compulsory to advertise for a new candidate at every general election as it is in most Ulster Unionist parties, but on this occasion the Management Committee decided to do so. A selection committee was set up which was composed of delegates chosen on the principle of one member for every 500 votes in each of the divisions. The Ulster Unionist Council (equivalent to Central Office) took no part in the controversy, simply providing the chairman for the committee. Cunningham received two out of every three votes from the selection committee, and his opponent asked that the nomination be made unanimous. At the ensuing general meeting of the South Antrim party Cunningham succeeded in removing his local chairman, vice-president, vice-chairman, and secretary. Afterwards Cunningham had easier relations with his local party, and he was re-elected for South Antrim in 1964.

Captain Lawrence Orr was first elected for South Down in 1950. The party regulations in that constituency require that before every election an advertisement must be inserted in the newspapers asking individuals to apply to be the Ulster Unionist candidate. If the incumbent intends to stand again this is included in the advertisement. Party cohesion is strengthened by the requirement that everyone who stands for nomination

[1] The case of George Forrest (Mid-Ulster) was discussed in chapter 9.
[2] Knox Cunningham, interview.

must sign a pledge stating that he will not stand as an Independent if he is not selected.

At the 1963 selection conference a candidate came forward to challenge the sitting Member, but he received only four votes out of approximately 1,000, and Captain Orr was easily readopted. There had been no serious complaints about Orr. This case was not like any of the readoption conflicts which have been discussed in this chapter. In South Down the MP simply has his readoption challenged before every election.[1]

North Down has almost the same political machinery as South Down, and it is therefore relatively easy for party members to challenge the sitting MP. Advertisements for candidates are automatically placed in the local newspapers before every election. In 1963 the North Down MP, George Currie, was accused of being out of touch with the views of many local people and of not answering mail from his constituents. In contrast to the Orr case discussed above, a serious attempt was made to defeat Currie at the 1963 selection conference. He survived by only 26 votes, but the party rallied behind his candidature and he was re-elected to parliament in 1964.

For Opposing Official Party Policy

Although Conservative MPs joined a considerable number of party rebellions during the years 1945 to 1964 very few of them had their readoption challenged. Four Members were challenged because they opposed the Conservative government's decision to attack Egypt, and two because they opposed other official party policies. Viscount Hinchingbrooke (South Dorset)

[1] The South Down Member's communication with his association is mainly with the Management Committee, which consists of 10 members. There is also a South Down Central Committee composed of a number of members from each division (about 44 members), but it meets only once a year to manage the finances.

got into trouble over German rearmament and Anthony Fell was condemned for his criticism of the party leadership. The four Members who had the most serious readoption difficulties were Anthony Nutting (Melton), Colonel Cyril Banks (Pudsey), Sir Frank Medlicott (East Norfolk), and Nigel Nicolson (Bournemouth East and Christchurch).

Viscount Hinchingbrooke was first elected for South Dorset in 1941. He was a very independent MP, and angered his local party by opposing Britain's involvement in the Korean War and by publicly abstaining over German rearmament. In October 1952 the South Dorset Executive Council passed a motion of no confidence in him by a vote of 46 to 9.[1] Hinchingbrooke asked the Central Office to intervene, but Lord Woolton replied that he would not become involved. The Area Agent attended all of the meetings about Hinchingbrooke's readoption but would not commit himself to either side. Moreover, Hinchingbrooke thought that in parliament the Whips adopted 'an air of neutral hostility'.[2]

Hinchingbrooke would not accept the decision of his Executive Council, and took the dispute to a meeting of the whole association where he was readopted by a vote of 836 to 468. Many members of the Executive Council then resigned, and Hinchingbrooke had them replaced with his own supporters. In the 1955 general election he was again elected as the Conservative Member for South Dorset. In 1956 Hinchingbrooke resigned the Conservative whip because he opposed the government's policy over Suez. An association meeting was called, but only six local members voted against him.[3] Later he took back the whip, was readopted, and re-elected in 1959.[4]

[1] He had earlier problems with his South Dorset Association because of a critical speech about National Savings.
[2] Viscount Hinchingbrooke, interview. Also see the *Dorset Daily Echo*, 9 Oct 1952, *The Times*, 26 Jun 1952, and Bulmer-Thomas, *Party System in Great Britain*, p. 273.
[3] The vote was 495 to 6. *Dorset Daily Echo*, 18 May 1957.
[4] In 1962, after becoming a peer, Hinchingbrooke supported an Independent candidate, Sir Piers Debenham,

Anthony Fell was first elected for Yarmouth in 1951. When he resigned the Tory whip over Suez his association gave him complete support, and the chairman said, 'We don't hamstring our candidates. They are entitled to give views they hold personally'.[1] However, according to Fell, some bitterness lingered over Suez.[2] In October 1962 he had a major dispute with his local executive because he opposed Britain joining the Common Market and called Harold Macmillan 'a national disaster'.[3] Fell received an almost unanimous vote of confidence from the Yarmouth Conservative Association, and his opponents on the executive resigned their positions.[4] Fell was elected again in 1964, and in 1966 he was the official Conservative Candidate for Yarmouth but was defeated in the large swing to Labour.

None of the eight Conservatives who resigned the whip over Suez were denied readoption because of their revolts against official party policy.[5] However, the Members who opposed Eden's decision to send troops to Egypt had trouble with their local parties, and four of them had their readoption challenged.[6]

in a South Dorset by-election. Hinchingbrooke and Debenham both opposed the official Conservative policy of joining the Common Market. Labour won the seat, possibly because of Hinchingbrooke's intervention. (Lab. 33·5%, Cons. 31·8%, Lib. 21%, Ind. 12·3%.)

[1] *Yarmouth Mercury*, 17 May 1957, and *The Times*, 20 Jun 1957.

[2] Anthony Fell, interview.

[3] *Ibid.*

[4] *Eastern Daily Press*, 15 Nov 1962, and *The Times*, 23, 24 Oct 1962.

[5] These eight were discussed in chapter 9. The other important right-wing Conservative rebel over Suez was Captain Charles Waterhouse. He resigned his seat in Leicester South-East, but not because he was in any trouble with his constituency party.

[6] For a summary of the history of MPs who did not have readoption difficulties, see Epstein, *British Politics in the Suez Crisis*: for J. J. Astor, pp. 112–14; Robert Boothby, p. 115; Sir Edward Boyle, pp. 110–12; Peter Kirk,

Anthony Nutting, who represented Melton from 1945 to 1957, was the most senior of the Conservatives who had difficulties with their local parties. During the Suez campaign he resigned his position as Minister of State for Foreign Affairs. Until that time he had not had any trouble with his local party, even though he had abstained on the capital punishment issue.

Eden and Nutting agreed that the resignation should not be made public until after the cease-fire. In order to keep his decision secret, Nutting stayed away from the House, and told reporters that he was ill. The resignation was first disclosed at a private meeting between Nutting and the president and chairman of the Melton Conservative Association and the Area Agent. Nutting thought that a decision had been made that no action would be taken, but the story of his resignation was given to the press.[1] When the Finance and General Purposes Committee held its regular meeting that week it repudiated Nutting and publicly supported Eden.[2] Before the end of the month Nutting resigned from the House of Commons.

There had been no time for Nutting to organize an opposition to the meeting of the Finance and General Purposes Committee. He had asked privately that no statement be made until he spoke to the association, but apparently this was refused. According to Nutting he had always been friendly with the chairman and president, and was surprised by their action. The only advice he had solicited was from the vice-chairman of the Conservative party at Central Office, to whom he had spoken about the proper procedure for a Member to adopt with his local executive. Later, Nutting declined a chance to speak to the local association, and decided to retire. This was partially due to the publicity given by the *Sunday Express* to his relationship with a Mrs. Vanderbilt.[3] Nutting's political career was

pp. 120–1; A. C. M. Spearman, pp. 119–20; William Yates, pp. 117–19. Also see Anthony Nutting, *No End of a Lesson.*
[1] Anthony Nutting, interview.   [2] *The Times*, 7 Nov 1956.
[3] *The Sunday Express*, 11 Nov 1956, and Nutting, interview.

not completely destroyed because of his resignation; he was adopted for Oldham and was defeated there in the 1964 general election.

Colonel Cyril Banks represented Pudsey from 1950 to 1959. He had been a friend of both Nasser and his Foreign Minister before the Egyptian revolution brought Nasser to power. Moreover, Banks developed a very successful business selling British products in Egypt both before and after the Suez controversy.[1] When British troops attacked Egypt Banks immediately declared his support for Nasser, and therefore allied himself with the Labour party. In September Banks openly abstained when the Labour party moved a vote of no confidence in the policy of the Conservative government.[2] The next month he abstained again, and subsequently resigned the Conservative whip. Although Banks had not joined any other revolts in his parliamentary career, the Pudsey executive immediately discontinued all communication with him, and began the process of selecting another candidate. The executive announced, 'The Association wishes to make it clear that Colonel Banks now has no connection with the Pudsey Division Conservative Association'.[3]

Later the Conservative whip was returned to Banks, but embarrassment prevented him from attending meetings of the 1922 Committee, and he played no part in parliamentary activities. He did not stand for parliament in 1959, and although he attempted to get a seat at a later date, he was told that he would not get one because of what he had done over Suez.[4]

Sir Frank Medlicott was first elected for East Norfolk in 1939, and he held Central Norfolk from 1950 to 1959 as a National Liberal candidate. Sir Frank experienced some minor difficulty because he opposed blood sports, but although he had liberal views on hanging and liquor he had no serious trouble with his local party before the Suez crisis. His independent judgement had been shown on 8 May 1940 when he joined the Con-

---

[1] Interview.   [2] *Pudsey and Stanningley News*, 27 Sep 1956.
[3] *Ibid.*, 22 Nov 1956.   [4] Interview.

servative rebels in forcing the resignation of Chamberlain and the consequent rise of Churchill.

On 8 November 1956 Medlicott abstained from voting on the government's confidence motion over Suez. The Central Norfolk Association immediately declared its support for Eden. The association did not tell Medlicott that they wanted a new candidate, but he was prevented from speaking to the branches and the local chairman sent him a letter which suggested he should retire from politics.[1] The Area Office stated that this was a local affair, and that they would not interfere. Central Office asked Medlicott not to involve them in the matter, but also said that he should not resign from parliament.[2]

In May 1957 the president of the Central Norfolk Association announced that Medlicott would not be standing at the next election, and stated that '. . . he was sure that all, including those who had been most angry with . . . [Medlicott] would recognize that for twenty years he had been a very good member'.[3] Sir Frank was angry that the statement did not give his reasons for standing down, and told the press: 'My reason reflects little credit on those who are running the affairs of the association'. They want 'to be free to choose a party hack, prepared to throw overboard everything in which he believes if only he can cling to his seat in parliament'.[4] Medlicott resigned the Conservative whip in November 1957, but took it back after a year as an Independent. He did not stand for parliament in 1959, and in 1962 he joined the Liberal party.[5]

The most familiar and best documented case of a MP having his readoption challenged is that of Nigel Nicolson. This is mainly because Nicolson forced his constituency executive to allow a postal ballot which somewhat resembled direct

[1] Sir Frank Medlicott, interview.
[2] *Ibid.*, *Eastern Evening News*, 2 May 1957.
[3] *The Times*, 2 May 1957.
[4] *Norfolk News*, 3 May 1957.
[5] *The Times*, 15 Nov 1957, and 22 Nov 1958.

primaries in the United States, and because he wrote a book about his difficulties.[1]

Nicolson was first elected in 1952 for Bournemouth East and Christchurch which had long been a safe Conservative seat. Early in his career he made a complimentary remark about Aneurin Bevan which lost him some support. He alienated more of his constituents when he seconded the bill to abolish capital punishment,[2] and when he later moderated his views he lost other supporters. Personal criticisms were levied against Nicolson for remoteness, carelessness in dress, and inability to remember constituents' names.[3] All of this meant that Nicolson had no reserve fund of goodwill on which he could draw when he was in trouble.

Nicolson, along with other Suez critics, tried various private methods of changing party policy before he actually rebelled in the House. When Anthony Nutting resigned his position in the government Nicolson wrote to the Chief Whip, Edward Heath, and said that as soon as the fighting was concluded he would have to declare his opposition to government policy. Although Heath tried to persuade him to the contrary, Nicolson replied:

> Dear Ted, Further to my letter of yesterday, I feel the time has come to make my protest public . . . Now that the Prime Minister has announced our cease-fire in Egypt, I do not think it could ever be said that I had acted unpatriotically. Please forgive me, but I still believe that it cannot be a bad thing for the Party that there should be at least one Conservative back-bencher who is prepared to state that he agrees with the very many eminent Conservatives outside this House who have

[1] See the various works by Epstein cited in chapter 6, and Laurence W. Martin, 'The Bournemouth Affair: Britain's First Primary Election'.

[2] Unpublished letter, local official to Nigel Nicolson, undated. It confirmed that nearly every branch of the local association favoured capital punishment.

[3] Unpublished letter, Nigel Nicolson to Anthony Nutting, 26 Sep 1957. Martin, 'The Bournemouth Affair', p. 660.

expressed their distress at the Government's action, however successful it may be. I need hardly add that whatever my feelings about the methods and motives of the Government, I will continue to support them in every other respect, including the securing of our national interests in the Middle East. The feeling in my constituency runs so strongly in favour of the Prime Minister's action that I do not expect that they will be greatly impressed by my demonstration, nor that I will politically survive![1]

Nicolson told Major Grant, chairman of his local association, that he would not be able to support Eden and would soon speak against the government's action. Grant tried to prevent Nicolson from speaking at a meeting of the United Nations Association. He wrote to Nicolson: '. . . I really cannot understand this indecent haste . . . I am bitterly disappointed in you. When the plaudits of the U.N.A. crowd are sounding in your ears tonight, I hope you will remember that thousands will look upon your action as a betrayal of those who trusted you to support the cause in which their deepest feelings are engaged'.[2]

Nicolson did not heed this advice; on 7 November he became the first Conservative backbencher openly to oppose the government, and the next day he and several other MPs abstained in the House.[3] That evening his views were repudiated by the officers of his local association, and the Executive Committee issued the following statement:

> Officers of Bournemouth East and Christchurch Conservative Association repudiate views expressed by Mr. Nigel Nicolson and maintain full confidence in and support of Government policy.[4]

The committee also called a special general meeting of the association to consider a resolution for choosing a candidate to

[1] Martin, 'The Bournemouth Affair', pp. 657–8.
[2] *Ibid.*, p. 659.
[3] *Bournemouth Daily Echo*, 8 Nov 1956. See chapter 6.
[4] *Bournemouth Daily Echo*, 9 Nov 1956, and see *Christchurch Times*, 16 Nov 1956.

replace Nicolson. At the meeting a vote of no confidence in Nicolson was passed (298–92), and the resolution instructed the Executive Committee to select a new candidate. Arguments about loyalty and conscience predominated in the debate. Mrs. G. Openshaw said that Nicolson had 'horrified our branch of the Primrose League with his socialist language'. Other arguments centred on the fact that the hall was too small and that this situation had prevented some members from attending the meeting.

Nicolson tried to persuade the executive to wait two years before selecting a new candidate, but Major Grant opposed this suggestion.[1] On 11 February 1957, immediately after his selection as candidate, Major J. A. Friend indicated his right-wing views by asserting, 'I greatly regret we did not occupy all the Canal'.[2] Nicolson encouraged his supporters to join the local association in order to prevent the adoption of Friend, but he was not able to rally enough support. On 6 March Friend was adopted by the whole association by a vote of 589–176. Nicolson accepted the defeat and suggested a public truce, but Friend responded,

> Dear Mr. Nicolson, I have read the letter which you sent to me from the House of Commons on April Fool's Day.

In order to strengthen his case Nicolson called meetings, co-operated with the local press, and wrote a book *People and Parliament*. The local executive instructed its branches not to allow Nicolson to speak to them, but the Boscombe East Young Conservatives rebelled, were suspended, and set up an independent organization.[3] The executive also issued a strict enrolment

[1] Leonard Allen resigned his position as vice-chairman of the association and chairman of the Young Conservative division council, and John Little announced that he would not seek re-election as vice-chairman of the Boscombe East Conservatives. *Christchurch Times*, 25 Jun 1957.

[2] *Bournemouth Daily Echo*, 12 Feb and 1 Mar 1957.

[3] *Bournemouth Times*, 21 Jun 1957, and *The Times*, 26 Mar 1957.

form which required all new members to 'abide by ... all resolutions of the Executive and General Meetings of the Associations'.[1] The complaints against this new pledge were so vociferous that it was not used.

The Conservative Chief Whip attempted to prevent MPs from becoming involved in this local dispute, and on one occasion he convinced a Member to withdraw a letter of support for Nicolson which had been sent to *The Times*. Central Office also followed the proceedings in Bournemouth very closely, and the Area Agent was present at every meeting of the executive.[2] The Area Agent relayed information to Central Office, and Major Grant sent further details directly to Lord Poole and the Prime Minister.[3]

On 11 February Major Grant told the Prime Minister that he had the full support of the Bournemouth East and Christchurch executive, and asked him to indicate his views on Nicolson. The Prime Minister answered that Oliver Poole had kept him informed of the situation, and asserted:

> It is a very long tradition of our party that the leader of the party should not intervene in matters between a Member and his constituents. I am sure that the Association, in deciding its action, will bear in mind the best interests of the Conservative Party, nationally as well as locally.[4]

Central Office was in a dilemma over the Nicolson affair. Party officials did not want to attract too much publicity, nor did they favour a by-election. Nicolson was assured by Poole that he should not resign from the House, and because of this Nicolson thought that Central Office was on his side.[5] However, he was later told by the new party chairman, Lord Hailsham, that 'This is a struggle for power between you and your

---

[1] *Bournemouth Daily Echo*, 8 Mar 1958.
[2] *Bournemouth Daily Echo*, 12 Feb 1957.
[3] Unpublished letter, Lord Poole to Nigel Nicolson, 3 Feb 1957.
[4] *Bournemouth Daily Echo*, 21 Feb 1957.
[5] Nigel Nicolson, *People and Parliament*, pp. 149–50.

Association, officially I must be neutral and accept the one who wins'.[1] The Area Agent does not appear to have remained as neutral as the officials at Central Office. He approved the local party's first repudiation of Nicolson, and told Grant that there was 'a certain amount of danger' in delaying a decision over Nicolson's readoption.[2]

In December 1958 suggestions were voiced that Major James Friend was a member of the League of Empire Loyalists. This was denied by both Friend and Grant in a letter to *The Times* on 17 December. The embarrassment caused by this statement led members of the Empire Loyalists to tell the press that Friend was a supporter of the League and that they had helped to organize the opposition to Nicolson. In view of this surprising disclosure Friend offered his resignation in early January 1959.[3]

Friend's resignation forced the executive to look for a new candidate, and for this reason a meeting between the executive and Lord Hailsham was arranged for 24 January 1959. Grant announced that Hailsham had been invited to their meeting, and that the executive would be prepared to accept his advice.[4] After the meeting Lord Hailsham announced that there would be a postal vote and that the ballot would be accompanied by a statement from each side. If Nicolson won the ballot he would automatically be readopted, but if he lost he would not stand in the 1959 general election.

Nicolson was allowed to speak to any branch which invited

[1] Notes made by Nicolson of a meeting with Lord Hailsham and Lord Poole on 2 Apr 1958.

[2] Martin, 'The Bournemouth Affair', p. 668.

[3] The chairman of the Bournemouth Empire Loyalists said, 'We went to a lot of trouble on Major Friend's behalf to cover up his association with us. We did everything short of lying.' *Daily Herald*, 31 Dec 1958. *Bournemouth Daily Echo*, 14 Jan 1959.

[4] *The Times*, 22 Jan 1959. Hailsham announced before the ballot that 'Mr Nicolson is in every way in good standing with the Whips of his party'. *The Times*, 27 Feb 1959.

him, but he was refused the party membership lists. New members were accepted into the association for two weeks, and during this period publicity about the dispute increased the membership by approximately twenty-five per cent. Central Office bore the cost of the election, and nominated W. H. L. Urton, General Director of Central Office, to be in charge of planning the poll, Ralph Homan, Central Office Agent for Wessex to conduct the poll, and Lord Hailsham to be arbitrator.

The result was very close: Nicolson lost by only 91 votes.[1] He immediately offered to resign from parliament, but was told to wait until parliament was dissolved. Lord Hailsham wrote to Nicolson: 'As a Conservative Member of Parliament in good standing with the Party you are also entitled to our good offices in Central Office should you desire now or later to be considered for any other constituency'.[2] However, Nicolson retired from politics, and the Bournemouth East and Christchurch Conservative candidate easily won the seat in 1959.

This chapter has examined the history of the MPs who were either refused endorsement by party headquarters or had their readoption challenged by their local parties between 1945 and 1964. This was done in order to ascertain whether these external controls had a significant effect on party cohesion in the House of Commons or were used to punish rebel Members.

In spite of the power of both parties to refuse the endorsement of any candidates, no Members and only one former Member were refused sponsorship after 1945. The Labour party's refusal

[1] 9,724 ballots were sent out, 60 were spoiled and 2,118 were not returned in time.
[2] Unpublished letter, Lord Hailsham to Nigel Nicolson, 26 Feb 1959.

to accept Tom Braddock was considerably due to his rebelliousness in the 1945 parliament. Since this is the only occasion on
which either of the party headquarters refused to endorse a
MP or a former MP and since there were a great many revolts,
it is evident that endorsement has not been used as a weapon to
control rebellion in the House.

Between 1945 and 1964 constituency parties very rarely
challenged the readoption of their Members, but when they
did it was usually because of personal factors such as divorce or
drunkenness. Members almost never had readoption difficulties
for speaking or voting against official party policy even though
these occurred with some frequency. No Conservative Members
are known to have had their readoption challenged for obeying
party policy. Some local Labour parties severely attacked their
MPs for opposing the Bevanites (in other words – for defending
official party policy), but when it was necessary the NEC intervened to protect these Members. Conservative associations
caused more trouble than their Labour counterparts when
their MPs engaged in such activities as spending too much time
travelling abroad, lecturing for the MRA, or attacking the
party leader. Moreover, Central Office intervened less than the
NEC in protecting MPs from readoption difficulties.

MPs very rarely had their readoption challenged for disobeying the party Whips. Even discounting the fact that every
Member who had readoption problems was accused of having
personal failings, only one Labour Member, Stanley Evans, had
his readoption challenged for revolting in parliament, and only
four Conservative MPs were forced out because they were
rebellious in the House of Commons. It takes only a few cases
of local party discipline to implant the idea in Members' minds
that they could lose their positions for rebelling. However, many
Members also realize how few times this power has been exercised in relation to the number of revolts that do take place in
the House.

Comparing the relatively few Members who have had their
readoption challenged to the much larger number who have

joined revolts without having trouble with their constituency parties makes one dubious of the assertion that local parties often act to enforce party cohesion. A member who decides to oppose the Whips will not usually be deterred by constituency threats – real though they may be – and after he revolts his local party generally upholds his right to rebel.

Even Members who rebelled consistently usually maintained good relationships with their local parties; undoubtedly the local organizations even encouraged some of the revolts. The wise MP 'cultivates' his constituency party, and the few Members who did have trouble with their local parties almost always survived. A senior member of the Conservative party aptly summarized the relationship between MPs and their constituency parties:

> Any Member can get away with a rebellion if he remembers three points. First, don't speak to anyone until you have explained your action to your local executive. Second, paper the cracks with your critics on the executive. Third, be patient.[1]

[1] Interview.

11 The Strategy of Rebels and Whips

The Whips' function is not to stifle genuine dissent, but to canalize it as far as possible along channels hidden from the public gaze.[1]

Parts II and III have shown that between 1945 and 1964 there were a great number of open revolts, and yet the rebels were almost never punished. In view of this fact it is important to assess the role of rebellions and party discipline in the British political system. This chapter analyses the various strategies employed by rebels and Whips in disputes over party policy.

Early in the twentieth century the British political system reached the stage where parties maintained almost complete solidarity in the division lobbies. Whereas revolts had been a way of upsetting governments or changing policy, they came to be merely a factor, but an important factor, in the dialogue between backbenchers and their leaders. The revolts and the few sanctions that were applied became part of the influence situation, which has been outlined in chapter 1, and contributed to communication within each party. It is important therefore to understand what role rebellions and discipline play in the strategy of Whips and rebels.

A chief objective of backbenchers is to influence, shape, and even determine party policy in the House of Commons. Of course, backbenchers are divided among themselves about which policies should be pursued, but most of the open revolts can be classified as: (a) revolts against very important new policies which have had no ideological history in the party, such as the Common Market proposals in the Conservative party; (b) revolts against policies which have had ideological

[1] Nicolson, *People and Parliament*, p. 75.

roots in the history of the party, but which party leaders have found necessary to qualify because of specific circumstances, such as conscription in the Labour party; (c) revolts against policies which have directly affected Members' constituencies, such as subsidies to the fisheries. Controversies over these types of policies and variations of them continued to erupt in both parties from 1945 to 1964, and they are very likely to continue to cause problems for party leaders. No amount of pressure has been able to eliminate these revolts; to adapt Zbigniew Brzezinski's conclusion about deviations in the Soviet bloc, revolts contained but not crushed are the handmaidens of history, stimulating an evolution of party thought.[1]

Backbenchers are usually badly organized for changing party policy. Therefore the first object of partisans is to form a group of like-minded Members. In this regard R. H. S. Crossman wrote that, 'Today the struggle for real power takes place secretly inside the government party, and shadow power inside the Opposition. Driven underground by the requirements of party discipline it is normally a conspiratorial matter of cliques and cabals'.[2]

Backbenchers who want to change party policy have to make decisions about what types of groups to form. In certain circumstances, it may be believed that influence will be best brought to bear on party leaders by a group composed of influential Members such as the 'knights of the shires' or the chairmen of certain backbench committees. Some groups go to great lengths to keep certain MPs from joining them; they believe that the addition of Members 'who revolt on anything' and 'cranks' does more harm than good to their cause. At other times dissident MPs may think it is important to form as large a group as possible in order to impress party leaders with their numerical strength.

[1] Zbigniew Brzezinski, 'Deviation Control: A Study in the Dynamics of Doctrinal Conflict', p. 22.
[2] Crossman, Introduction to Bagehot, *The English Constitution*, pp. 44-5.

Some of these groups become almost permanent alliances, such as Keep Left, the Bevanites, One Nation, and the Expanding Commonwealth group. Some of them ally themselves with pressure groups outside parliament such as the Campaign for Nuclear Disarmament, Victory for Socialism, and the Howard Society.[1] Less permanent are the various dining clubs, such as the Monday Club in the Tory party, which serve as meeting places for discussion of policy and sometimes become the centres of organized party revolts. The least permanent but possibly most important groups are simply based on acquaintances in the House. Of course, one of the main factors in the formation of these latter groups is personality, but many of these 'circles of friends' come together to protest against party policy because they hold similar ideological beliefs. Ian Mikardo explained that when an MP wants to promote a cause he phones his friends, and they contact their friends. This continues until a large, effective group is formed.

After the leaders of the dissidents know which MPs wish to join their protest against party policy they may proceed to form an *ad hoc* organization. They may have meetings in discreet places or even in the House of Commons. Sometimes they elect a chairman and secretary to keep records of their meetings and to forward information to members. The leaders of the

[1] Most Members, of course, have loyalties to groups outside parliament and some of them find that they are unable to reconcile their duty both to their party and to these groups. Sir Ian Fraser had some difficulties with the British Legion, of which he was president, because he would not consistently rebel over war pensions. However he was not forced to resign as president, and the Whips did not punish him when he did rebel. On the other hand, Dr. Hyacinth Morgan found that his duties to parliament and to the council of the British Medical Association were incompatible, and in 1946 he resigned from the council. See John H. Millett, 'The Role of an Interest Group Leader in the House of Commons'. Also interesting is Potter, *Organized Groups in British National Politics*, p. 292.

rebels often act on two assumptions. They believe that on any given policy the Cabinet or Shadow Cabinet will be divided, and that there will be someone in it who will privately support their opinion. Secondly, they think that when leaders want to accommodate backbenchers' opinions they will have 'something to give' on every policy. That is, the rebels believe that party leaders are usually in a position to make compromises with the rebel point of view when they so desire. 'The government may have to give some compensation when it nationalizes steel, but how much will the shares be worth? That is the question!' The object of dissidents, therefore, is to make leaders believe that they should compromise.

Once a rebel group is organized, its members have to decide whether to act privately, semi-privately, or publicly. The dissidents normally use private methods of persuasion first. They approach ministers and their PPSs about the controversial policy, and inform them about their views and the strength of their group. There is considerable 'trading on information' in the House of Commons, and it is not long before the Whips find out about the dissatisfied Members. Moreover, the recalcitrants often want the Whips to know about their dissatisfaction so that their views will be communicated to party leaders other than those directly in charge of the policy. Rebels try to convince Whips and party leaders that their group is quite large and representative, and that its views should be taken into consideration. Backbenchers generally believe that leaders try to prevent revolts because they think that open disputes have adverse electoral consequences. Therefore, dissatisfied Members often imply that they may have to revolt in the division lobbies unless a compromise can be arranged.

Probably the dissident MPs will next take their complaints about party policy to the 1922 Committee, PLP meeting, or one of the appropriate backbench committees. Complaints aired in these semi-private meetings are more apt to have a direct effect on committees dealing with technical subjects such as changes in corporation and capital gains tax, and are less likely to affect policy in the general party meetings and in the major committees dealing with subjects such as foreign affairs. But, regardless of their effectiveness in directly influencing policy, the complaints undoubtedly help the Whips to discover which MPs are dissatisfied with party policy.

The dissident movement may disappear if the dissatisfied Members are successful in changing or influencing policy. Or the group may not endure if party leaders will not change their policy and the dissident MPs are not adamant in the espousal of their cause. However, the rebels may be persistent enough to rebel openly against their party. They do not rebel because they think that by doing so they will change the policy in question; in fact, an open split is usually a sign of certain failure for the rebels. Of course, many dissidents 'go on hoping' for a concession from party leaders, but more important is the fact that rebel Members believe that they must show the Whips that they 'mean business'. Thus, they rebel openly both to show that they believe in their policy and to make it clear to party leaders that on the next occasion they may cause another open revolt if they are not allowed to have some influence on party policy.

Before rebels revolt publicly they invariably consider the consequences of their action. They may take into consideration the views of their local executives, local constituents, the Whips, other MPs, and the historical ideology of their party. The attitudes and fears of whipless MPs provide some enlightenment on this topic, especially in view of a former Chief Whip's comment that 'the idea of rewards and punishments is in the minds of the rebels, not in the minds of the Whips'.[1] All Labour Members who lost the whip expressed the view that the most important sanction of the party was that it could prevent rebels from being MPs. None of them expected to be expelled, but they thought that the NEC might prevent their endorsement or cause trouble with their local GMCs. As William Baxter put it 'the question is to be or not to be an MP'. Many Conservatives

[1] Patrick Buchan-Hepburn, interview.

who resigned the whip declared that the important thing was that the party 'controls the career of every MP'. Most Conservatives thought that there was a direct link between the Whips and the local parties, and said that when they rebelled the Whips' Office contacted their local executives, and raised the question of their readoption. This concern about readoption by rebel MPs in the Tory party was reinforced by the fact that few of them thought they could obtain more than 1,500 votes if they stood as Independents in their former constituencies. Less understood is the fact that some rebels are also apt to consider how their revolt will affect public opinion. Viscount Hinchingbrooke reported 'All of my rebellions were when it was safe for the party – long before an election'.

After a decision is made to rebel openly, the leaders of the recalcitrants may try to convince other MPs to commit themselves to joining the rebellion. They may ask dissident Members to provide verbal assurances that they will join the revolt, or they may ask them to sign a paper indicating their intention to participate in the demonstration. These assurances fulfil two purposes. Firstly, some Members will not revolt unless they are convinced that a number of other MPs intend to join them. Such Members will be more likely to participate if they are shown a list of Members who are already committed to the cause. Secondly, if a specified number of MPs do not indicate their intention to rebel the demonstration will be cancelled, thus assuring that no rebel Members will be left in isolation.

The form a revolt takes is also important. Rebels may cross-vote, abstain, sign critical EDMs, or use extra-parliamentary methods such as publishing pamphlets critical of party policy. The methods by which dissident MPs decide which form of rebellion to choose may be rather 'higgledy piggledy' as one persistent Labour rebel maintains, but the rebels must bear certain factors in mind. If they are in the government party they will have to consider the size of the majority. They obviously will not want to bring down the government so they will not be able to cross-vote to any extent if the majority is small. If the government's majority is large the dissidents will be able to show their dissatisfaction in the division lobbies. On both the government and opposition sides the decision to cross-vote or abstain is usually dictated by how the other party intends to vote. There is always a bias towards joining a revolt which sets an MP apart from his own party, but which does not associate him with another party. The leaders of the recalcitrants will also bear in mind that Whips are much less concerned with a critical motion than with a cross-vote or abstention. Moreover, it is much easier to organize the tabling of a hostile EDM than it is to arrange other forms of rebellion, and many Members will sign a motion, but will never cross-vote or abstain.

Experienced parliamentarians also know how to avoid danger of retaliation when they revolt. It is well known that it is easier for leaders to punish one than a number of MPs, and therefore Members usually try to avoid being isolated when they rebel. Dissidents attempt to make their revolts 'just the right size' so that they damage neither the party nor their political careers. Experienced MPs also attempt to build up a 'reserve fund' of goodwill with their local parties and other MPs in case they want to rebel. They especially avoid trouble with their local officials when they are in difficulties with their parliamentary party. Furthermore, rebels seem to have an excuse or alibi for joining revolts; they always defend their actions in terms of the national interest, their constituents' interests, or a great matter of principle.

At the same time as backbenchers are trying to find a way to influence party policy, Whips are attempting to prevent overt disputes. All Whips conceive their main function as being to preserve unity in the party by liaison work in carrying opinions between backbenchers and frontbenchers. Whips generally hope that party leaders will be able to accommodate the views of their backbenchers so that open disputes can be avoided. In order to stem dissatisfaction before it causes open revolts Whips try to elicit the private opinions of their backbenchers, and one Chief Whip reported that he 'always took a consensus of views, but I never let this be found out by the backbenchers'. Since the Second World War not only have backbenchers been able to make their views more fully known through their party committees and sub-committees,[1] but as chapter 2 has shown the Whips' Offices have become more highly developed for discovering Members' opinions and complaints about party policy.

Whips try to convince MPs that their views are being carefully weighed by party leaders, and one Chief Whip commented that his function was to make backbenchers 'think they have influence even when they really have very little'. They also perform functions such as arranging for ministers to see dissident MPs. One Chief Whip asserted that 'ministers are responsible for revolts, not Whips'. The Whips spend a considerable amount of their time talking to persistent rebels because it is thought in the Whips' Offices that these individuals 'hate not to be noticed'. Whips hope that their constant efforts to 'maintain good temper' and to communicate the views of dissatisfied MPs to party leaders will help maintain a cohesive party. R. T. McKenzie succinctly summarized the relationship between leaders and their backbenchers when he said that party leaders:

> ... have to take into account at every stage the clearly defined currents of opinion within their party. Blind appeals to loyalty (either to the person of the leader or to the party itself) are frequently resorted to, and often they achieve their purpose. But they are rarely successful in bridging a real gulf when one does develop between leaders and their followers.[2]

Regardless of the constant conflict of opinion within each party, MPs do stick consistently with their leaders in the

[1] These backbench committees first became linked to the Labour party organization in 1944 and to the Conservative party organization in 1946.

[2] McKenzie, *British Political Parties,* p. 644.

division lobbies. What factors do Whips conceive as causing this consistency? When the Whips responded to this open-ended question in interviews, they did so in terms of the importance of parties in British political life. They spoke about the need to maintain party loyalty in order to obtain success either in winning elections or in satisfying one's general emotional attachment to one's party. Labour Whips, who stressed the relationship between party cohesion and emotional attachment, used such phrases as 'they feel part of a movement' to somewhat more sophisticated responses like 'they grow up in a party and develop certain emotional attachments which make for party loyalty'. Conservative Whips tended to answer more in terms of the importance of informal personal relations than in concepts of group loyalty. Only very rarely were mechanical factors such as the size of the majority or withdrawal of the whip mentioned as replies to this general question.

Practically every Whip articulated his assertions about party loyalty along with statements about winning elections. Two themes were usually interwoven in the Whips' responses. They argued that individual Members are only elected because they are members of a party, thus highlighting the fact that electoral behaviour has thwarted the election of Independent candidates in Britain. On a higher level most of the Whips asserted that the success or failure of their whole party at the polls depended to a very great extent on maintaining the appearance of a united and confident party.

Whips and leaders exaggerate public awareness of parliament and its activities. The great majority of Whips believe that the electorate is aware of proceedings in the House of Commons, and this gives rise to a belief that large rebellions in parliament and the accumulation of small revolts should be discouraged because they will have adverse electoral consequences.[1] The average Whip commented in words such as 'revolts make a

[1] Moreover, revolts are especially disliked in the government party because they take up valuable parliamentary time.

party look unstable' and a perceptive Chief Whip of the
Labour party related:

> I think at the time revolts occur they are known by the public
> because of the press, radio, and especially television. Splits
> develop when morale is low and morale worsens when there
> are splits. Uncertainty is what hurts a party, but a split does
> not always hurt morale. The public is not aware of the precise
> nature of the splits on say Rhodesia or capital punishment, but
> it is aware of the tone and feeling aroused by a split.[1]

In view of the importance Whips place on eliminating open
disputes it is important to know what means they feel can be
used by a party to discourage a Member who wants to abstain
or vote against his colleagues. Generally speaking Whips believe
that there are no specific means of preventing rebellion other
than by the use of persuasion. Labour MPs more often than
Conservatives cited means such as reporting rebels to the
Liaison Committee and withdrawal of the whip, but they were
only mentioned as the last possible alternatives for the party
to take.

---

[1] There is some evidence that the public is aware of dissension in the party. Mark Abrams and Richard Rose
made a study based on 724 people interviewed between
January and February 1960. They found that 20% of
Labour supporters and 29% of non-Labour supporters
in the working class thought that the question 'Which
party has a united team of top leaders?' was the most
important of the 16 questions asked. They also found
that 65% of the non-Labour party supporters thought
that the Conservatives had the most united team of top
leaders and that only 4% of them thought the same about
Labour. More important, even Labour supporters
thought that the Conservatives were more united than
Labour; 38% maintained that the Tories had a united
team of top leaders, and only 18% thought the same
about Labour. Mark Abrams and Richard Rose,
Must Labour Lose?, pp. 12–30. Also see the analysis of
poll data in Butler and King, *British General Election 1964*
and *British General Election of 1966*.

In chapters 9 and 10 it was shown that punishments such as expulsion, withdrawal of the whip, and demotion were used very sparingly between the years 1945 and 1964. Labour Whips all regarded the threat of expulsion as an effective device, but asserted that it can only be used on extremely rare occasions. Conservative and Labour Whips are totally split on the question of whether a threat to withdraw the whip would be effective in preventing rebellion. The Conservative party has not withdrawn the whip since 1942 and its Whips do not believe this device will prevent open disputes. On the other hand, Labour Whips believe that it has an effect and as we have seen the party has employed this method. However, and this is of special importance, few Labour Whips believe withdrawal of the whip is nearly as significant as the public appears to think it is. Most of them declared that it has not had 'harsh' consequences.

It is not surprising after this account to discover that Conservative Whips do not think that the whip should ever be withdrawn while many Labour Whips propose that it should be used in certain extreme circumstances. Labour Whips generally agreed that a MP should not be excluded from the parliamentary party for occasional deviations from the party line, but that the Member should be ostracized if he is following a 'pattern' of serious revolt against official policy. A few of the Labour Whips admit to actually having strong emotional 'hatred' against all rebels, but rationally they assert it would be unwise to pursue a policy based on this feeling.

Significantly, few Whips on either side of the House believe that taking the whip away from rebels has actually had much effect in maintaining party cohesion in the various cases that have occurred in the past. They assert that the basic difficulty in withdrawing the whip is that it has to be returned before the next general election. Moreover, the act of withdrawing the whip receives considerable publicity from the daily press and it is thought that this has an adverse effect on the public's opinion of the party. Martin Redmayne told the author that he sometimes asked Harold Macmillan if he could withdraw the whip from persistent rebels but that Macmillan always objected. Apparently party leaders agree with the general opinion in the Whips' Office that withdrawal of the whip causes bad publicity and has little effect in maintaining party cohesion.

The earlier analysis in chapter 10 of the effect of pressures from the national party headquarters and from the local organizations showed that these techniques were used very rarely. Whips are totally agreed that party cohesion cannot be affected by the NEC or SACC making use of their right to veto candidates for elections. They do not agree however on the effect that local party officials can have on their Members' activity in the House. Labour Whips do think that their Members are affected by their local parties but they assert that the pressure may encourage Members to revolt or refrain from revolting depending on the circumstances. Conservative Whips were split on this question; half thought that local associations sometimes did discourage revolts whereas the remainder declared flatly that this never happened.

Whips on both sides were generally agreed that it was 'unlikely' that a Member who voted against his party would have difficulty being readopted. It is very difficult to judge the effectiveness of Whips' attempts to convince local party organizations that they should discipline rebellious MPs. These attempts may or may not prevent party rebellion, but in the period between 1945 and 1964 there were extremely few occasions when rebellious MPs had their readoption challenged. Sometimes Whips suggested to MPs that their local parties would be informed of any rebellion against party policy, but Whips usually try to avoid referring parliamentary matters to local parties because they think that this results in even greater troubles for the party.

Although rebel MPs were rarely punished for disobedience, the statistics have shown that a number of Members possibly did receive rewards for loyalty. Most of the Whips thought that there were no rewards which could be used to entice MPs to stick consistently with their party in the division lobbies. They

tended to agree with the mood struck by one of the inter-
viewees: 'Many MPs who will never get office still stay loyal
and some who have been kicked out of office stay loyal'.
They agreed unanimously that occasional revolts did not in
any way affect the possibility of promotion. One Whip, men-
tioning Harold Wilson and R. H. S. Crossman, said, 'You need
to be outrageous to be seen.' However, Chief Whips are always
consulted about the appointment of PPSs and junior ministers,
and there is no doubt that they consider party loyalty an
important factor in the selection of MPs for these positions.
Every Chief Whip declared that regular abstainers were never
thought to be suitable for office.

Minor enticements such as honours and trips abroad are
often thought to constitute rewards for loyalty. Whereas
Labour Whips stated dogmatically that honours should not be
given for political service of any kind, many Conservatives said
that these enticements should be awarded for party loyalty.
But Conservatives argued that honours could never be arranged
to help prevent revolts because they are almost always given
after the event and that on the few occasions on which they
were used before the revolt occurred the strategy backfired.
The statistics in chapter 9 suggest that this last assertion is correct.

When the Whips were asked if trips abroad were used to
entice MPs not to abstain or vote against their party in the
division lobbies, they responded that rebels were often given
trips abroad, even those trips that were controlled by the Whips'
Offices. Whips tended to agree that occasional trips abroad for
Members helped maintain party fellowship and hence strengthened party solidarity. The Whips were also adamant that
helping MPs with 'financial difficulties' or 'women troubles'
strengthened attitudes of loyalty to the party and might conceivably influence party cohesion.

The basic images that the Whips hold of their own party
are shared by the Whips of the other party. Both sides, for
example, agree that the Labour party has written regulations
and that the Conservatives do not. However, when they per-

ceive each other's use of rewards or punishments they do so through the ideologically coloured glasses which have become so much a part of British life. The Conservatives regard themselves as freer and less disciplined because they do not employ punishments as Labour does to ensure cohesion. They insist that the formality and the employment of regulations prevent individual initiative on the Labour side. Labour Whips tend to view the Tory party as buying Members by awarding honours or offering financial awards to their Members. Labour Whips think their Members are free and use their initiative because they have regulations for ordering decision-making within the party. With the exception of two Whips, they all condemn their opponents for using devices for maintaining cohesion and congratulate their own side for not having to employ the same ones.

Whips see their role as the management of men and do not consider themselves to be rigid disciplinarians. They believe that a cohesive party is best promoted by keeping party leaders aware of backbench opinion. Thus, they do not regard the collection of information about backbenchers as spying, but as a legitimate exercise to keep leaders aware of current opinion within the party. Members also perceive the Whips' function as relaying backbench opinion to leaders, and often give the Whips information which they want to be imparted to the leaders. The Whips' job of preventing open revolts is not usually conducted in the language of threats. Most of the time Whips can employ the criticisms of one group to offset those of another. Dissidents are simply told that their views cannot be accepted because there are other contradictory groups in the party who want their opinions made official policy, and consequently party leaders have had to accept a compromise. Among other things, Whips suggest to dissatisfied Members that a revolt will 'rock the boat', 'force a dissolution', or 'cause a run on the pound, and a possible devaluation'. Leaders realize that Members are somewhat concerned that they may be punished if they join a revolt, and Whips no doubt make use of this fear, but it is not the major factor. It is very difficult for a dissident MP to justify joining a revolt when the Whips declare that by doing so he is damaging the party, and going against the wishes of his fellow party members. It is pointed out that a party involves a relationship of mutual dependence. MPs are aware that at some time and in some degree the furthering of their ambitions depends on the party remaining a cohesive body. It is therefore relatively easy for the Whips to convince them that avoiding overt revolts is in their own as well as the party's best interest.

Since Whips tend to believe that the best way to change party policy is to work privately behind the scenes it is not surprising that Martin Redmayne has asserted that the Whip's main function is to keep all party controversies as private as possible. They advise critics to make their points in the secrecy of party meetings or behind the closed doors of a committee room. If this fails they advise the writing of a letter to the editor or the making of rebellious speeches, but they still assert that the Member must not abstain or vote against his party. If all else fails the Whips will finally suggest that the critic should pair and abstain quietly to avoid publicity. There are more of these unpublicized abstentions than is generally realized. Martin Redmayne explained that there were between one and twelve abstentions every week in the Conservative party when he was Chief Whip, and that many of these were not made public.

These various forms of pressure must sometimes affect policy or there would be even more revolts than there are at the present time. Whips maintain unanimously that party leaders are willing to 'shift emphasis' on any policy if enough MPs are dissatisfied. One Whip proffered: 'Party leaders must be willing to change their policy. If they will not change they should not be leaders; they can't afford to be too rigid'. And another asserted that this process of backbench influence and leaders willing to shift their emphasis on an issue is 'the way policy is formed'.

When dissatisfied Members cannot be persuaded to keep

private their opposition to official party policy the Whips try to convince them to voice their criticism in the House of Commons, but not to revolt in the division lobbies. This suggestion is not always successful as the preceding chapters have shown. While there is a fairly well-defined scale of revolt in the Whips' minds, which runs from a relatively mild criticism of official policy to a Member actually voting against his party, Whips have no consistent definition of a rebel. Some believe a rebel is anyone who utters a word against the party, while others say it should only be used to depict persistent critics. Whips especially dislike these persistent rebels whom they often describe as being 'crackers' or 'self-interested'. A letter from Churchill to the Conservative Chief Whip in 1954 concerning a persistent rebel expressed his dislike of MPs who use 'cheap ways of getting self-advertisement'. Whips assert that habitual rebels carry little weight within the parliamentary party, but harm the party in the country.

Dissatisfied Members who do openly rebel will be subject to some criticism. If the aberration has been small the area Whip will give a 'fatherly talk' to the rebel, but if there has been a major revolt the rebels may be summoned to a meeting with the Deputy or Chief Whip, and possibly the party leader. Sometimes even this does not happen; Martin Redmayne reported that frequently he had not got round to reprimanding one group of rebels before another revolt occurred. In the Labour party, on the other hand, the Whips tend to believe that a cross-vote should at least always raise the question of withdrawal of the whip even if the punishment is not actually used.

By using these criticisms Whips hope to convince Members that if they revolt on future occasions they may lose favour with the party. Much of this talk is in the realm of threat and bluff. Chapters 9 and 10 have shown that very few persistent rebels ever got into grave difficulties with their parties, and that those who did were nearly always successful in combating the party pressures. As a Whip has said, 'We have no real sanctions, but we don't tell that to rebels.'

12 Stability in Change

Members of parliament believe so much that rebellions and discipline damage their party that a self-correcting process occurs.

There is certainly more solidarity in British than in United States' parties, but the significance of this contrast should not be exaggerated. British parties need to be looked at in their own context. Within the two major British parties there are innumerable stresses and strains, pushings and pullings, arguments and counter-arguments, and sometimes these disagreements lead to overt rebellions. There have been more of these revolts than has usually been acknowledged in studies of British political history. Moreover, when Members did rebel they rarely got into any serious trouble. Dissident Members in both parties realize this fact, and one persistent rebel even asserted that 'Party discipline never stopped anyone from rebelling'.

The revolts that occurred in parliament and the very few punishments that were used against the recalcitrants were important in the dialogue between party leaders and followers. It is through the interaction of informal rebel groups with parties' formal groups and leaders that policy evolves. Since a party is a vessel for reconciling diverse interests it is not surprising to find that individual Members sometimes think it necessary for them to revolt while at the same time they do not desire to harm their party. Nor is it surprising to discover that although party leaders threaten to punish recalcitrants they usually think that it is impractical to take any action against them. As long as these two beliefs are held concurrently, the British political system will retain its cohesive parties with their built-in compromise mechanisms.

These beliefs in the politicians' political culture are based on their appraisal of the party system and the electorate's voting habits. Since MPs conceive of politics only in terms of 'parties' and believe that the public reacts against 'disunity' in parties, neither loyalists nor critics can afford to disregard the need for harmony and unity. But harmony and unity require a sensitive communications system for transmitting attitudes to and from leaders and backbenchers. Stability and cohesion cannot be maintained without change or adaptation which occurs by a process of accommodation. Most of the time the ideas of those in authority will predominate but at other times the critics will have to be satisfied to some degree or the necessary harmony and unity will be destroyed. Backbenchers must feel that they have influence even if they do not continually exercise it. The seemingly contradictory state of affairs where there is a subtle relationship between influence and deference must exist to maintain stability in democratic countries and cohesion in political parties. The adjustments in policy may often be so slight that they escape the eyes of the public but the politicians notice them and believe that only this process of accommodation will result in highly cohesive parties. Rebellions and discipline are but part of the flow of information in this process.

Appendix I
Methodological Problems

1. The rebellions used for the statistics were chosen as follows:

   (a) all known cross-votes where more than one Member voted against his party whip were included;

   (b) all known public abstentions where more than one Member was concerned were included. Of course, there are many unknown private abstentions;[1]

   (c) all EDMs with more than six signatures were included if they criticized well defined party policy; (these EDMs are unwhipped backbench manifestoes, but they are demonstrations of dissent.)[2]

   (d) also included were other MPs' activities which were condemned by party leaders.

2. Official party policy is defined as being parliamentary policy, not policy enunciated by the mass party. It was usually impossible to discover the reasons and motives that Members had for joining rebellions, but the rebel Members must have been aware that their actions were disliked by party leaders. Fur-

[1] Martin Redmayne explained in an interview that between one and twelve Members may abstain privately in any given week. *The Listener*, vol. 70 (26 Dec 1963), p. 1056. Attempts to have abstentions recorded have failed. 663 *H.C. Deb.*, col. 430.

[2] See Finer *et al. Backbench Opinion in the House of Commons, 1955–1959.*

thermore, Members were excused when they unwittingly acted against their leaders' wishes.

3. The statistics used in the tables indicate which Members were usually loyal and which were usually rebellious. The percentages in the text were determined by dividing the number of times a Member revolted by the number of revolts which occurred while he was a Member. All by-elections, deaths, etc., have been taken into consideration in the statistics. Given a number of issues and a constitutionally equal chance of joining rebellions, some types of MPs did so more than others. The most significant categories in the tables are those at the extreme ends – i.e., MPs who did not join any rebellions, and MPs who were involved in a large number of them. Moreover, the categories are 'contingent'. If more information was available, it might have been possible to introduce more categories, and change the number of MPs in each category.

4. The fact that it was impossible to assign weights to particular rebellions caused certain difficulties. A Member's rebelliousness had to be equated with the number of rebellions he joined. Furthermore, a Member's personal involvement in a rebellion could not be incorporated in the statistics. For example, the fact that a Member organized a group of friends to rebel could not be quantified, but where possible such information has been described in the text.

Appendix II
Labour Party Candidates
Application Form

To: Miss Sara E. Barker
NATIONAL AGENT
THE LABOUR PARTY

I agree to accept the Parliamentary Labour Party Standing Orders now in operation, a copy of which has been supplied to me.

SIGNED..

ADDRESS..

....

....

....

Date..

Appendix III
Standing Orders
of the PLP

1945 Standing Orders

The Parliamentary Party have the authority to withdraw the Whip on account of things said or done by Members of the Party in the House, such decision to be reported to the NEC.

Outside activities, whether in writing or speech, which are contrary to the discipline or constitution of the Party shall be dealt with by the NEC.

1. For the purpose of securing concerted action in the House, Members shall consult the officers of the Parliamentary Party before tabling any Motion, Amendment or Prayer, or other proposal which may involve Party policies or decisions and shall not vote for any Motion, Amendment or Prayer contrary to the decision of the Party Meeting.

2. Where there is persistent refusal to observe the decisions of the Parliamentary Party, it shall be the duty of the Liaison Committee to bring a recommendation to the Party Meeting to report the Member to the NEC, who shall consider the matter in its constituency and other aspects with which the NEC is concerned. The Member concerned shall have the right to be heard both by the Parliamentary Party and the NEC.

3. It is recognized that on certain matters, for example religion and temperance, Members may have good grounds for conscientious scruples, and in such cases they may abstain from voting.

(The above Standing Orders may be amended, rescinded, altered, added to or suspended for such period and under such conditions as may be determined upon by a duly constituted meeting of the PLP).[1]

1952 Standing Orders

1. The privilege of membership in the PLP involves the acceptance of the decisions of the Party Meeting. The Party recognizes the right of individual Members to abstain from voting on matters of deeply held personal conscientious conviction.
2. The Parliamentary Party have the right to withdraw the Whip on account of things said or done by Members of the Party in the House. The Member or Members concerned shall have the right to be heard at the Party Meeting before the Whip is withdrawn.
3. The NEC shall be informed of any decision to withdraw the Whip.
4. It is the duty of the Parliamentary Committee to bring before the Party Meeting cases of serious or persistent breaches of Party discipline, and in appropriate cases to recommend to the Party Meeting that the Member or Members concerned shall be reported to the NEC. The Member or Members concerned shall have the right to be heard by the Parliamentary Committee and the Parliamentary Party.
5. For the purpose of securing concerted action in the House, Members shall consult the Officers of the Parliamentary Party before tabling any motion, amendment or prayer, or other proposal which may involve Party policies or decisions.[2]

1959 Party Code

1. In making this recommendation the Parliamentary Committee points out that such rescinding does not affect the right of the Parliamentary Party to withdraw the whip from

[1] *LPCR*, 1946, p. 221.   [2] *LPCR*, 1952, p. 201.

any member should the occasion require, nor the right of the Parliamentary Party to take any steps calculated to ensure the well-being of the Parliamentary Party.

2. If the party is to be an effective force politically, its activities must be co-ordinated and collective decisions taken. Members are expected to observe those decisions.

3. This applies especially in the matter of voting, although the right of individual members to abstain on grounds of deeply held personal conscientious convictions is recognized.

4. Members are requested, before tabling any motion or amendment, to consult the party officers so that confusion, misunderstanding, and contradiction can be avoided.

5. Membership of the Parliamentary Labour Party is a privilege involving responsibilities and obligations as well as rights and opportunities. We are relying now not on formal standing orders but on a spirit of good friendship, co-operation, and comradeship for the acceptance of these responsibilities and obligations.[1]

1961 Standing Orders

1. If the party is to be an effective force politically, its activities must be co-ordinated and collective decisions taken. The privilege of membership of the PLP involves the acceptance of these decisions.

2. The party recognizes the right of Members to abstain from voting in the House on matters of deeply-held personal conscientious conviction, but this does not entitle Members to cast votes contrary to a decision of the Party Meeting.

3. It is the duty of the Parliamentary Committee to bring before the Party Meeting cases of serious or persistent failure by Members to act in harmony with the Parliamentary Labour Party, including a bad record of attendance in the division lobbies.

[1] *The Times*, 23 Nov 1959.

4. The Parliamentary Party has the right to withdraw the Whip on account of things said or done by Members of the party in the House. The Member or Members concerned shall have the right to be heard at the Party Meeting before the Whip is withdrawn.

5. The NEC shall be informed of any decision to withdraw the Whip.

6. In appropriate cases the Parliamentary Committee may recommend to the Party Meeting that the Member or Members concerned shall be reported to the NEC. The Member or Members concerned shall have the right to be heard by the Parliamentary Committee and by the Parliamentary Party.

7. For the purpose of securing concerted action in the House, Members shall consult the Officers of the Parliamentary Party before tabling any Motion, Amendment or Prayer. The tabling of such Motion, Amendment or Prayer shall be delayed for one sitting day should the Officers so request. Where the Officers are unable to give approval to the tabling of any Motion, Amendment or Prayer, this must be made known by the sponsor or sponsors to such other Members as may be approached in seeking support of the Notice of Motion.

8. Minutes of meetings of the PLP shall be kept and shall be available for inspection on application to the Secretary of the PLP.

9. These Standing Orders may be amended, rescinded, added to, suspended, or re-instated for such periods and under such conditions as may be determined, after due notice, by a duly-constituted meeting of the PLP.[1]

[1] *LPCR*, 1962, p. 85.

Bibliography

I. Government Publications

Much of the material for this study has been taken from the *Official Report of the House of Commons Debates, House of Lords Debates*, and the *Order Paper of the House of Commons* for the years 1945 to 1964. The author gratefully acknowledges a significant debt to the authors of *Backbench Opinion in the House of Commons 1955–59* for use of their copies of the *Notices of Motions*, and for their aid in selecting the rebellious EDMs. A few other government publications are cited in the footnotes. They are:

Lord Denning's Report, Cmnd 2152, H.M.S.O., 1963.
The Public General Acts, 1957. London, 1958.
Report of the Committee of Privileges. H.M.S.O., 23 Jul 1947, appendix 4.
Report of the Committee of Privileges, H.M.S.O., 17 Jun 1947.
Report of House of Commons Standing Committee C, 1950–1951.
Report of the Select Committee on Procedure. H.M.S.O., 1947.

II. Official Party Literature

The most important sources of information about the working of the Labour and Conservative mass party organizations are the reports of their annual conferences. In addition, both parties have published innumerable pamphlets and leaflets about their organizations and party policies. The pamphlets which were published without an author are listed below. The author is indebted to the Research Departments of the Labour and Conservative parties for allowing him to make extensive use of their facilities at party headquarters.

Conservative Party Campaign Guides. 1959, 1964.
Conservative Party Committees, 1946–51. Conservative Research Dept.
Conservative Party Daily Notes. 1950, 1951.
Labour Party, Notes for Speakers. 10 Feb 1939.
Labour Party Talking Points. No. 9. 1956.

III. Unpublished Sources

A. *Interviews*

The most important source of information about the activity of the Whips' Offices, constituency organizations, and rebel MPs has come from interviews. An attempt was made to see every MP who lost the whip, was expelled, had readoption difficulties, or experienced other disciplinary problems. Moreover, a number of Whips, party officials, and civil servants in the Whips' Offices and the Speaker's Office have been interviewed. The following individuals were interviewed at least once, and those with an asterisk following their names also loaned the author their private papers and letters. Where positions or offices are specified, they are those at the time of the interview.

Colonel Cyril Banks, MBE
 (MP 1950–59)
Sir Frank Barlow
 (Secretary to the PLP)
Mr. B. C. C. Batsford, MP
Mr. William Baxter, MP
Rt. Hon. Anthony Wedgwood
 Benn, MP
Mr. Humphry Berkeley, MP
Mr. John Biggs-Davison, MP
Mr. Edward Bishop, MP
Mr. Peter Blaker, MP
Rt. Hon. Sir Edward Boyle
Mr. Tom Braddock*
 (MP 1945–50)
Mr. R. W. Brown, MP
Mr. Paul Bryan, MP

Mr. Ivor Bulmer-Thomas*
 (MP 1942–50)
Mr. Robert Chichester-Clark,
 MP
Mr. Percy Collick
 (MP 1945–63)
Sir Knox Cunningham, Bt, MP
Colonel Alan Vincent Dower
 (MP 1931–50)
Sir William Duthie, OBE*
 (MP 1945–64)
Mr. I. L. Evans, MP
Mr. Stanley Evans
 (MP 1945–56)
Mr. Reginald Eyre, MP
Mr. Anthony Fell, MP
Mr. Ernest Fernyhough, MP

Mr. Nigel Fisher, MP

Mr. E. A. Fitch, MP

Mr. Anthony Fletcher
(Private Secretary to Conservative Chief Whip 1961–)

Mr. Michael Foot, MP

Mr. Geoffrey Gibson
(Labour Party Research Department)

Mr. H. Gourlay, MP

Mr. Anthony Grant, MP

Mr. Charles Grey, MP

Mr. Michael Hamilton, MP

Mr. J. Harper, MP

Sir Charles Harris, KBE
(Private Secretary to Government Chief Whip 1919–61)

Rt. Hon. Denis Healey, MBE, MP

Mr. Anthony Howard
(Political Correspondent for *The Sunday Times*)

Mr. W. Howie, MP

Mr. Emrys Hughes, MP

Mr. H. Montgomery Hyde*
(MP 1950–59)

Dr. Donald Johnson
(MP 1955–64)

Captain Henry Kerby, MP*

Mr. G. M. Lawson, MP

Major Sir Harry Legge-Bourke, MP*

Hon. Patrick Maitland
(MP 1951–59)

Mr. James Margach
(Political Correspondent for *The Sunday Times*)

Mr. I. A. McArthur, MP

Mr. Neil McBride, MP

Mr. Jack McCann, MP

Sir Frank Medlicott, CBE*
(MP 1939–59)

Sir John Mellor, Bt
(MP 1935–55)

Mr. Ian Mikardo, MP

Mr. Victor Montagu
(Viscount Hinchingbrooke)
(MP 1941–62)

Mr. Jasper More, DL, MP

Sir Thomas Moore, BT, CBE
(MP 1925–64)

Mr. Charles Morris, MP

Lord Morrison of Lambeth

Mr. Nigel Nicolson, MBE*
(MP 1952–59)

Rt. Hon. Anthony Nutting
(MP 1945–56)

Captain Lawrence Orr, MP

Mr. John Platts-Mills*
(MP 1945–50)

Lord Hailes of Prestonkirk

Mr. F. L. Pym, MP

Sir Victor Raikes, KBE
(MP 1931–57)

Rt. Hon. Sir Martin Redmayne, MP

Sir Francis Reid, CBE
(Secretary to Mr. Speaker)

Sir David Robertson
(MP 1939–64)

Mr. Andrew Roth

Mr. Peter Shore, MP

Rt. Hon. Edward Short, MP

Rt. Hon. John Silkin, CBE, MP

Mr. Arthur Skeffington, MP

Mr. Colin Turner
(MP 1959–64)

Mr. Lawrence Turner*
(MP 1950–59)

Mr. A. H. Warren
  (Private Secretary to Government Chief Whip 1961–)
Rt. Hon. W. S. Whitelaw, MC, MP
Mr. Paul Williams
  (MP 1953–64)

Mr. Patrick Wolrige-Gordon, MP
Mr. Victor Yates, MP
Mr. George Younger, MP
Mr. Konni Zilliacus, MP

The following individuals corresponded with the author about certain aspects of party discipline.

Mr. Francis Boyd
  (Political Correspondent of the *Guardian*)
Mr. John Brewis, MP
Rt. Hon. James Callaghan, MP
Mr. Robert Cooke, MP
Mr. Hugh Delargy, MP
Mrs. Sybil Edwards
  (Daughter of the late Mr. Alfred Edwards)

Mr. John W. Lett
Mr. John Maginnis, MP
Mr. P. Rogers
  (Cabinet Office)
Mr. J. Willcox
  (Clerk in Charge of Divisions)
Mr. Mark Woodnutt, MP

B. *Theses*

Coates, C. M. 'The course of party discipline in Parliament and the constituencies over the past thirty years, and its effect on the worth of the backbencher in British government.' Unpublished Master's Thesis. Bristol, 1959–60.

Jones, Russell. 'Party Voting in the English House of Commons.' Unpublished Master's Thesis. Chicago, 1933.

McNevin, M. 'The Left Wing in the British Labour Party.' Unpublished B.Litt. Thesis. Oxford, 1964.

Rose, Richard. 'The Relation of Socialist Principles to British Labour Foreign Policy, 1945–51.' Unpublished D.Phil. Thesis. Oxford, 1959.

Saloma, John. 'British Conservatism and the Welfare State.' Unpublished Ph.D. Thesis. Harvard, 1961.

IV. Newspapers and Periodicals

Many newspapers and periodicals have been consulted for various aspects of this study. The following are cited in the footnotes:

Belfast Telegraph
Bilston and Willenhall Times
Birmingham Evening Dispatch
Birmingham Mail
Bournemouth Daily Echo
Bournemouth Times
Cambridge Independent News
Cambridge Times
Carlisle Journal
Christchurch Times
Consett Chronicle
Consett Guardian
County Advertiser
Cumberland Evening News
Daily Express
Daily Graphic
Daily Herald
Daily Mail
Daily Mirror
Daily Sketch
Daily Telegraph
Daily Worker
Dorset Daily Echo
Eastern Daily Press
Eastern Evening News
Economist
Essex and Thurrock Gazette
Evening Gazette
  (*Middlesborough*)
Evening Standard
Forward
Glasgow Evening Citizen
Govan Press

Hampstead News
Hertfordshire and Bedfordshire
  Express
Irish Times
Islington Gazette
Keighley News
Listener
(*Manchester*) *Guardian*
Middleton Guardian
New Statesman
Newcastle Journal and North Mail
Newcastle Times
News Chronicle
Norfolk News
Northern Dispatch
Northern Echo
Observer
Oldham Chronicle
Oxford Mail
Prestwich and Whitefield Guide
Pudsey and Stanningley News
Reynolds News
Socialist Commentary
Socialist Outlook
South Oxfordshire Standard
Star
Sunday Empire News
Sunday Express
Sunday Times
Surrey Herald
The Scotsman
The Statist
The Times

Tribune   *Yarmouth Mercury*
Western Mail   *Yorkshire Post*
Wimbledon Boro' News

V. BIOGRAPHIES AND AUTOBIOGRAPHIES

Allen, Walter Gore. *The Reluctant Politician: Derick Heathcoat Amory*. London, 1958.

Attlee, C. R. *As It Happened*. London, 1954.

Baker, Capt. Peter. *My Testament*. London, 1955.

Blackburn, Fred. *George Tomlinson*. London, 1954.

Blackburn, Raymond. *I Am an Alcoholic*. London, 1959.

Boothby, Lord. *My Yesterday, Your Tomorrow*. London, 1962.

Boyd, Francis. *Richard Austen Butler*. London, 1956.

Braddock, Jack and Bessie. *The Braddocks*. London, 1963.

Brockway, Fenner. *Socialism Over Sixty Years: The Life of Jowett of Bradford*. London, 1946.

Churchill, Randolph. *The Rise and Fall of Sir Anthony Eden*. London, 1958.

Coote, Colin R., ed. *Sir Winston Churchill: A Self Portrait*. London, 1954.

Cowles, Virginia. *Winston Churchill: The Era and the Man*. London, 1953.

Dalton, Hugh. *High Tide and After, Memoirs 1945–1960*. London, 1962.

Denman, Sir Richard Douglas. *Political Sketches*. Carlisle, 1948.

Dickie, John. *The Uncommon Commoner, A Study of Sir Alec Douglas-Home*. London, 1964.

Driberg, Tom. *The Best of Both Worlds: A Personal Diary*. London, 1953.

Eden, Sir Anthony. *Full Circle, The Memoirs of Sir Anthony Eden*. London, 1960.

Estorick, Eric. *Stafford Cripps*. London, 1949.

Foot, Michael. *Aneurin Bevan*. Vol. 1. London, 1962.

Horner, Arthur Lewis. *Incorrigible Rebel*. London, 1960.

Hughes, Emrys. *Macmillan: Portrait of a Politician*. Leicester, 1962.

Hunter, Leslie. *The Road to Brighton Pier*. London, 1959.

Hyde, Douglas. *I Believed*. London, 1950.

Jenkins, Roy. *Mr. Attlee, An Interim Biography*. London, 1948.

Johnson, Dr. Donald. *A Doctor in Parliament*. London, 1958.

Kilmuir, Lord. *Political Adventure*. London, 1964.

Kirkwood, David. *My Life of Revolt*. London, 1935.

Krug, Mark. *Aneurin Bevan: Cautious Rebel*. New York, 1961.

Mann, Jean. *Woman in Parliament*. London, 1962.

Morris-Jones, Sir John. *Doctor in the Whips' Room*. London, 1955.

Morrison, Lord. *Herbert Morrison, An Autobiography*. London, 1960.

Nicolson, Nigel. *People and Parliament*. London, 1958.

Parker, C. S. *Sir Robert Peel*. Vol. 3. London, 1899.

Rees-Mogg, William. *Sir Anthony Eden*. London, 1956.

Rodgers, W. T., ed. *Hugh Gaitskell 1906–1963*. London, 1964.

Shinwell, Emanuel. *Conflict Without Malice*. London, 1955.

Smith, Dudley. *Harold Wilson, a Critical Biography*. London, 1964.

Toole, Millie. *Mrs. Bessie Braddock, M.P.* London, 1957.

Wedgwood, C. V. *The Last of the Radicals*. London, 1951.

Williams, Francis. *Ernest Bevin*. London, 1952.

—— *A Prime Minister Remembers: The War and Post-War Memoirs of the Rt. Hon. Earl Attlee*. London, 1961.

Winterton, Earl. *Orders of the Day*. London, 1953.

Woolton, Earl of. *The Memoirs of the Rt. Hon. The Earl of Woolton*. London, 1959.

Wyatt, Woodrow. *Distinguished For Talent*. London, 1958.

—— *Into the Dangerous World*. London, 1952.

VI. Historical and Special Studies of British Politics and Party Discipline

The most useful reference books for this work were *Dod's Parliamentary Companion*, *The Times House of Commons*, *Vacher's Parliamentary Companion*, *Whitaker's Almanack*, and D. E. Butler and Jennie Freeman, *British Political Facts 1900–1960*. There is a profusion of books and articles which mention party discipline.

A. *Books*

Abraham, L. A., and S. C. Hawtrey. *A Parliamentary Dictionary*. London, 1956.

Bibliography

Abrams, Mark and Richard Rose. *Must Labour Lose?* London, 1960.

Allen, V. L. *Trade Unions and the Government.* London, 1960.

Amery, L. S. *Thoughts on the Constitution.* Oxford, 1948.

Attlee, C. R. *The Labour Party in Perspective – And Twelve Years Later.* London, 1949.

Bagehot, Walter. *The English Constitution.* Introduction by Earl Balfour, London, 1928.

—— *The English Constitution.* Introduction by R. H. S. Crossman, London, 1963.

Bailey, Sydney D. *The British Party System.* London, 1952.

Barker, Ernest. *Essays on Government.* 2nd ed. Oxford, 1951.

Barker, S. *How the Labour Party Works.* London, 1955.

Bealey, Frank *et al. Constituency Politics: A Study of Newcastle-under-Lyme.* London, 1965.

Beer, Samuel H. *Modern British Politics.* London, 1965.

Belloc, H., and G. K. Chesterton. *The Party System.* London, 1911.

Beloff, Max. *The Party System.* London, 1958.

Birch, A. H. *Small Town Politics.* Oxford, 1959.

Birch, Nigel. *The Conservative Party.* London, 1949.

Blondel, J. *Voters, Parties, and Leaders.* London, 1963.

Boardman, Harry. *The Glory of Parliament.* London, 1960.

Boyd, Francis. *British Politics in Transition, 1945–63.* London, 1964.

Boyd-Carpenter, John. *The Conservative Case: Choice for Britain.* London, 1950.

Braine, Bernard. *Tory Democracy.* London, 1948.

Bromberger, Merry and Serge. *Secrets of Suez* (trans.), London, 1951.

Bromhead, P. A. *The House of Lords and Contemporary Politics, 1911–1957.* London, 1958.

—— *Private Members' Bills in the British Parliament.* London, 1956.

Brown, Alan. *The Tory Years.* London, 1963.

Brown, R. Douglas. *The Battle of Crichel Down.* London, 1955.

Buck, Philip W. *Amateurs and Professionals in British Politics 1918–59.* Chicago, 1963.

Bulmer-Thomas, Ivor. *The Party System in Great Britain.* London, 1953.

Butler, D. E. *The British General Election of 1951.* London, 1952.

—— *The British General Election of 1955.* London, 1955.

—— *The Electoral System in Britain Since 1918.* 2nd ed. Oxford, 1963.

Butler, D. E., and R. Rose. *The British General Election of 1959.* London, 1960.

Butler, D. E., and Anthony King. *The British General Election of 1964.* London, 1965.

—— *The British General Election of 1966.* London, 1966.

Cambray, P. G. *The Game of Politics: A Study of the Principles of British Political Strategy.* London, 1932.

Campion, Lord, ed. *Parliament: A Survey.* London, 1952.

Carter, B. E. *The Office of Prime Minister.* London, 1956.

Chapman, Brian. *British Government Observed.* Birkenhead, 1963.

Chester, D. N., and Nona Bowring. *Questions in Parliament.* Oxford, 1962.

Childers, E. *The Road to Suez.* London, 1962.

Christoph, James B. *Capital Punishment and British Politics.* London, 1962.

Churchill, Randolph S. *The Fight for the Tory Leadership.* London, 1964.

Comfort, G. O. *Professional Politicians, a Study of the British Party Agents.* Washington, 1958.

Crick, Bernard. *Reform of Parliament.* London, 1964.

Crossman, Richard. *Palestine Mission: A Personal Record.* London, 1947.

Driver, Christopher. *The Disarmers.* London, 1964.

Duverger, Maurice. *Political Parties.* trans. 2nd ed. London, 1962.

Eckstein, H. *Pressure Group Politics.* London, 1960.

Epstein, L. *Britain – Uneasy Ally.* Chicago, 1954.

—— *British Politics in the Suez Crisis.* London, 1964.

Fienburgh, Wilfred. *No Love for Johnnie.* London, 1959.

Finer, S. E. *Anonymous Empire.* London, 1958.

Finer, S. E., et al. *Backbench Opinion in the House of Commons 1955–1959.* London, 1961.

Fitzsimons, M. A. *The Foreign Policy of the British Labour Government, 1945–1951.* Notre Dame, 1953.

Foot, M. *Parliament in Danger!* London, 1959.

Friedrich, C. J. *Man and His Government: An Empirical Theory of Politics.* New York, 1963.

Guttsman, W. L. *The British Political Elite.* London, 1963.

Gwyn, W. B. *Democracy and the Cost of Politics.* London, 1962.

Hanson, A. H., and H. V. Wiseman. *Parliament at Work.* London, 1962.

Harrison, Martin. *Trade Unions and the Labour Party Since 1945.* London, 1960.

Harrison, W. *The Government of Britain.* 4th ed. London, 1957.

Harvey, J., and L. Bather. *The British Constitution.* London, 1963.

Herbert, A. P. *Anything But Action.* London, 1961.

—— *Independent Member.* London, 1950.

Hill, Andrew, and Anthony Whichelow. *What's Wrong With Parliament?* London, 1964.

Hoffman, J. D. *The Conservative Party in Opposition, 1945–51.* London, 1964.

Hollis, Christopher. *Can Parliament Survive?* London, 1949.

Hollis, Christopher, *et al. The Ayes and the Noes.* London, 1957.

Hopkins, Harry. *The New Look: A Social History of the Forties and Fifties in Britain.* London, 1963.

Howard, Anthony, and Richard West. *The Making of a Prime Minister.* London, 1965.

Irving, Clive, *et al. Scandal '63.* London, 1963.

Jackson, J. A. *The Irish in Britain.* London, 1963.

Jenkins, R. *Pursuit of Progress.* London, 1953.

Jennings, Sir Ivor. *Parliament.* 2nd ed. Cambridge, 1957.

Johnson, Dr. Donald. *On Being an Independent M.P.* Carlisle, 1964.

Johnson, Paul. *The Suez War.* London, 1957.

Keeton, G. W. *The Passing of Parliament.* London, 1952.

Laski, Harold J. *Parliamentary Government in England.* London, 1938.

—— *Reflections on the Constitution.* Manchester, 1951.

Leiserson, A. *Parties and Politics: An Institutional and Behavioral Approach.* New York, 1958.

Leonard, R. L. *Guide to the General Election.* London, 1964.

Liggett, E. *British Political Issues.* 2 vols. London, 1964.

Lipset, S. M. *Ostrogorski and the Analytical Approach to the Comparative Study of Political Parties.* Institute of International Studies, General Series, Reprint no. 140.

Lipset, Seymour Martin. *Political Man.* London, 1963.

Low, Sydney. *The Governance of England.* London, 1904.

Lowell, A. Lawrence. *The Government of England.* 2 vols. New York, 1908.

McCallum, R., and A. Readman. *The British General Election of 1945.* Oxford, 1947.

McDonald, N. A. *The Study of Political Parties.* New York, 1955.

Mackenzie, K. R. *The English Parliament*. London, 1945.

McKenzie, R. T. *British Political Parties*. 2nd ed. London, 1964.

Mackintosh, John P. *The British Cabinet*. London, 1962.

MacLeod, Iain. *The Future of the Welfare State*. C.P.C. Lectures. Oxford, 1957.

Marshall, Geoffrey, and Graeme C. Moodie. *Some Problems of the Constitution*. 2nd ed. London, 1961.

Mathiot, A. *The British Political System*. London, 1958.

Mayo, H. B. *An Introduction to Democratic Theory*. New York, 1960.

Michels, Robert. *Political Parties*. New York, 1959.

Miliband, R. *Parliamentary Socialism*. London, 1964.

Mitchell, Joan. *Crisis in Britain 1951*. London, 1963.

Morrison, Lord. *Government and Parliament: A Survey From the Inside*. 2nd ed. London, 1962.

Neumann, S., ed. *Modern Political Parties: Approaches to Comparative Politics*. Chicago, 1956.

Nicholas, H. G. *The British General Election of 1950*. London, 1951.

Northedge, F. S. *British Foreign Policy*. London, 1962.

Nutting, A. *No End of a Lesson: The Story of Suez*. London, 1967.

Ostrogorski, M. *Democracy and the Organization of Political Parties*. 2 vols. London, 1902.

Parliamentary Reform, 1933–1960. London, 1961.

Pelling, H. *A History of British Trade Unionism*. London, 1963.

—— *A Short History of the Labour Party*. London, 1962.

Potter, Allen. *Organized Groups in British National Politics*. London, 1961.

Pritt, D. N. *The Labour Government, 1945–51*. London, 1963.

Ranney, Austin. *The Doctrine of Responsible Party Government*. Urbana, 1962.

—— *Pathways to Parliament*. Madison, 1965.

Ranney, Austin, and Willmoore Kendall. *Democracy and the American Party System*. New York, 1956.

Richards, Peter G. *Honourable Members: A Study of the British Backbencher*. London, 1959.

—— *Patronage in British Government*. London, 1963.

Roberts, B. C. *Trade Union Government and Administration in Great Britain*. London, 1956.

Rogow, A. A., and Peter Shore. *The Labour Government and British Industry 1945–51*. Oxford, 1955.

Rose, Richard. *Politics in England*. Boston, 1964.

Runciman, W. G. *Social Science and Political Theory*. Cambridge, 1963.

Shinwell, Emanuel. *The Labour Story*. London, 1963.

Sissons, M., and P. French, eds. *The Age of Austerity*. London, 1963.

Smith, Barbara, and Geoffrey Ostergaard. *Constitutional Relations Between the Labour and Co-operative Parties: An Historical Review*. Hansard Society. London, 1959–60.

Snyder, William P. *The Politics of British Defence Policy, 1945–1962* Columbus, 1964.

Stewart, J. D. *British Pressure Groups*. Oxford, 1958.

Stout, Hiram Miller. *British Government*. New York, 1953.

Taylor, E. *The House of Commons at Work*. 2nd ed. London, 1955.

Thomas, Hugh, ed. *The Establishment*. London, 1962.

Thomas, N. P. *History of British Politics from the Year 1900*. London, 1956.

Thomson, David. *England in the Twentieth Century*. London, 1963.

Truman, David B. *The Congressional Party*. New York, 1959.

Turner, J. *Party and Constituency: Pressures on Congress*. Baltimore, 1951.

Utley, T. E. *Not Guilty: The Conservative Reply*. London, 1957.

Weber, Max. *The Theory of Social and Economic Organization*. New York, 1947.

Wheare, K. C. *Government by Committee*. Oxford, 1955.

—— *Legislatures*. Oxford, 1963.

Wilson, H. H. *Pressure Group: The Campaign for Commercial Television*. London, 1961.

Wood, Neal. *Communism and British Intellectuals*. London, 1959.

Young, Roland. *The British Parliament*. London, 1962.

Young, Wayland. *The Profumo Affair: Aspects of Conservatism*. London, 1963.

Zilliacus, K. *Why I Was Expelled*. London, 1949.

B. *Articles*

Alderman, R. K. 'Discipline in the Parliamentary Labour Party, 1945–51', *Parliamentary Affairs*, vol. 18 (Summer 1965), pp. 293–305.

Alderman, R. K. 'The Conscience Clause of the Parliamentary Labour Party', *Parliamentary Affairs*, vol. 19 (Spring 1966), pp. 224–32.

Andrews, William G. 'Some Thoughts on the Power of Dissolution', *Parliamentary Affairs*, vol. 13 (Summer 1960), pp. 286–96.

Ashe, Geoffrey. 'Bevan vs. Bevanism', *Commonweal*, vol. 56 (Jul 1952), pp. 311–3.

Astor, W. W. 'The Conservative Party in Opposition', *The New English Review*, vol. xii (Apr 1946), pp. 344–8.

Attlee, Earl. 'Party Discipline is Paramount', *National and English Review*, vol. 148 (Jan 1957), pp. 15–16.

—— 'The Art of Being Prime Minister', *The Times* (15 Jun 1957).

—— 'The Attitudes of M.P.s and Active Peers', *The Political Quarterly*, vol. 30 (Jan–Mar 1959), pp. 29–32.

—— 'The Role of the Member of Parliament', *Fabian Journal*, no. 26 (Nov 1958), pp. 5–8.

Beales, H. L. 'The Labour Party in its Social Context', *The Political Quarterly*, vol. 24 (Jan–Mar 1953), pp. 90–107.

Beer, Samuel. 'The Conservative Party of Great Britain', *Journal of Politics*, vol. 14 (Feb 1952), pp. 41–71.

—— 'Democratic One-Party Government for Britain', *The Political Quarterly*, vol. 32 (Apr–Jun 1961), pp. 114–23.

—— 'The Future of British Politics', *The Political Quarterly*, vol. 26 (Jan–Mar 1955), pp. 38–9.

—— 'Pressure Groups and Parties in Britain', *APSR*, vol. 50 (Mar 1956), pp. 1–23.

Beloff, Max. 'Executive and Legislature in Britain', *Calcutta Review*, vol. 109 (Dec 1948), pp. 161–8.

—— 'The Leader of the Opposition', *Parliamentary Affairs*, vol. 11 (Spring 1958), pp. 155–62.

Berrington, Hugh. 'The Conservative Party: Revolts and Pressures – 1955–1961', *The Political Quarterly*, vol. 32 (Oct–Dec 1961), pp. 363–73.

Biffin, John. 'The Constituency Leaders', *Crossbow*, vol. 4 (Autumn 1960), pp. 27–32.

Biffin, W. J. 'Party Conference and Party Policy', *The Political Quarterly*, vol. 32 (Jul–Sep 1961), pp. 257–66.

Birch, A. H. 'The Labour Party's Real Split', *Manchester Guardian* (24 Nov 1960).

Blondel, Jean. 'The Conservative Association and the Labour Party in Reading', *Political Studies*, vol. 6 (Jun 1958), pp. 101–19.

Bonner, J. 'The Four Labour Cabinets', *Sociological Review*, vol. 6 (Jul 1958), pp. 37–48.

Boyd, Francis. 'Mr. Bevan in Search of Power', *Spectator*, vol. 191 (25 Sep 1953), pp. 318–9.

—— 'The New House at Work', *Spectator*, vol. 187 (14 Dec 1951), pp. 810–11.

Boyle, Sir Edward. 'No, Not Quite . . .', *The National and English Review*, vol. 148 (Jan 1957), pp. 17–18.

Bromhead, Peter. 'How Should Parliament be Reformed?' *The Political Quarterly*, vol. 30 (Jul–Sep 1959), pp. 272–82.

Brzezinski, Zbigniew. 'Deviation Control: A Study in the Dynamics of Doctrinal Conflict', *APSR*, vol. 56 (Mar 1962), pp. 5–22.

Bulmer-Thomas, Ivor. 'How Conservative Policy is Formed', *The Political Quarterly*, vol. 25 (Apr–Jun 1953), pp. 190–203.

Burns, J. M. 'The Parliamentary Labor Party in Great Britain', *APSR*, vol. 44 (Dec 1950), pp. 855–71.

Butler, Arthur. '1951–1959: The Conservatives in Power', *The Political Quarterly*, vol. 30 (Oct–Dec 1959), pp. 325–35.

Butler, D. E. 'American Myths About British Parties', *Virginia Quarterly Review*, vol. 31 (Winter 1955), pp. 46–56.

—— 'The Redistribution of Seats', *Public Administration*, vol. 33 (Summer 1955), pp. 125–47.

—— 'Some Notes on the Nature of British Political Parties', *Occidente*, vol. 10 (Mar–Apr 1954), pp. 137–53.

Cassinelli, C. W. 'The Law of Oligarchy', *APSR*, vol. 67 (Sep 1953), pp. 773–84.

Chester, D. N. 'Critique of Mackintosh's Cabinet Government', *Parliamentary Affairs*, vol. 15, no. 4 (1962), pp. 519 ff.

Clarke, David. 'The Organization of Political Parties', *The Political Quarterly*, vol. 21 (Jan 1950), pp. 79–90.

Crick, Bernard. 'Two Theories of Opposition', *New Statesman*, vol. 59 (18 Jun 1960), pp. 882–3.

Crossman, R. H. S. 'Left of Centre', *Guardian* (8 Feb 1963).

—— 'The Party Oligarchies', *New Statesman*, vol. 48 (21 Aug 1954), pp. 200–1.

—— 'Reflections on Party Loyalty', *New Statesman*, vol. 49 (2 Apr 1955), pp. 460–1.

Crossman, R. H. S. 'Socialism and the New Despotism', *Fabian Tract*, no. 298 (Feb 1956), pp. 1–24.

'The Decline of Parliament', *The Political Quarterly*, vol. 34 (Jul–Sep 1963), pp. 233–9.

Devons, Ely. 'Government on the Inner Circle', *The Listener*, vol. 59 (27 Mar 1958), pp. 523–5.

Dowse, Robert E. 'The MP and his Surgery', *Political Studies*, vol. xi (Oct 1963), pp. 333–41.

—— 'The Parliamentary Labour Party in Opposition', *Parliamentary Affairs*, vol. 13 (Autumn 1960), pp. 520–9.

—— and Trevor Smith. 'Party Discipline in the House of Commons – A Comment', *Parliamentary Affairs*, vol. 16 (Spring 1963), pp. 159–64.

Epstein, Leon D. 'British Mass Parties in Comparison with American Parties', *Political Science Quarterly*, vol. 71 (Mar 1956), pp. 97–125.

—— 'British M.P.s and their Local Parties: The Suez Cases', *APSR*, vol. 54 (Jun 1960), pp. 374–90.

—— 'Cohesion of British Parliamentary Parties', *APSR*, vol. 50 (Jun 1956), pp. 360–77.

—— 'New M.P.s and the Politics of the PLP', *Political Studies*, vol. 10 (Jun 1962), pp. 121–9.

—— 'Partisan Foreign Policy; Britain in the Suez Crisis', *World Politics*, vol. 12 (Jan 1960), pp. 201–24.

—— 'Politics of British Conservatism', *APSR*, vol. 47 (Mar 1954), pp. 27–48.

Fienburgh, W. 'Put Policy on the Agenda', *Fabian Journal*, no. 6 (Feb 1952), pp. 25–33.

—— 'The Future of Labour's Organization', *Fabian Journal*, no. 17 (Nov 1955), pp. 10–14.

—— 'The Tory Machine', *New Statesman*, vol. 43 (31 May 1952), p. 636.

Finer, S. E. 'The Individual Responsibility of Ministers', *Public Administration*, vol. 34 (Winter 1956), pp. 377–96.

Fulford, Roger. 'The Member and his Constituency', Ramsay Muir Memorial Lecture, 1957.

Hanham, H. J. 'The Local Organization of the Labour Party', *The Western Political Quarterly*, vol. ix (Jun 1956), pp. 376–88.

Harman, N. 'Minor Political Parties in Britain', *The Political Quarterly*, vol. 33 (Jul–Sep 1962), pp. 268–81.

Healey, Denis. 'Aneurin Bevan does it Again', *New Republic*, vol. 130 (3 May 1954), p. 5.

Heasman, D. J. 'Parliamentary Paths to High Office', *Parliamentary Affairs*, vol. 16 (Summer 1963), pp. 315–30.

Hindell, Keith and Philip Williams. 'Scarborough and Blackpool', *The Political Quarterly*, vol. 33 (Jul–Sep 1962), pp. 306–20, and corrections (Oct–Dec) p. 347.

Hitchner, Dell G. 'The Labour Government and the House of Commons', *The Western Political Quarterly*, vol. v (Sep 1952), pp. 417–44.

Hollis, Christopher. 'Can Parliament Survive?' *Encounter*, vol. 4 (Feb 1955), pp. 12–20.

—— 'Has Parliament a Future?' *Unservile State Papers*, no. 1 (London, 1961).

—— 'The Tactics of Abolition', *Spectator*, vol. 195 (25 Nov 1955), pp. 706–7.

Hornby, Richard. 'Parties in Parliament 1959–1963: 1. The Labour Party', *The Political Quarterly*, vol. 34 (Jul–Sep 1963), pp. 240–8.

Hunt, Norman. 'The Commons in Action', *The Listener*, vol. 70 (19 Dec 1963), pp. 1011–13.

—— 'The Commons in Action II', *The Listener*, vol. 70 (26 Dec 1963), pp. 1056–7.

Jenkins, Roy. 'Party Discipline in the House of Commons', *The Listener*, vol. 55 (26 Jan 1956), pp. 127–8.

King-Hall, Commander Stephen. 'The Independent in Politics', *Parliamentary Affairs*, vol. 5 (Winter 1951), pp. 103–15.

Kirchheimer, Otto. 'The Waning of Opposition in Parliamentary Regimes', *Social Research*, vol. 24 (Summer 1957), pp. 127–56.

Lane, Davis. 'British Socialism and the Perils of Success', *Political Science Quarterly*, vol. 69 (Dec 1954), pp. 502–16.

Laski, H. 'The Position of Parties and the Right of Dissolution', *Fabian Tract*, no. 210 (Mar 1924).

Lewis, G. K. 'The Present Condition of British Political Parties', *The Western Political Quarterly*, vol. v (Jun 1952), pp. 231–57.

Loewenberg, G. 'The British Constitution and the Structure of the Labour Party', *APSR*, vol. 52 (Sep 1958), pp. 771–90.

McKenzie, R. T. 'Parties, Pressure Groups and the British Political Process', *The Political Quarterly*, vol. 29 (Jan–Mar 1958), pp. 5–16.

McKenzie, R. T. 'Policy Discussion in Opposition: A Rejoinder', *Political Studies*, vol. 5 (Jun 1957), pp. 176–82.

McKitterick, T. E. M. 'The Membership of the [Labour] Party', *The Political Quarterly*, vol. 31 (Jul–Sep 1960), pp. 312–23.

Mallalieu, J. P. W. 'The Trade Union M.P.', *New Statesman*, vol. 58 (28 Nov 1959), p. 734.

Martin, Laurence, W. 'The Bournemouth Affair: Britain's First Primary Election', *Journal of Politics*, vol. 22 (Nov 1960), pp. 654–81.

Miliband, R. 'Parliamentary Democracy and Parliamentary Government', *Political Studies*, vol. 6 (Jun 1958), pp. 170–4.

Millett, John H. 'The Role of an Interest Group Leader in the House of Commons', *The Western Political Quarterly*, vol. 9 (Dec 1956), pp. 915–26.

Newman, Frank C. 'Reflections on Money and Party Politics in Britain', *Parliamentary Affairs*, vol. x (Summer 1957), pp. 308–28.

Nicholas, H. G. 'The Formulation of Party Policy', *Parliamentary Affairs*, vol. 5 (Winter 1951), pp. 142–53.

O'Leary, Cornelius. 'The Wedgwood Benn Case and The Doctrine of Wilful Perversity', *Political Studies*, vol. 13 (Feb 1965), pp. 65–78.

Pennock, J. R. 'Responsiveness, Responsibility, and Majority Rule', *APSR*, vol. 46 (Sep 1952), pp. 790–818.

Plowman, D. S. 'Allegiances to Political Parties', *Political Studies*, vol. 3 (Oct 1955), pp. 222–34.

Potter, Allen M. 'The English Conservative Constituency Association', *The Western Political Quarterly*, vol. 9 (Jun 1956), pp. 363–75.

—— 'British Party Organization (1950)', *Political Science Quarterly*, vol. 66 (Mar 1951), pp. 65–86.

Powell, J. Enoch. '1951–1959 Labour in Opposition', *The Political Quarterly*, vol. 30 (Oct–Dec 1959), pp. 336–43.

Raikes, Victor. 'The Outlook for the Conservative Party', *New English Review*, vol. xiii (Nov 1946), pp. 478–9.

Ranney, Austin. 'Inter-Constituency Movement of British Parliamentary Candidates, 1951–1959', *APSR*, vol. 58 (Mar 1964), pp. 36–45.

Rees-Mogg, William, T. E. M. McKitterick, Philip Skelsey. 'Selection of Candidates', *The Political Quarterly*, vol. 30 (Jul–Sep 1959), pp. 215–29.

Rose, Richard. 'Complexities of Party Leadership', *Parliamentary Affairs*, vol. xvi (Summer 1963), pp. 257–73.

—— 'Parties, Factions and Tendencies in Britain', *Political Studies*, vol. 12 (Feb 1964), pp. 33–46.

—— 'The Bow Group's Role in British Politics', *The Western Political Quarterly*, vol. 14 (Dec 1961), pp. 865–78.

—— 'The Political Ideas of English Party Activists', *APSR*, vol. 56 (Jun 1962), pp. 360–71.

—— 'Who are the Tory Militants?', *Crossbow*, vol. 5 (Autumn 1961), pp. 35–9.

Rose, S. 'Policy Discussion in Opposition', *Political Studies*, vol. 4 (Jun 1956), pp. 128–38.

Schenkman, Alfred S. 'The British Election Agent', *Parliamentary Affairs*, vol. 5 (Autumn 1952), pp. 449–54.

Silverman, S. 'Standing Orders and Democracy', *New Statesman and Nation*, vol. 48 (4 Dec 1954), p. 729.

Singer, J. David. 'Inter-Nation Influence: A Formal Model', *APSR*, vol. 57 (Jun 1963), pp. 420–43.

'Socialist Rifts and Revolts', *Notes on Current Politics*, no. 11 (31 May 1948), pp. 1–24.

'Special No. – The Conservative Party', *The Political Quarterly*, vol. 24 (Apr–Jun 1953).

'Special No. – The Conservative Party', *The Political Quarterly*, vol. 32 (Jul–Sep 1961).

'Special No. – The Labour Party', *The Political Quarterly*, vol. 31 (Jul–Sep 1960).

Stephenson, T. E. 'The Leader-Follower Relationship', *Sociological Review*, vol. 7 (Dec 1954), pp. 179–95.

Strauss, Rt. Hon. G. R., and Richard Hornby. 'The Influence of the Back-Bencher: I. A Labour View, II. A Tory View', *The Political Quarterly*, vol. 36 (Jul–Sep 1965), pp. 277–94.

Thomson, George. 'Parties in Parliament 1959–1963, II, The Conservatives', *The Political Quarterly*, vol. 34 (Jul–Sep 1963), pp. 249–56.

Tivey, Leonard. 'The System of Democracy in Britain', *Sociological Review*, vol. 6 (Jul 1958), pp. 109–24.

Voigt, F. A. 'Twenty-One "Rebels" and a Letter', *The Nineteenth Century and After*, vol. 141–2 (Jan 1947), pp. 1–9.

'Whips of Parliament', *The Economist*, vol. 200 (15 Jul 1961), pp. 220–1.

Wilcox, R. W. J. 'Probables and Possibles, 1963', *The Political Quarterly*, vol. 34 (Jul–Sep 1963), pp. 300–5.

Willenz, Eric. 'The Conservative Party in Britain since 1945', *Social Research*, vol. xvi (Mar 1949), pp. 12–30.

Williams, A. L. 'Expelled for Opinions?' *Labour Organiser*, vol. 34, no. 393 (Jan 1955).

Williams, Francis. 'Labour's Rifts', *Spectator*, vol. 189 (8 Aug 1952), pp. 177–8.

Williams, P. M. Letter to the Editor, *Economist*, vol. 161 (8 Dec 1951), p. 1395.

Willson, F. M. G. 'Routes of Entry of New Members of the British Cabinet', *Political Studies*, vol. 7 (Oct 1959), pp. 222–32.

Windlesham, Lord. 'The Communication of Conservative Policy 1963–64', *The Political Quarterly*, vol. 36 (Apr–Jun 1965), pp. 164–180.

Yates, Ivan. 'Power in the Labour Party', *The Political Quarterly*, vol. 31 (Jul–Sep 1960), pp. 300–11.

Index